Praise for *In The Land O

"*In The Land Of Shiva* is a marvelous book, literally, a book filled with marvels. Not only is it a poignant and often amusing, true adventure story, it's also a profound journey inward into the 'unseen world.' *In The Land Of Shiva* invites us to take this fascinating spiritual excursion in the company of a wonderfully observant and emotionally sensitive man, a journey leading ultimately to an extraordinary and totally convincing place 'beyond religion.'"
~ Jeremy Taylor

"Jim is a fine storyteller who offers light humor and deep wisdom along with his tale of how he, as a Catholic Brother in India and Nepal, discovered not only pieces of those countries, but characteristics of himself in those exotic lands. His inner task is nothing less than determining where spiritual authority really resides. I highly recommend this journey to India, Nepal, and the human spirit."
~ Betty Dietz

"Every page drew me in further, taking me deeper into the far-away India and Nepal that transformed O'Hara in his quest for spiritual evolution. He brings India to life, pairing its frenetic beauty with his own life's journey, and sprinkling it with a cast of characters that he illustrates with humor, soul, and wit."
~ Dave Casuto

"O'Hara paints a vivid picture of his seven years in India and Nepal, where his travels find him re-examining his most closely-held beliefs about God, religion, and personal connections. Told with honesty and compassion, he shows us the land of Shiva— and his own heart—in all its grit, glory, and contradictions."
~ Sandra Krakowski

"The dynamic of Shiva-energy destroying what is old and no longer useful in order to make way for the new, is the story of every person's inner journey. Don't miss this compelling tale in which the Indian subcontinent comes alive on every page, and personal growth and challenge is the order of the day. And Jim got this narrative right. I know. I was there."

~ Joseph Sheehan

IN THE LAND OF SHIVA

IN THE LAND OF SHIVA

A Memoir

JAMES O'HARA

LEANDROS PUBLISHING

Leandros Publishing
www.leandrospublishing.com

Copyright 2014 by James O'Hara
www.jamesohara.com

ISBN: 0991241606
ISBN 13: 9780991241606
Library of Congress Control Number: 2014905169

Leandros Publishing
Berkeley, CA

Cover design: Victoria Davies
Map: Tlielaxu Miykel
Author photo, contemporary: Jo LaRoque

Printed in the United States of America

For All My Teachers

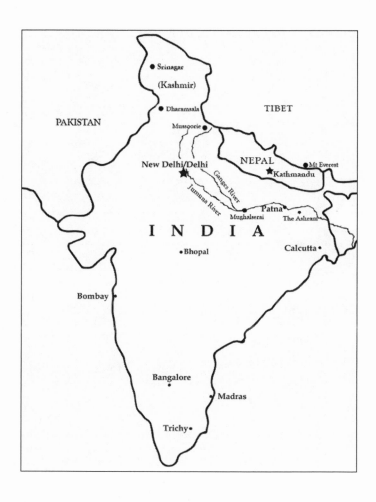

Srinagar

(Kashmir)

PAKISTAN

Dharamsala

Mussoorie

New Delhi/Delhi

TIBET

NEPAL

Mt Everest

Kathmandu

Ganges River

Jumuna River

Patna

Mughalserai

The Ashram

I N D I A

•Bhopal

Calcutta

Bombay

Bangalore
•

•Madras

Trichy•

CHAPTERS

LONG AGO AND FAR AWAY

MORE THAN A generation of time has wheeled across the sky since I first lived on the Indian subcontinent, and I sometimes wonder how much the years have reshaped my memories of those far-off places and events. My letters and photos, however, stare at me and confirm that I've gotten most of the facts right. The bazaars sparkled with brass pots next to strands of gold flowers for temple worship, elephants walked past my house, and monkeys clambered in nearby trees. I bathed in jungle streams and trudged across rice paddies, and my Kathmandu home peered into the snowcaps of the Himalayas. It was a landscape made for adventures.

There is another story, however, that is not portrayed in those pictures and only hinted at in the letters. The account of the inner journey thrust upon me by that foreign land is altogether another narrative, one with its own unique challenges. How does one chart in a linear fashion, one page after another, the spiraling and labyrinthine flows of the mind and heart?

While many people no doubt learn their major life lessons in their own home and backyard, I seemed to have required the conspiracy of another culture—a culture that was fascinating, seductive, and frustrating—to move my life forward and deeper.

The India and Nepal of that time have already drifted into history, like gusts of Himalayan air dispersed on the plains. It was a time when Nepal was still called Shangri-La, when India's chimes came only from ornate temples rather than from mobile phones. But much of Asia is indeed timeless, and the smell of sandalwood still perfumes the bazaars, the muezzin's call to prayer is still heard, and the land and its people still have the power to enchant, stir up, and ultimately transform one's soul.

DEATH

Our Lady of the Pillar Church
St. Louis, Missouri
1964

A LARGE BLACK cloth—a shroud, symbol of our dying—settled slowly onto me and my companions lying face down on the sanctuary floor. In that dark space, the cold marble pressed into my body and I squirmed slightly. A few moments later the sanctuary floor had sucked the warmth from my chest and I knew I couldn't avoid the cold sinking into my bones.

"*De profundis, clamo ad te Domine.*" Out of the depths I cry to you, O Lord. A hundred brothers in black suits behind me sang the centuries-old chant. It was a prayer for forgiveness usually reserved for funerals.

"From today forward you will be *in* the world, but not *of* the world," Father Superior said to us, still under the cloth. "You are dead to sin, to the world, and to yourselves. You live only for God. Your vows of poverty, chastity, and obedience will support complete dedication to God, self-sacrifice, and service to others. You shall be called 'Brother,' a description of how you shall relate to all with whom you come in contact. This important step must be taken only after full deliberation on your part, because it is forever."

I had heard it all before during my previous four years as a brother with temporary vows. I knew what I was getting into with taking vows for life, and I wished that Father would finish his sermon quickly. The longer I stayed under the cloth, the more claustrophobic I felt.

"Rise, my sons, to profess your vows, and step forward freely and of your own accord," Father Superior concluded, "for these vows are irrevocable."

MOTHER INDIA

Delhi, India
January, 1980

"NOT GOING, NOT going, some problem ahead," the taxi driver said to me and my three companions. The taxi, which had been inching along for miles, came to a complete stop behind half a dozen cycle rickshaws, three horse-drawn carts, and two buses spewing black exhaust. I had expected the streets of Old Delhi to be crowded, but this was complete blockage.

My first day in India. I was eager to get to the seminary, move in, settle down, see the land and its people. A traffic jam was not my idea of the exotic East.

"Definitely not going," the taxi driver said again, then spoke rapidly in Hindi, waved his arms left and right, and finally pointed straight ahead. I could see nothing from my position in the back seat, though I heard shouts and drumming not far away. Was it a festival? In any case, we weren't moving, so I settled back and practiced waiting, a virtue I was told I must cultivate in order to survive life on the subcontinent.

Other taxis and autorickshaws pulled up alongside our vehi-cle, hemming us in, and making retreat to a side street, if any existed, impossible. Two taxi drivers, both wearing bright red turbans and full beards, stepped out of their cars and joined in the shouting, which seemed more like chanting than the arguing

I had expected over vehicle right-of-way. The drivers walked past our taxi, leaving their own abandoned in the middle of the street. Maybe this wasn't a simple traffic jam.

A street disturbance could be a friendly or unfriendly encounter, and I instinctively pulled my shoulder bag closer to my body, for it contained precious documents—my American passport and a letter from my Superior, Father Dave.

Father Dave had written to the Dean of the Delhi seminary, explaining who I and my companions were and why we had come to India. "Better take a copy with you," he had said. "You can't depend on the letter arriving by mail before you do. And become familiar with its contents, so if you lose it, just retype what you remember and sign my name."

Dean of Studies
Light of Wisdom Seminary, Delhi
Dear Father John,

Thank you for accepting the following men as students at your institute. As their Superior, I have charged them with the task of establishing a branch of our religious order in India. They have entered your country on student visas, and my hope is that living with your seminarians will enable them to acclimate gradually to India while they plan how to develop the mission assigned to them.

Brother Jim, age 38, the Superior and my representative in India, is an experienced administrator and teacher. He will handle all official communication, coordinate the running of the local community and keep me informed on all developments. I trust you will find him a clear communicator and sensitive leader.

Father Gerry, age 37, is appointed Novice Master and is in charge of the training of any young men wishing to join our community. There are already several young Catholic Indians who wish to join our order, having come in contact with our Father Bill, who arrived in India last year to do village development work.

Brother Joe, age 36, an excellent teacher, and Brother Steve, 26, a gifted artist, complete the community and will assist in transmitting the spirituality of our order to the Indian candidates.

I thank you in advance for any assistance you may render these men and our mission. May God and His Holy Mother bless you and keep you well.

Sincerely,

Father David, Religious Superior

Society of Mary

St. Louis, Missouri, U.S.A.

Just a few years older than me, and someone I knew well, Dave had promoted the mission from its very inception and appointed me the Superior. I had promised to keep in close contact with him about the progress of the mission. He was, however, halfway around the world, and letters took nearly two weeks to travel in each direction. Clearly, the four of us in India would make most decisions ourselves. I, not Dave, was effectively in charge here. I would negotiate with bishops, the seminary, and the government, and my vote would break a tie in our group's decision-making process. The position of Superior carried much responsibility, but also power and influence. A smile crept over my face. I was the Superior—I liked that.

"I'm tired of sitting," Joe said. "Let's look around." Always ready to see new sights, Joe pushed open the car door and stepped out. I glanced at Steve who sat between us. His eyes were closed and his head lay back against the seat, his stomach evidently still churning from the spicy food on Air India and from a bumpy airport landing.

From the front seat, staring straight ahead, Gerry said, "I'm not getting out. You go, I'll stay with Steve and the taxi."

Another glance at Steve assured me he didn't want to be disturbed, and I opened the taxi door. The noonday sun that greeted me was mild. This was, after all, winter, and there was even a slight chill in the air. Many Indians in the street and on nearby sidewalks wore shawls over their shoulders. When I looked more closely, I realized they were mostly men. Where were the women?

An immense mosque, with minarets and dome that pointed heavenward, stood a short distance away, looming large over a bazaar cluttered at its feet. On the other side of the street, a red sandstone fort stretched ahead for at least half a mile, adorned with bright flags and banners that waved over the people gathered on its lawn. The crowd, like revelers, milled in all directions, the men in Western clothing—collared shirts in solid colors and light-colored slacks—or baggy shirts and billowy pants. The few women present were adorned in saris of many hues—soft pink, dark blue with gold trim, deep green, and bright orange saris caught my eye.

In spite of harsh exhaust fumes, the smell of sweet, cloying incense from burning sticks that sidewalk clothing vendors placed near their wares assailed my nose. Beyond the vendors, more people were shouting, drumming, and piercing the air with trumpet blasts, all in a festive tone. Suddenly my jet-lag was gone—I felt excited. This was India! I had arrived.

I drank it all in, then joined Joe in snaking our way past rickshaws and bystanders to get closer to the activity. Surprisingly, I could see fairly well over the crowd, and assumed Joe could also. Though both of us were of similar, average height, I realized that most men in the crowd had a similar stature. What a pleasant surprise not to crane my neck so much!

Soon the crowd thickened and forced us to stop in front of a thin elderly man pumping water from what resembled an ice cream cart. While Joe looked out over the crowd, the vendor offered me a glass of water, which I refused with a shake of my head and a smile.

"Very good, sir. I wouldn't drink that water either. Visiting from which country, please?" A man near the water vendor, wearing polyester pants, a white shirt, and a light green sweater-vest, had spoken to me. Of course I would be taken for a tourist, dressed, as we brothers were, in the ordinary street clothes of a Westerner.

"America. The United States," I replied. "Are you from Delhi? Can you tell me what's going on?"

"Yes, indeed. I live here. But what you are seeing is not limited to Delhi. People are dancing in the streets in many parts of India. All India Radio has just announced that Mrs. Gandhi's party has swept the election. So, she is once again our Prime Minister."

As the shouting and drumming grew louder, people around us opened a path, and drummers and dancers, all men, stood in front of us. Behind the dancers, other men held placards that read, "Mother India—Mother Indira." The dancers circled Joe and me, their arms above their heads, their fingers snapping, their faces grinning broadly with the invitation to join them. To their delight, Joe imitated their dance movements, and after only a moment's hesitation I followed suit. I raised my arms, let my head fall back, and circled slowly with the other men. The crowd blocked all air circulation, and the moderate heat of the day pressed in, close and throbbing. Though no one touched me, a physical feeling pushed against my chest, the feel of India, the pulse of its people—warm, humid, vibrating. Blood rushed through my body. The drums reverberated in my chest. My eyes saw only a swirl of dancers. The chanting continued. After we circled again, the men smiled and nodded farewell to us, a placard carrier said, "Bye, bye," and all the dancers moved on.

The stranger near the water cart spoke to me again. "I think you will like India. Please enjoy your stay, but be careful. Many Westerners come here seeking something. A few find it, but others get lost. All the best to you." He shook my hand, and disappeared into the crowd.

What a strange thing to say! He must be referring to hippie-types who came to India seeking enlightenment and ended up on drugs. Yes, I was curious about India and Eastern spirituality, but I had not come to India to find something, but rather to give something. I knew what I was here for.

LIGHT OF
WISDOM SEMINARY

THE GATE SWUNG open at Light of Wisdom Seminary, and we stepped out to see our new home. Father John, the Dean, emerged from a cluster of seminarians in front of the modern-looking building and greeted us. A small, stocky man, he wore a short-sleeved shirt, Western pants, and sandals of the plastic-thong variety. Though a few of the seminarians—young men studying to be priests—wore brightly colored wraparounds that reached to their ankles, most of them were dressed like Father John in slacks and shirts. It appeared I would not feel out of place in my American clothing in a large city like Delhi.

After a smiling welcome and offer of tea, Father John led us from the residence to the classroom building, took us to the second floor, pushed open a classroom door and said, "This will be your room, both for sleeping and study. I'm sorry we don't have individual rooms for you in the residence building, but with almost one hundred seminarians, we are filled to capacity."

Before us lay a room with gray concrete walls, four cots in the center, and several small tables and chairs at the far end. The smell of dust and stale air permeated the chilly room. High windows lined one wall, and a layer of grime tempered the light streaming through. No sound of drumming and shouting dancers filtered through the closed windows, no bright flags could be seen nearby. At night, light would be provided by the institutional fluorescent tubes that lined the ceiling. This too was India, I was forced to conclude—colorless and dull.

While I thanked Father John for the accommodations, I couldn't help noting to myself the contrast between the crowded seminaries of India and the empty religious houses in almost every city in America. The recruiting of priests, brothers, and nuns was at an all-time low in the States. Young men just weren't interested anymore, it seemed. What was different in India? I would find out before too long.

"We use English as our house language, so you will be feeling at home immediately," Father John said in a lilting accent. He explained that India had eighteen official languages, and while Hindi was the national language and the language of Delhi, it was really only spoken in northern India. English, therefore, was used all over India as the language of higher education. Before he left, he invited us to join everyone at five o'clock that afternoon for Mass. "Perhaps you wish to take rest before then. I'll send a seminarian over to be sure you are awake in time."

We thanked him, and turned to claim a bed for much-needed rest. Within a few minutes, Joe lay still. Steve and Gerry, with their six-foot frames, tossed for several minutes before falling asleep in the rather small beds. Steve still looked pale, and his shoulder-length golden-brown hair lay carelessly about his face, but at least he had claimed the much-needed sleep.

I was tired, but the steady stream of thoughts that rushed through my mind would not let me sleep. How had I, a Catholic brother from the American Midwest, come to be halfway around the world in a Hindu land?

Perhaps even religious brothers were prone to mid-life crises, for after years of teaching math and being in school administration, I wanted something new. In fact, I was bored and wanted adventure and excitement, even though we brothers were supposed to be satisfied with any job at all. When the call for volunteers for India went out, I was more than ready to jump at the challenge.

The "India Mission" had intrigued me for it was different from any mission we had started in the past. Usually, when the brothers arrived in a new country, they started a school first and then attracted local men to join the order. In India, the situation would be different. It wasn't easy to start a school because the Indian government was reluctant to grant visas, even for humanitarian purposes, to any foreigners who were associated with churches. India might call itself a secular country according to its Constitution, but it was Hindu-dominated and appeared to see all Christians as proselytizers and any spread of "Western" religion as an encroachment on Indian culture.

The Indian government didn't have to worry about us proselytizing, for that was not our intent. Our order—a "teaching" order, not a "missionary" order—had been founded in the nineteenth century with the express purpose of providing education, especially to poor youth. Our plan in India was to recruit from Catholic Indian men, educate them, and train them to be brothers who would then teach the children of the poor, no matter their religious affiliation.

Christianity had flourished in small pockets throughout India for centuries and Catholics alone now numbered in the millions. As far back as the first century, many South Indians—said to have been converted by the Apostle Thomas—had embraced Christianity, and another wave of conversion occurred in the sixteenth century when the Portuguese settled along India's west coast. A third period of conversion, by both Protestants and Catholics, had taken place in the nineteenth century during British rule. For good reason, then, Christians were seen as proselytizers.

The previous year, however, one of our own priests had come to India to develop literacy programs and cottage industries for the poor. His badgering the government for a non-tourist visa finally paid off, and they granted him the coveted stamp. Soon Father Bill had been approached by several young Catholic Indians who wanted to join his order. He temporarily placed four such young men in a rural ashram several hundred miles from Delhi for training with an Indian priest, and requested our order to send more members to continue the young men's education. These four hopeful young Indians represented the beginning of our humble mission. Soon, others would join them. After their own training, they would run schools for the needy, provide technical training for the poor, perhaps administer orphanages—all works legally difficult for the foreign brothers to do. It was a grand and ambitious vision.

The "visa issue," not surprisingly, had plagued me ever since I first accepted the role of religious Superior of the mission. As expected, the Indian government would not issue us resident visas, but a chance meeting with an Indian priest visiting the U.S. provided a glimmer of hope. "Apply for student visas," he suggested. "They are more easily granted." Once we were settled in India for a year or so, he said, we could visit various bishops and ask them to intervene with the government to grant us longer-term visas. Indian bishops often provided social services that officials wished to see continued, and so had some influence with the government. Light of Wisdom Seminary in Delhi, he added, would be a good base for our operations. The student visas, good for one year and renewable for several more, had in fact been issued. And here we were, at Light of Wisdom Seminary.

An hour later, a rap on the door awakened us. A soft-spoken young man, probably in his late twenties, rather thin, but with a ready smile and energetic face, greeted us. "Hello, I'm Santosh. Please come for tea and Mass."

On the way to the other building for tea, Santosh assured us that if we needed any assistance for shopping, or had questions about India, about the seminary, about anything, he would be happy to help us. "Indeed, you must learn some Hindi," he said. "It will help you feel more at home in North India." Santosh offered to teach us basic Hindi for shopping and to find us a good tutor for further study. This man, I could see, would be a gold mine of information and assistance.

Entering the seminary dining room, Santosh advised us that teatime would be a good occasion to catch anybody we wanted to talk to. "A person might miss morning prayers or Mass, but he won't miss tea time, unless he's out on an errand," he confided.

Three large metal teapots sat on a serving table at the far end of the cavernous dining room. Joe sampled the beverage and whispered, "It's got milk and sugar in it! Oh, what I'd give for a good cup of coffee." Seminarians streamed in and out of the room, picking up their tea, and nodding and smiling in our direction. A few stopped to welcome us and introduce themselves. Their names, for the most part, were Christian—Sebastian, Matthew, and Joseph—these I knew I could remember. Other names, like Subash, Raju, Pradeep, and Chacko, would take more getting used to, and I hoped I wouldn't make too many mistakes.

A few seminarians stood chatting around the teapots, while others gathered at small tables that seated four. While Santosh conversed with Gerry and Steve, and Joe searched the room for a coffee pot, I took my tea to one of the tables. The three other men at the table welcomed me in English, then continued their conversation, glancing and smiling in my direction to include me, though they had switched back to Hindi. Suddenly their heads all turned toward me, apparently expecting some response to a question. "I'm sorry, I don't speak Hindi," I apologized. The others stared while the seminarian to my right exclaimed rather loudly, "Vee are not speaking Hindi—vee are speaking English!"

My mouth fell open hoping a gracious reply would come forth, but none did. Santosh rescued me by pulling me away from the table and announcing that it was time for Mass. "You will get used to our English. I suppose it must sound quite strange to your ears," he consoled.

"Quite frankly, yes. Do you have difficulty understanding us Americans?"

"Not at all. Whenever possible, we see American films."

Santosh led us to the chapel door where a sea of sandals faced us. The plastic thongs closest to me had paper-thin soles and the imprint of each toe outlined in accumulated dust. The pair next to it was made of shiny, new leather, but neither pair was fit for the house of God. In India, one entered a place of prayer barefoot. I thought of God telling Moses to take off his shoes in front of the burning bush because he was standing on holy ground. The body clearly needed to acknowledge what the mind and heart accepted.

While I struggled to pull off my own shoes and socks, other seminarians arrived, slid out of their sandals and padded softly into the chapel. I made a mental note to pick up sandals the first chance I had.

The smell of incense floated through the open door, a sweet, heavy, musky scent, not at all like the more subdued scents I was used to. The chapel itself was a large, low-ceilinged room, covered with carpeting, and dotted with small round cushions. The ceiling fans remained immobile, though I imagined they would spin continually during the summer heat that Delhi was famous for. The seminarians sat cross-legged on the floor throughout the chapel, their backs erect, their loose shirts and pants or wrap-arounds— *lungis* Santosh had called them—comfortably draped over their limbs. I found a place next to a side wall I could lean against, and lowered myself slowly to the floor. I noticed that my American companions had also chosen to prop themselves against the wall.

The tuk-tuk of small drums beat a steady rhythm accompanied by nasal organ music from a small harmonium, a squat keyboard instrument resting on the floor and powered by hand-worked bellows. A cantor near the harmonium chanted a flowing melody in Hindi that was repeated by the entire group. Moments later, the priest entered, alone, barefoot, in Western clothing, but wearing a saffron-colored shawl over his shoulders. Seating himself on the floor behind the altar, he greeted us.

"The Lord be with you."

"And also with you," we responded in the customary English phrases of the Mass, a ritual identical in structure throughout the Catholic world. Prayers memorized decades earlier poured out of my mouth in concert with the Indians around me. I felt, however, both at home and a foreigner at the same time. I was accustomed to incense and organ music in church, but not in the way Indians used them. I understood English, but much of that tongue escaped me here. It seemed I had plunged down the hole after the White Rabbit into a realm where the seemingly familiar suddenly made no sense.

India was, on a broad scale as well, a land of confusion and contradictions. It was of the East, yet its people were not considered Oriental. Its people were dark-complexioned, yet Caucasians. Though proud of their ancient culture, Indians had no problem making the customs, language, and architecture of both their Muslim and British rulers their own. The native Indian languages, and even their alphabets, varied from state to state, as did food, music and customs, yet together the regions formed one Republic. Severe internal strife often plagued India, but that was no surprise given its vast differences. The surprise was that it functioned at all as a nation. India was the ultimate hybrid.

What kind of hybrid would I be in a few years' time? I was as far away, physically and culturally, from my previous life as I could be. For almost twenty years I had lived a life circumscribed by teaching mathematics in the brothers' schools in American Midwest cities and living in the brothers' house located on the same property as the school. I was ready for something new, ready to take in India's music, her ancient wonders, her food, her wisdom. I could make it mine, I was sure, quite easily. Of course I couldn't make *all* of it mine. India was primarily a Hindu country and though I had respect for other religions I knew that Catholicism was the True Faith, the most certain path to God. This was the faith of my parents and grandparents and much of the Western world. It was as core to my being as the way I walked, talked, and breathed.

A few more songs in Hindi and English filled the chapel and, before I knew it, the Mass was over, and the seminarians were getting up to leave.

"Come, Jim, come," Santosh leaned down and whispered as he passed. Outside the chapel doors, he grasped my hand and pulled me toward the dining room. "Let us sit together. We have a very nice meal tonight. You will find it refreshing. And again, very good welcome to India. We are all happy you and your brothers are here."

Church Ties

The winter morning chill still hung in the air the next day as I made my way to the Dean's office, and to the surprise that waited there for me. Joe and Steve had left for the bazaar with Santosh, Gerry was writing letters home, and it was my job to make certain that expectations of our stay at the seminary were clear on both sides.

"Please sit down." Father John motioned toward a chair and sat opposite me, a dark brown shawl wrapped over his shirt. We exchanged pleasantries and I gave him more background on the four of us and reiterated our reasons for being in India. I told him quite frankly that we were at the seminary primarily as a way of entering India to fulfill our mission. We already had four novices and we hoped to visit them some time soon.

"In short," I said, "since none of us is studying for the priesthood we aren't really seminarians. But please don't worry, we'll be serious about our classes. We wouldn't think of jeopardizing our visas or the reputation of the school."

"Very good," Father John replied, nodding his head. "But you're not here to convert Hindus are you?"

After I assured him we had no intention of proselytizing, he seemed satisfied and suggested that we sign up only for reading courses after we finished our first semester. That would leave us more time to travel and recruit. We could focus on the seminary's courses on Islam, Hinduism and Buddhism to better understand the religious milieu of India.

"Why, that's perfect for us!" I said. "Four years as a student might be more interesting than I thought."

"Four years?" Father John raised his eyebrows. "In the past, our foreign students have received a maximum of two-years' stay from the government, most often just one year. Better that you count on one. You can pray for two."

Just one year! *Maybe* two. Might we be forced to leave the country in the middle of establishing the project? And if the government could send us packing at the end of just one year, why pour blood and sweat into the work? Suddenly I felt defeated, and we hadn't even begun.

"You must find a bishop to sponsor you and use his connections with the government to allow you to stay. That is a challenging search, so prepare yourself to travel extensively."

I knew all along that enlisting official Church help was necessary, but until now, I didn't realize that it was urgent.

"Let me suggest one thing," Father John said. "When you travel, it will help your cause not to advertise that you are Catholic brothers. Just tell people you are students, which you are. That will be best, and you will not raise so many suspicions. And don't worry if classes prevent you from visiting your novices right away. From what you've told me, they are village boys, just learning the basics of English and the routines of prayer in a religious house. Give them time, yourselves also. Just settle down here in Delhi, get to know India."

As I rose to thank Father John, my mind was nevertheless spinning. I would have to carve time out of weekends, summer recess, and national holidays to travel across India in search of bishops who could help. Father John could supply me with names, Santosh could help me with travel plans, and the seminarians could give me inside information about each diocese.

Father John must have read my thoughts, for as he shook my hand warmly, he added, "Above all, let me give you this advice. Take things slowly. This is India, not America. Please, take things slowly."

I had no experience in dealing with bishops. In the U.S., my Superiors had handled all communication with them, but now I would be forced more directly into the inner workings of the Church. Part of me liked getting closer to the Church's power center, while another part of me felt like a commoner having to approach the royal court. I wasn't even sure how I felt about the "successors of the Apostles," as bishops everywhere were called. While they might be compassionate leaders, at other times they appeared to be mainly official administrators, carrying out company policy.

When I returned to our room, Steve and Joe were unpacking treasures from the bazaar—shawls and sandals for everybody, a bright tablecloth to add color to the room, and a large covered kettle that Joe was certain could serve as a coffee pot. The four beds nestled in the corners of the room, and a table and chairs in the center served as a gathering point while I recounted my conversation with Father John.

"You'll have to go 'hat in hand,' begging to the bishops. A new role for you, Jim," Steve teased.

"I'll do my best, but I won't be kissing any bishops' rings, I can assure you of that," I replied, referring to the old custom still practiced in some church circles.

Each man had his own take on what to do next. Joe offered to travel with me and lay the groundwork for later recruitment trips. Steve was pleased with seminary courses and was eager to study world religions and Indian art, while Gerry—having recently completed seminary training—was less enthusiastic about studies. He wanted to see the novices as soon as possible, for their training was his main purpose.

"This means, of course, another thing," I told the group. "We'll have to be content right now with a daily life that seems quite removed from our goal." Our classes would keep us from seeing the novices right away, and we wouldn't recruit other candidates until we had a more secure status in the country. That left us without much to do, tough medicine for Americans. "We'll have to take things slowly. This is India, not America," I echoed Father John's words but my heart wasn't fully in them.

After a few moments of silence, Gerry brought us back to immediate matters. "What about our daily schedule?" he asked.

Ever since St. Benedict created monasteries in the sixth century, the timetable had governed a religious community's whole life, dividing the day between prayer and work, *ora et labora*, and necessary rest. At least we modern brothers didn't arise at three in the morning to chant Matins, though I was perennially sleepy even at six o'clock morning prayers. At Light of Wisdom Seminary, our meal times and class times were already determined, though we could set our own prayer times. We scheduled the recitation of Psalms and our practice of meditation at the reasonable hour of seven-thirty in the morning, before classes.

"We could have Mass every afternoon in this room, or in the small chapel downstairs, right before dinner," Gerry suggested.

"Oh, not everyday," Steve disagreed. "I want to attend the seminary Mass, learn Hindi songs, and practice their style of music."

Steve was an artist with talents in many arenas—pottery, cooking, music, singing—and I knew he could quickly pick up the basics of Indian music.

"Sounds good to me," I said, "especially since our novices are learning Hindi hymns too."

Joe agreed, though Gerry was less enthusiastic. As a recently ordained priest, Gerry no doubt saw presiding at daily Mass as a major role for himself, and now his own little community wasn't looking to him for that service. He said no more, but I was certain that his face was registering real disappointment.

"How about inviting a few seminarians over in the evenings?" Joe asked, changing the topic and the mood. It would be, he said, a good chance to show our hospitality, play cards, and get to know them better. "And have a beer. On holy days, that is." We all laughed, knowing that neither Joe nor any of us needed the excuse of a holy day for a beer.

The schedule generally sounded good, though one aspect gnawed at me—meditation. I felt I was a failure at it. As instructed, I tried to empty my mind altogether and experience God's presence, but I felt nothing. Other brothers, and especially nuns, would speak in warm terms of their "personal relationship with God," and I would feel like an outsider. That sense of missing something had gone on for years, but I never expressed those concerns to anyone. Who wants to admit to feeling like an imposter?

That evening as Steve turned off the room light, I felt for my bed in the darkness and my hand hit its metal frame with a clang. The sound came from the ring I wore, a simple gold wedding band that signified I had taken Perpetual Vows. Because we wore no distinctive habit, occasionally a stranger in America had assumed I was married. A simple explanation about being a brother usually clarified the situation. In India, the ring might again elicit such questions and explanations. I recalled Father John's admonition not to announce that we were part of the Church, and I wondered if I should wear the ring at all. In the twenty years that I had worn it, the ring had never once come off my finger. The need to be prudent and practical, however, overcame the utter strangeness of having a bare hand for the first time in my adult life.

My suitcase lay under the bed, and I opened it as quietly as possible to place the precious symbol in a side pocket. In that semidarkness, I tugged at my gold band, which was harder to remove than I expected.

January 6, 1980
Delhi, India
Father David
St. Louis, Missouri
U.S.A.

Dear Dave,

We'll definitely have to depend on letters for our communication from now on because international phone calls can't be
made from a private residence. Yesterday, before we were unfortunately disconnected, I was calling from downtown Delhi, a
half-hour bus ride from here.

I'll be visiting the bishop of Delhi, whom you said requested
the brothers to come here some years ago to run an English
school. I don't want us to get stuck running his school for Delhi's
upper classes, but I'm nevertheless hoping he will sponsor us in
some way. The solution to our visa situation may be right here
in Delhi!

Already the bureaucracy here is getting to me. Yesterday
afternoon, I had to first present papers to three different officials before I could pick up an extra piece of luggage at the
airport warehouse. Then the warehouse agent said it hadn't
arrived though I could see it clearly on a rack in the storeroom.
I brushed past him, pointed it out to his assistant, and refused
to pay the "service charge" (that is, bribe) the scowling agent
asked for. I might not be an "old hand" in India, but I expect I
can take care of myself. If I can plough through problems like
this, I think I'll be able to handle anything else India throws at
me.

Because of our daily class schedule, it will be a month or more
before we can travel to meet the novices Father Bill recruited last

year. Meanwhile, we are studying Hindi—Steve and I like it, Joe and Gerry do it solely out of a sense of duty.

Will close for now. I'll write every few months to keep you updated on our progress.

Sincerely,

Jim

Mustaches And Commitment

A WEEK PASSED AND the days quickly formed a routine. The first thing I heard each morning just below our window was the gardener's deep and prolonged coughing. A small, wiry man, he labored all day on the lawns and flowerbeds, making his own bed in a lean-to at the far end of the yard. From his cough, I guessed he had tuberculosis, the major killer of adults in India. I knew tuberculosis was transmittable, and when Steve, who had begun to practice "bazaar Hindi" with the gardener, began coughing, I thought the worst. It turned out to be only a cold, most likely a result of Steve's taking early morning showers in the unheated building.

Steve had seen the gardener eating *pooris*—round, oily, fried wheat bread—and discovered they were available in the food bazaar at Kashmiri Gate, less than a ten-minute walk away. Soon he was supplying us *pooris* for snacks, heating them up on the grill of a space heater found in the bazaar. The space heater had proved inadequate to heat the large room, but had redeemed itself as a toaster.

We spent our mornings in classes, and used the afternoons for exploring the city, often with Santosh. Though a serious student, Santosh was always ready to leave his books and serve as our guide in the back streets of Delhi. He guided us through the labyrinthine Chandni Chowk bazaar, a maze of alleys and lanes where one could find goldsmiths, ivory workers, and silk traders, as well as vendors of ordinary necessities like shawls, sweaters and scarves—useful for winter in Delhi. He broadened our experience of Indian food by introducing us to *masala dosa*, a South Indian crepe made of lentil flour and stuffed with curry-flavored potatoes. He joined us in our room for card games, like *Oh Hell*, grinning broadly when someone else took his desired cards and he got to yell, "Oh, hell!"

Lunches and dinners at the seminary were almost identical—water buffalo stew with potatoes, rice, and a vegetable. Dessert was always a banana. Surprisingly, I looked forward to that same meal every day, though I thought I would quickly tire of it.

One afternoon Santosh said, "Jim, Sister Thelma asked me if you were really a brother." Sister Thelma, a serious and self-composed person, was the lone woman taking classes at the seminary, preparing herself to teach theology to her own nuns. "She says that you look more like a film hero."

"Why on earth did she say that?"

"It's your mustache." Santosh pointed out something I hadn't really noticed. All the seminarians were either clean-shaven or, an occasional few, had full beards. In Indian society, Santosh explained, a mustache was cultivated as a young man "came of age" and wanted to appear attractive to women. Dashing film stars—or film "heroes" as they were called in India—men looking for a wife, and *dacoits*—highway robbers—might sport a mustache, but not brothers or priests. Full beards had been made acceptable by the tradition of wandering holy men whose beards sometimes reached great lengths, a sign of asceticism.

"Are you suggesting I change my appearance?"

"Not at all," Santosh said. "Maybe you'll set a new style here at the seminary. I just thought you'd want to know that about your appearance."

"What about the rest of the Americans? What impressions do they give?"

Gerry was clean-shaven and would fit nicely into any group of priests, Santosh said, though Gerry would always stand out because of his taller stature. Steve, with his long hair and full beard, would look like a holy-card picture of Jesus to Christians, and like a hippie to everyone else. Joe's full beard would blend into Indian society easily, though his fair skin and light brown hair would clearly set him apart as a foreigner.

"With your mustache and dark hair, Jim, you might even be taken for a lighter-skinned North Indian," Santosh concluded.

I couldn't imagine being mistaken for an Indian, but I assumed I would at least be taken as the Superior of our little group by all at the seminary.

"You can't possibly be the Superior of your community," a voice behind me said as I left the dining room one evening. I turned to the speaker. Father Vincent, an opinionated Jesuit, had addressed me in his usual high-pitched voice.

"Says who?" I said as evenly as possible.

"Church law," he responded. "My graduate studies are in Canon Law, and there can't be a layperson, as a brother is, as Superior over priests. We Jesuits never have that."

As if what the Jesuits did was the norm for all others! I had always had a problem with the superior attitude of some Jesuits. As the largest male religious order in the Church, they wielded significant influence and power. And, composed mainly of priests, with brothers historically invited in to cook and care for the house, many Jesuits seemed to look down on the role of the non-ordained brother.

"There's a distinction you've forgotten." I reminded him that Canon Law distinguished between the older religious "orders," such as the Benedictines, Franciscans, and Jesuits, whose regulations had been molded by the rigid feudal systems of their times, and the newer religious "congregations," such as the many teaching congregations, like my own, which had grown out of a more democratic culture in the nineteenth century. The newer groups, though often referred to as "orders" as well, had more flexible rules. A brother could be the Superior even over priests in my religious congregation.

"Well, perhaps," Father Vincent replied, rubbing his chin. "I'll have to check that out."

"Yes, why don't you?" I pointed out to Vincent that our brothers wore ordinary street clothes, and were to make decisions as a group when possible. In our daily living, there was to be no distinction between brothers and priests. In fact we usually referred to ourselves, brothers and priests alike, as "the brothers." And we all took the same vows—poverty, chastity, and obedience—for life.

"But," he continued to object, "once a person is ordained by a bishop, he is a priest forever. That's real commitment."

"Vincent, commitment comes from the heart, not from the oils pressed on your forehead by a bishop," I said, a slight sharpness entering my voice as I walked away. Yes, I did bristle at clerical superiority, a fundamental aspect of the Church in which the Brotherhood, my true heart-felt commitment, nestled.

That Church had been an integral part of my life as long as I could remember. With parents of Polish, French, and Irish background, and two aunts who were nuns, Catholicism was taken for granted in our home on Milwaukee's South Side. Prayers before meals and at bedtime, Sunday Mass, Baptisms, First Holy Communions—all these customs were the infrastructure of the day and, over time, of the years.

My three sisters and I all attended Catholic grade school, a significant bus ride away, even though a public school sat a mere block down the street. In second grade, Sister Juliana chose several of us scrubbed-faced boys to memorize Latin prayers and train as altar boys—a goal my father had considered important though I did not. However, as the shortest boy in the group, I and my usual partner, Bobby, were placed right up front to lead many church processions, and on one occasion, carry the bishop's train when he visited the parish. That task was quite an honor, Sister Juliana informed us, and if we were lucky His Excellency would permit us to kiss his ring. He did, I did, and my father was proud.

As we moved through grade school, we memorized the catechism and learned, in the seventh grade, what seemed to be the most important rule of conduct—no sex outside the sacrament of marriage. Unrepentant failure in this matter meant hell for eternity. Much lecture time, though no discussion, was devoted to that topic. Though in retrospect I sometimes thought my Catholic upbringing a bit stern, it was a familiar structure in which I moved through the world, and it brought me a sense of security and comfort.

In that same year, when I turned twelve, my father went off to work one day and never returned. There had been an explosion at the factory where he worked, and my sisters and I huddled around the radio for hourly updates on his condition, for we were not permitted at the hospital, where my mother sat by his side. Mercifully, the final sad news was announced on the radio only after my mother had spoken to us herself.

Throughout high school, taught by the brothers, I had watched those men of commitment and marveled at their generosity. They seemed genuinely happy with their lives, they were there for me when I needed someone to talk to, and they gave me a glimmer of an idea for my future. And so, at age eighteen, I had knocked on their door and asked to be admitted to their company. Now, twenty years later, I was on the verge of giving that opportunity to young men so far away from my land of birth. To that I was committed.

THE LEMON SELLER

I SAT IN THE last row of Father John's class on Hindu scriptures and took notes studiously. Everything he had explained over the previous three weeks concerning Hinduism had been interesting to me, even the name Hindu. Travelers approaching India from the West had given the name *Hindu* to all the inhabitants living on the other side of the Indus River. Over the centuries, those inhabitants had meshed local gods into a syncretic religion whose pantheon continued to increase with every wave of new arrivals sweeping into India. Father John said that, because of that history, Hindus were more accepting of other people's religious icons than any other group. "You may even see a picture of Jesus next to Krishna's in a Hindu home," he had once stated.

"Today," Father John announced, "we shall begin our study of the Bhagavad Gita, the scriptures that contain the core premises of Hinduism." In the Gita, God in the form of Krishna explains the prime importance of fulfilling one's given role in life, whatever that may be. Krishna addresses the warrior, Arjuna, urging him to fight for just causes since that is his designated function in life. He must, however, be completely detached from the results, the second great lesson of the Bhagavad Gita.

A Hindu's duty, Father John said, meant accepting one's caste and status. Unfortunately, this philosophy led many Hindus to believe they were poor by God's design, and that attitude had restrained the social justice movement in India. Christians, on the other hand, believed in only one lifetime and often tried to improve conditions for humanity.

"It's no surprise," Father John pointed out, "that Mother Teresa is such a strong symbol of Christianity in India—she embodies the Christian characteristics of service to others and a conviction that social conditions can and must be changed. But perhaps we think we have more power to change and control situations than we actually do. And, in changing things, do we always know what is best?"

That afternoon, I walked the short distance to the Kashmiri Gate bazaar for *pooris*, which Steve had asked me to purchase. The arched Gate and high walls, designed at one time to protect the old Moghul city, stood crumbling and in disrepair, with garbage heaped against the walls. But the area itself contained modern shops and open-air markets, rickshaw stands, and taxi drivers. As usual, there was the unending blast of noise and pollution from the many vehicles funneling in and out of the walled city.

Entering the Old City, I walked past the barbers squatting along the wall—their straight edged razors waving at me or settled near a customer's throat—continued beyond the Khyber Restaurant where I had several times enjoyed tandoori chicken, and entered the busy bazaar. The heavy odor of grease used to deep-fry orange, pretzel-shaped dough called *jilaybee* assailed my nose, as did the ever-present sweet incense. Vendors' stalls crowded next to each other, vying for precious space. One counter was laden with pyramids of sweet rice balls sprinkled with coconut shavings. Another counter displayed pans of milk-and-sugar squares next to mounds of shiny dates—both attended by a cloud of flies.

The afternoon warmth drew me to the fruit-sellers' stalls where a rainbow of oranges, lemons, apples, and bananas lined the counter and filled baskets hung on the sides of the stall.

Teenaged boys stuffed oranges into blenders and offered juice chilled with chipped ice. The juice looked refreshing, but wary of the purity of the ice, I bought whole oranges, then found a small portion of curb on which to sit.

My eyes swept the area in front of me, coming to rest on an old man sitting cross-legged on the ground perhaps fifteen feet away. He stared impassively at the eight or ten lemons that lay on a cloth in front of him. No bountiful pile for him, such as the ones at the fruit stalls, just a paltry few lemons to represent his day's wares. He sat so still, his gaze so steady, that I wondered if he were blind. Shoppers milled around him and occasionally glanced at his wares, though no one stopped to buy.

How could he possibly make a living selling those few lemons? His thin body looked nearly starved. He needed customers. I would buy some lemons from him.

I walked over to him, knelt down and asked in Hindi how much the lemons were.

"*Ek rupia, char nimbu,*" he replied quietly. Four for a rupee, about two cents each. I was pleased I had understood him. Santosh's lessons in "bazaar Hindi" were paying off. "Four, please," I told him in Hindi.

In unhurried movements, he picked up four lemons and placed them in a paper bag made from old newspaper. There were only six lemons left now.

"Six more, please," I said, deciding he needed more business. No doubt everybody was going to the larger stalls for their lemons for there they could buy other fruit at the same time.

"Not today," he replied. He held out his hand to receive the one rupee for the lemons and continued to stare in front of himself.

His answer gave me pause. Why on earth didn't he want another sale? No Westerner would turn down a customer that way. I handed him the single rupee and returned to my place on the curb. For another fifteen minutes I watched him. People passed by but no one else bought lemons. Mostly he sat in perfect stillness. Occasionally, he rearranged the remaining lemons—lonely ovals of yellow, shining brightly in the afternoon sun—placing them farther apart. He never glanced in my direction and, after a few more minutes, still confused about his response, I got up and left.

I headed back to the seminary through the Kashmiri Gate, and could not stop thinking about the lemon seller. The old man appeared to practically *want* his condition, not selling many lemons, not making much money, staying poor. He seemed like the Hindu resigned to his habitual status in life and doing his karmic soul work in the state of poverty apparently assigned to him.

The word detachment came to my mind. The brothers' Rule of Life said that we were to do our work, and leave the outcome to God. I knew myself well enough to realize I had not learned the wisdom of detachment. I had worked hard to get to India. I would work even harder to set up the mission, and I did not want to fail.

It was only when I returned to our room that I realized I had four lemons, of little use to me, and no *pooris*.

FORBIDDEN TERRITORY

DUSK AND THE glare of kerosene lanterns blurred the figures that crowded the Old Delhi train station. Wrapped in gray shawls, men and women pushed through the gates and headed toward the platforms as steam-driven trains hissed into the domed shed. Where were the diesel trains and bright electric lights like those at the New Delhi station? New Delhi station, home to the fastest, long-range overnight trains, had looked relatively modern when I had recently accompanied Santosh there to greet a seminary guest. At the Old Delhi station, however, I almost expected to see saber-wielding British soldiers keeping the trains of the empire running on time. Passenger lists were posted in Hindi only, a sure sign that few government officials and fewer businessmen frequented the station. Old Delhi station served primarily local trains and narrow-gauge trains going, as Steve and I were, shorter distances to the north. We were headed to the hinterlands, not to a city like Bombay.

A national holiday had provided a three-day weekend and Steve, who had been in a small study-group on Buddhism at the seminary, suggested we visit Dharamsala, the home in India of the Dalai Lama. Though Gerry and Joe opted to stay in Delhi, I jumped at the opportunity to get my first view of the Himalayas and to, hopefully, encounter one of Asia's holy men.

The overnight train, crowded with men perched like vultures on overhead luggage racks and women squatting on the floor cradling babies, passed through the fertile Punjab. By morning it had reached the base of the Himalayas. Light shone into the compartment and Steve pulled himself upright. "My bones ache from this wooden bench," he said. "I think I've got a bruise on my hip."

"This is a spiritual journey, a pilgrimage. Offer it up," I said, quoting the traditional Catholic advice given to help someone bear his hardships. One could "offer up" his suffering to God to help cleanse himself of past sins.

Steve replied, "Who should I offer it up to? There's no God in Buddhism."

No God at all. It sounded cold. To whom did one pray? Although I had felt little success in establishing a personal relationship with God through prayer, belief in a paternal God comforted me and made me feel cared for. I believed in Him and his watchful presence. I believed I was following His will when, as far back as high school, I had this inner sense that "God wants me to join the Brotherhood." I knew that in doing so, I would be "doing something for other people." It was from that that I derived meaning. The fact that I didn't have a strong heart connection to God never bothered me because my sense of purpose was so resolute. I was not made for hours of meditation in a monastery. I was a man of action.

The train deposited us in a sleepy town in the plains, from which a connecting bus ascended the winding mountain road, carrying us to Dharamsala at 4000 feet. After a hike upward another 1000 feet, we checked in at the Green Guest House, recommended by the guidebook. Hanging on the edge of a cliff, the budget hotel supposedly afforded spectacular views of the Himalayas, but the morning mist allowed only a glimpse of immense, gray, pyramid shapes that loomed a few miles away.

While Steve wandered off to hike the mountain paths, I headed toward the Buddhist monasteries. Descending the path again, past low vegetation and an occasional hut, I came upon a collection of temples, all of them flying Tibetan prayer flags. The tiny white flags, perhaps eight or ten of them attached to long poles atop the buildings, fluttered in the breeze, sending heavenward the prayers written on them. I liked the idea of the wind carrying messages to heaven. We Catholics sent ours through fire as we lit vigil candles whose flames somehow beseeched heaven even after we had left the church.

A rumbling sound emanated from the first building, a dark, wooden structure with a golden dome, surrounded by a small crowd. From my position on the road, higher than the onlookers, I could see a dozen or more monks clad in purple and yellow robes, squatting on the floor of the open-air temple. The low, guttural sound, almost like gargling, came from the monks— Tibetan chanting. Having heard of Tibetan chanting before and thinking of Gregorian chant, I had expected a melodic sound. It wasn't melodious, but it was hypnotic in its repetition and sounded more earthy than the crystalline, high-pitched tones of Gregorian chant. After a few minutes, the monks' incantations had lulled me into a peaceful state of mind.

The other observers stood quietly at the edge of the temple, straining to see inside. I followed their gaze and saw a small boy weaving through rows of monks with a large teapot. He replenished the small cups in front of each monk, then moved farther and farther back into the temple. Finally, he stood before a raised platform draped in gold brocade—and bowed. Upon the platform sat the 14th Dalai Lama.

In a cross-legged position, his body quite motionless, the Dalai Lama did not chant with the others, and his eyes seemed to look far into the distance. I thought I saw a slight smile on his face, but the darkness of the temple prevented certainty on that point. During a pause in the chanting, the Dalai Lama brought his eyes into focus, swept his gaze over the monks, and looked toward us in the crowd. He smiled gently, and seemed to nod at each person individually. Far from acting like the near-god that some said he was, he appeared to show as much interest in us as we did in him. I wondered what he was really like.

The wind picked up suddenly, loudly flapping the overhead prayer flags, and I looked upward. Behind the temple's golden roof, the snowy peaks had emerged from behind the clouds. Row upon row of massive, white-clad peaks loomed surprisingly close by, dwarfing any man-made structure in the foreground, and guarding the unseen plateau beyond—Tibet. It was easy to see why Tibet had been inaccessible for so many centuries. Only the bravest or most desperate would have attempted to breach that snowy barrier. And for centuries Tibet was not only highly inaccessible, but expressly forbidden to Westerners. In the past, stepping across that border could mean torture and death if one were found out, yet, any number of Westerners—usually disguised as local pilgrims—had taken on that perilous journey.

For some reason, that which is "forbidden" has a seductive pull on many of us, like the apple in the Garden. What was forbidden for me? My vows proscribed personal wealth, a sexual life, and making all my own decisions. That I knew, but I had accepted it all for the support and companionship I had found in the Brotherhood. Something, however, about standing in front of the biggest barrier in the world, the Himalayas, and knowing that there was a land and people on the other side who didn't believe what I took to be fundamental—that there is a personal God and He created the world—made me see that, above all else, not believing in God was *the* forbidden fruit.

I simply took for granted the belief in God. Even before I could recite prayers, every trip to church and every religious picture in my childhood home assured me of His existence. I also knew that if you believed in God, and in Jesus His only Son, you were *virtuous*. "Blessed is he who has not seen but believed."

If you did not believe, you were an atheist or a pagan—words almost synonymous with depravity. Only an immensely egocentric person would not accept what the elders of the Church pronounced to be true.

And I *wanted* to believe it all. It gave me great comfort. Yet the people of Tibet and Buddhists everywhere lived beautiful lives without those beliefs. Just how certain *was* I about my beliefs? For a second, the fear of falling into the abyss of doubting my most fundamental creeds was truly frightening. Without a God, there's no safety net, there's no caring father to look out for you. There is nothing.

It was too strange, too foreign a place. I couldn't go there.

The chill of late afternoon had rolled down the mountain. I stuffed my hands into my pockets and left the chanting monks behind.

Early the next morning, Steve and I lined up with Buddhists and other pilgrims in front of the Dalai Lama's residence to be received by him. Vendors walked up and down the queue hawking the traditional white scarves that one customarily presented to the Dalai Lama. Not certain of its significance, we nevertheless purchased scarves.

"We'll just watch what everyone else does with these scarves, Jim," Steve said. "Here, you go in front of me."

Large, double doors opened into the compound of the residence, and tall Tibetan guards respectfully searched us as we entered. The Dalai Lama stood in the courtyard in front of a ceremonial platform, receiving everyone at close quarters. Each visitor presented the scarf draped over his palms. The Dalai Lama received it with both hands and a nod. The visitor then touched the feet of the Dalai Lama, and moved on.

It would be simple to present the scarf, but I was not comfortable with the second part. Touching someone's feet seemed like subservience, perhaps appropriate for a Buddhist in this case, but I was a Christian. Yet I didn't want to be disrespectful. I was standing in front of Steve, and all those before me had been Tibetans or Indians and the gesture was commonplace to them. But not to me. I was next.

I held the scarf in both hands, momentarily had eye contact with the Dalai Lama, then bowed my head as I offered up the gift. He received the scarf, quickly handed it to his attendant, and before any moment of awkwardness could lapse, gave me a firm handshake. "I am pleased you have come. May peace be in your soul," he said in English.

"Thank you," I mumbled back, my words slightly choked by the gratitude I felt toward the great man who had adapted to *my* ways. I bowed again, and moved on.

The sun was now gaining strength and warming the long line of pilgrims who waited patiently. I walked past the faithful and looked at them more carefully now. Each person seemed prayerful, focused on living out the customs of his religious tradition. I was filled with a sense of awe that, despite our different belief systems, we were all striving to do our soul work. I was on holy ground.

Farther away, over Tibet, clouds had once again formed, blotting out the sun and obscuring those snowy peaks.

26 February 1980

Dear Dave,

The four of us went, with high hopes, to see the Archbishop of Delhi last week.

Neither the hard wooden chairs in his reception room nor his demeanor were very welcoming. A tall, lanky man, he looked down through his glasses and reminded us that he had requested our brothers to come to his diocese several years ago, but we hadn't sent anyone. "You missed the train, and now you're trying to catch the bus, heh, heh," he said, waving his hands in the air, almost in dismissal of us. I'm afraid I disliked him immediately.

We spent the rest of the visit in small talk, and it was clear we would get no help from that quarter. Father John at the seminary said that the Archbishop may be under special scrutiny right here in the country's capital, and is cautious about sponsoring foreigners. Other bishops may be freer to act. I'm sure he was right, but I thought the archbishop would have given us more encouragement. He seemed less like a church leader and more like a politician securing his place at the table.

Bill came in from his village work last week to talk about the four candidates he recruited. He says he's pleased that we are taking full charge of their training, thus freeing him to organize economic and health programs in the villages. However, in the same breath, he tried to tell us exactly how we should run things. He wants us to create a very simple community, live in mud huts, be vegetarians. He even suggested that we accept illiterate candidates. I asked him if he could do the work he's doing if *he* were illiterate. He didn't like that. The conversation made me wonder what kind of candidates he has recruited. I'll soon find out.

We live on the north side of Delhi in a tree-lined area called Civil Lines, the section of Delhi used by the British administration before New Delhi was constructed. It's really a pleasant area, much more attractive than the newest residential sections of modern Delhi, where concrete high-rise apartments crowd each other on dusty streets.

After morning classes, we spend an hour in the afternoon with a Hindi tutor. The rest of our time, I don't know where it goes. Everything takes longer here. To buy a train ticket you wait for overcrowded buses to get to the station, wait in a long line at the ticket window, pray that tickets are available for the date you want, and pray again for patience when the agent closes his window to leave for tea. Santosh, a seminarian, looks at my frustrated face and says, "Oh, Jim, you're so American." Well, I *am* American.

Tomorrow, the beginning of our semester break, is the day I've been waiting for—Gerry and I leave to visit the four novices Bill recruited. I'm excited to meet them. At the ashram, Father Sevanand is teaching the novices Scripture studies, meditation, and basic English. As an Indian himself, he understands the novices' mentality better than we could, so I know they are in good hands.

Sincerely,

Jim

THEY WILL BE
MY BROTHERS

THE LATE AFTERNOON train sped southeast from Delhi across the vast Gangetic plain carrying Gerry and me to the ashram where the four novices lived. I was eager to meet the young men who had agreed to join an organization they had little acquaintance with. Earlier, Santosh had informed me of one reason why seminaries in India were packed—village boys were ready and happy to escape a dead-end future in rural India. They wanted an education, proficiency in English, and a chance to rise above a seemingly preordained low station in life. That didn't mean, Santosh had assured me, that they weren't genuinely good young men. "We join for certain reasons, but stay for others," he had reminded me.

Armed with a page of Hindi phrases and a map from Santosh, Gerry and I alighted the next morning at a small station in Bihar, India's poorest state.

"Santosh said we'd take a bus from here, but I don't see any buses at all," Gerry said, scanning the area and pulling his jacket closer to himself in the chilly morning air.

I practiced my Hindi with several people milling around an old jeep, only to find out that that vehicle was our "bus," and we were off down a dusty road.

The jeep bounced past tea stalls and vegetable markets, past villages of mud huts rising like brown islands on the flat terrain, and past the ever-present field workers that are part of rural India. A few men, bent low, pulled winter harvest from the rice paddies, and women behind them carried bundles of firewood on their heads. Despite the rough ride, I relaxed and let myself sink into the slower pace of the countryside.

Finally, the jeep driver turned to shout something at me as we slowed to a stop. I didn't completely understand his words, but he pointed to a side dirt road and said "Gobadda," the name of a village I knew was close to the ashram.

We set out on foot and soon caught sight of a low brick building, the first sign of the ashram. In only a few moments I would meet the young men who wanted to become brothers. Suddenly I was anxious. These four young men were the rock our mission would be built on. Were they solid enough? Did they have what it took to be leaders and teachers? The quality of this first group of Indian brothers was crucial. I also worried how we American brothers would measure up. I had never been part of a project that depended on so few people for its success. Were we up to the task? I used to feel confident I was—now I wasn't so sure.

"Namaste, welcome," said a thin man of moderate height, wearing black plastic-rimmed glasses, who had come to the gate. "I'm Father Sevanand. You must be the brothers. You are most welcome." After Gerry and I introduced ourselves, Father Sevanand, the local priest training the novices in Bible studies, offered us a seat under a shady arbor and said he would bring the novices to us. I was too excited to sit down and murmured something about not upsetting the day's schedule.

"Schedule?" Father Sevanand replied. "Please, don't worry. Nothing is more important than welcoming travelers from afar. Even prayer can wait when Christ comes to us in this manner."

He returned a moment later with four young men and introduced them as Johnny, Benedict, Juel, and Barto. Each young man made the gesture of namaste and smiled, but said nothing. My first impression was that two of them were too young to have left home, one appeared thin and sickly, and the fourth man's rough features and serious demeanor made him look like a highway robber. I knew I had a tendency to be overly critical, so I tried to pull back from my snap judgments—but I felt uneasy.

"Now, please sit and let us have tea together," Father Sevanand offered, waving us to benches under the arbor. I sat down and leaned back, letting leafy vines brush against my head, and accepted the milky tea. Father Sevanand asked about our trip, and, while Gerry recounted the details, I took a closer look at the novices.

The novices all wore the loose, waist-to-ankle wraparounds called *lungis*, thong sandals, and short-sleeved shirts. The two youngest, Benedict and Johnny, listened intently, though I could not tell how much they understood. When Gerry looked their way to include them, they cast their eyes downward, probably a cultural habit. I knew that young Indians were taught it was impolite to look directly at their elders.

Benedict had collar-length wavy hair, a tendency to lean away from the group, and at nineteen seemed rather unsure of himself. Johnny was also shy, though in the few seconds of eye contact he permitted, he smiled broadly. His movements were slow and graceful, no doubt a natural consequence of living his twenty years in a quiet village. Barto, though slight of build, had alert eyes that followed the conversation. At thirty-two, he appeared self-assured, his gaze direct. Juel, also thirty-two, was the most difficult to read. His squared-off face and intense eyes reminded me of a ritual mask—purposeful, yet set in a fixed mode. They all were polite, attentive, and sincere—all important qualities. For the moment, I contented myself with the belief that that was enough to start with. The only thing I could do was practice Christian patience, and wait and see.

The novices were North Indians but "tribals," so their features were darker and more rounded than the North Indians of Aryan heritage. The tribals, early indigenous peoples, had been pushed into the forests and remote hill areas with the arrival of Aryan clans from central Asia around 1700 B.C. The tribals had not intermarried with the Hindu majority—who had considered them "casteless"—and had maintained their tribal culture. Their native religion was animism, a rich nature-religion replete with sacred groves and woodland spirits.

In the nineteenth century, European missionaries had found fertile fields for conversion in the tribal areas. The tribal emphasis on communal living and its lack of a caste system meshed well with the group worship and service to others emphasized in Christianity, and many tribals had left animism behind to become Christians. The missionaries had also provided the tribals with education, often denied them by mainstream Hindu society, further cementing the tribals' allegiance to the Church. Over the decades, many tribals had joined religious orders and were considered to have "solid" vocations. I had been told to plan on recruiting more such young men.

After tea, Barto showed us where we would sleep for the next three nights—on string cots at one end of the brick building—then gave us a tour of the ashram property. His crisp English, which flowed effortlessly, told me that he would be the main spokesman for the novices. During the tour, Johnny and Benedict were generally silent, though Juel finally spoke up. "Now we are going to the well. You need to know where to take bath."

An open well, perhaps fifteen feet in diameter, was located at the edge of the property. Some twenty feet down, a pool of dark water supported moss and other green vegetation. Frogs croaked, their echoes convincing me they were legion. Barto explained that the water would be boiled before drinking, and one could take a morning bath by hauling up a single bucketful. "You then use these small plastic cups to pour it over yourself. It is no problem to take a bath outside. Do you need *lungis*?"

I had seen men on the streets of Delhi pouring water over themselves from sidewalk pumps, washing their bodies through their *lungis*, but neither Gerry nor I possessed one.

"Yes, we need *lungis*," Gerry said.

Johnny spoke slowly and deliberately. "Please, you are coming to the bazaar."

"Okay," Gerry said. "Do you mean now?"

"No, later," he replied.

Gerry glanced at me, and I knew we thought the same thing: conversation was going to be slower and more labored than we had expected. I might be forced, against my nature, to follow Father John's advice of "taking things slowly" after all.

After lunch Johnny, with Ben standing quietly at his side, announced, "The bazaar now please. They have *lungis*."

Villagers and water buffalo passed us on the road. All nodded to us, even the buffalo, so it seemed. Low hills covered with scrubby trees rose in the distance, and from that direction a slight breeze descended to cool us. Rural India definitely had its charm. The people were less hurried. There were no noisy taxis, and the cleaner air almost tasted sweet. A palm tree thrust its branches above a nearby village, cows bent over a nearly dry stream, and two small boys rolled a rusty hoop down the road.

We walked in silence for a while, then a few chickens ran across our path prompting me to ask Johnny what the Hindi word for chicken was.

"*Murghi*," he replied.

"I should learn more Hindi words. What about dog, and cow?"

Just then a cow looked up from its grazing and bellowed at us. I said "moo" right back to her. I often liked to bark back at dogs and respond to animals in kind—let them know I wasn't afraid.

"Moo?" Johnny repeated, a little confused.

"That's the sound a cow makes... right?"

"Not Indian cows. Our cows do this." Johnny took a deep breath and exhaled a nasal "uuhhh."

"What about ducks? They say 'quack, quack,' right?"

"Quake, quake?" Benedict chimed in. "I know what is a duck. It makes this sound, 'aaach, aaach.'"

Gerry agreed with me—ducks definitely went "quack, quack," not "aaach, aaach." Soon we were all laughing and comparing the sounds of "English-speaking" animals and "Hindi-speaking" animals.

"'Old MacDonald' is a song I'll teach you about this man and the animals on his farm. We'll use the English sounds for now. Here we go," I said.

I led the song, and with Gerry's help, the novices were soon singing the refrain to "Old MacDonald Had a Farm." The surrounding fields provided chickens and ducks and cows who paraded in front of us practically on cue, and to which I pointed as I gave an animal sound. The boys learned quickly and soon the four of us were walking down the road singing, "...a moo-moo here and a moo-moo there, a chick-chick here and a chick-chick there." A worker in a field a short distance away lifted his head but seemed unsurprised. Even while walking alone, Indians often sang out loud.

"Thank you, Brother Jim. Very nice song," Benedict said when we ended the song.

"You're welcome. And you both sang very well!"

That evening, the sun had already set over the low hills when Juel rang a bell that called us to the chapel for evening prayers.

The mud structure had a low altar with a wooden crucifix, a candle and a flower. The beauty of the room was its simplicity, and the simplicity was an unspoken invitation to go inward, toward prayer.

After fifteen minutes of silence, Father Sevanand explained that evening prayer time at the ashram was fairly informal and invited each person to share whatever he wished.

More silence. Then, one by one, the novices all spoke in Hindi. I caught words like "bazaar" and "*lungi*" and then, quite incongruously, "chick-chick here" and "moo moo there." The smiles on Ben and Johnny's faces were a delightful reward.

As I sat listening to everyone speak, it hit me even harder— this group was the foundation of our future. They trusted us, and they had faith. And they had already begun to endear themselves to me. I always had a strong commitment to the India mission, but now it was more personal. These men had put a face on it. And I was content, for the moment.

10 March 1980

Dear Dave,

Finding a way to stay in India long-term appears to be a real challenge. After a satisfying visit with the novices, Gerry and I paid a visit to the bishop of Jamshedpur, thinking that he might sponsor us. I like him. He's outgoing and friendly, but I fear he has more enthusiasm than practicality. He said he wanted us there, but was vague about convincing the government to issue us resident visas. Unlike the Archbishop of Delhi, this man *wanted* us, but it still appeared there was nothing he could do. I don't want to admit this, but I'm starting to feel discouraged.

Jamshedpur is a unique Indian city, owned almost completely by a large steel works and a coal mining company, and is located in the center of the eastern tribal area. Cheap coal is readily available to everyone and, as night falls, you can smell the smoke of a thousand fires cooking the evening meal. You can also see it. The cool evening air keeps the smoke low, and it spreads across the land like wispy fingers of death. I heard a lot of coughing. Jamshedpur, I'm afraid, doesn't hold much promise for us. Besides, I didn't come to India to get black lung.

At one train station on the trip, I was purchasing tickets at a window facing the outside platform, when something caught my attention. A swarm of large black flies were circling an object on the ground, just off the edge of the platform. I looked down and saw a headless body. The hands had also been severed and, along with the head, lay in the blood-splattered folds of the man's *lungi*, between his knees. Blood matted the hair, and the eyes were open. The man in line behind me said that he wasn't sure what had happened, but the body would stay there until nightfall when, in the dark, a certain caste would collect the corpse.

Dave, India is as harsh and callous as it is spiritual and intriguing. This country is not just snow-capped mountains in the north, palm trees in the south, and people everywhere seeking a spiritual path. India is also severe weather, terrible poverty, and violent death. I don't know how that accident happened, and it's hard to get the sight out of my mind. It may be what has upset me the most so far—certainly the accident itself, but also the cavalier attitude toward the life and body of that man.

Overall, however, I'm fine but I want to organize India, learn everything at once, and get things done, on time!

Did you know that October 2, our own Foundation Day, is a national holiday here? It's Gandhi's birthday. I'm sure the coincidence is a good sign.

Sincerely,

Jim

MONKEY BUSINESS

DRY, DUSTY APRIL blew into Delhi. Father John advised us to keep our windows closed so the concrete building could retain some of its coolness, and dust from the Gangetic Plain would temporarily be kept at bay. The seminarians told us to be prepared for noonday heat in excess of one hundred fifteen degrees within weeks.

Fortunately, by mid-April the seminary started its summer break, and I prepared to travel with Joe and Santosh to South India, where the weather was more temperate, and where I could visit bishops who might have influence with the government. Santosh was headed south to visit his family, and it felt good to be in the company of someone who knew the area.

Steve volunteered to brave the Delhi heat and move our meager belongings to the new apartment we had found, and furnish that two-floor residence. Gerry would serve as chaplain for a convent in the Himalayas during April, and would find a house in the hills where we could all rendezvous later during the worst of the Hot Season. With specific assignments for each of us and no classes to attend, our spirits were high as we ended the school year.

On the first day of the trip to South India, I gazed out the train window, watched the barren Deccan plateau pass by—a plain with desert-like open spaces, interspersed with sandy red arroyos and occasional towns—and recalled what I knew of my destination. South India was practically another country, a land of palm trees, softer climate and slower-paced living. Also, in certain areas, Christians constituted twenty-five percent of the population, ten times higher than the national average. These South Indians claimed a two thousand-year-old tradition of Christianity, and provided the Church with the majority of its priests, brothers, and nuns. Most of these religious orders had houses in Bangalore, a pleasant city that would be the first stop for Joe, Santosh, and myself.

At three thousand feet, Bangalore had a moderate climate and was called the "Garden City" of India for its greenery, and also called the "Rome of India" because of the presence of so many Catholic institutions—schools, hospitals, training centers for religious personnel. I looked forward to visiting Bangalore because one day we brothers would surely want to have our own house in that Catholic center.

The train lacked air-conditioning, and with all its windows thrown open, I soon began to mop my soot-covered forehead. Overall, however, I felt good. Away from a rich American diet for several months, I had lost a few pounds and was more energetic than ever. The trip to the South would help move the mission forward, and I enjoyed seeing new parts of the country. In general, India seemed to be agreeing with me.

That night I slept soundly, and didn't stir until the train came to a long, full stop. When I looked up the early morning sun had filled our compartment, though Joe and Santosh still slept. A conductor informed me that we had a two-hour layover, and that Bangalore lay yet another four hours to the south. With time on my hands, I decided to venture out to the main platform, several train tracks away, and find fresh fruit. On the way out, I passed other passengers in various stages of early morning activities. A Sikh man, his turban removed and his hair flowing well past his waist, ran a comb through his locks. An elderly gentleman in a loose-fitting long shirt sat cross-legged on his berth, eyes closed, meditating. Two college-age boys still slept, entwined on the narrow berth made for one person, one snoring into the other's ear.

The morning breeze was mild, and palms trees, some with monkeys scampering up their slopes, dotted the station area. We had definitely arrived in South India. A covered bridge crossed the tracks and provided access to the main platform, where I discovered bananas, small hard oranges, and coconut slices covered in dust. The bananas looked the most appealing, so I chose several bunches and headed back toward the bridge.

On the tracks, workers waved energetically at me as I passed. Most were red-turbaned coolies, making their way across the tracks with suitcases balanced on their heads. Though I didn't understand the words they shouted, their gestures indicated I should cross the tracks rather than take the bridge to return to my train. The tracks seemed like a dangerous shortcut. Indians did things like that, even when it was risky. No doubt the headless man I had seen several weeks earlier had crossed the tracks recklessly and paid for it with his life. No, I would take the long way on the bridge.

In front of me, not another soul was in sight. Only thin shafts of light streamed through the wooden slats of the bridge covering, so I was halfway across before I saw them—three monkeys standing abreast of each other, blocking my way. *O my God. Monkeys should be in trees, not here.* My heart thumped, but I reminded myself of the old saying about never showing fear to an animal. I would just breathe deeply and walk past them calmly, imagining they weren't there.

My bravado seemed to work. The monkeys let me pass, my arms laden with bananas. I had almost gained the end of the bridge when two of them screeched, startling me. One monkey screamed again, closer to me. Suddenly I felt a sharp slicing on the back of my right leg, and I dropped the bananas. While the monkeys scrambled for the fruit, I stumbled toward the stairs. Although I had little pain, I felt a sticky warm fluid running down my leg.

The next few minutes were hazy, but somehow Joe, Santosh, and the stationmaster appeared at my side. As I leaned, light-headed, against a pillar, the stationmaster tried to examine the wound, but my blood-soaked jeans prevented him from seeing the laceration. Within a few minutes, a large circle of Indians had surrounded me, pushing, peering, and pointing toward the bridge. The stationmaster decided to send me to the railway clinic a few blocks away with a young man to escort me. Since the area was Santosh's home state and he knew the language, he chose to accompany me while Joe remained with the train and our luggage.

I still felt dizzy and weak, but, supported by Santosh and the young man, I limped to the clinic. Two nurses greeted us at the door and told Santosh the doctor would arrive in another half-hour.

"Not to worry," Santosh tried to reassure me. "Our train does not leave for another hour and a half. Now, the nurses say you must remove your jeans, so they can clean the wound before the doctor comes."

I did as he asked and lay on the table. A moment later when Santosh got a good view of the gash, I heard him mutter, "The blood...the..." He crumpled to the floor in a faint, his eyes rolling back in his head. When he came to, the nurses helped him into the next room, then returned to finish swabbing my injury and to ask me questions in a language I did not understand.

The doctor arrived shortly, and I was relieved to find that he spoke English. "Everything will be fine. I shall clean this wound thoroughly, give you a tetanus shot, and sew you up. I am quite good at this. You are the sixteenth person this month who has been bitten by the monkeys in the station."

"Why don't you get rid of the monkeys?" I asked.

"Mr. James! The monkeys are sacred! There would be a riot if we tried to remove them." Later on, we brothers were to coin the phrase: In India, all forms of life are sacred, except human forms.

With my leg sewn up and Santosh revived, we made our way back to the station and toward our train—across the tracks this time. I was well aware now of the searing pain in my leg, but I wasn't aware yet of the consequences of treating an animal bite in a Third World medical system. As we approached the train, its whistle blew and the train began to pull away.

"Hurry, Jim! You can make it—I'm sure of it," Joe said, hanging out from the train door and offering me a hand. With a push from Santosh, I crawled onto the steps of the slow-moving train and, once again, we were on our way.

At St. Joseph's School in Bangalore, a priest answered the door and apologized that our rooms were not ready. One of the priests had died that morning and they were busy making funeral arrangements. "What a pity," he added. "Father was only thirty-eight years old. And he died from tetanus that he contracted while in the hospital."

Thirty-eight—my own age. Much too young to die, and from a hospital mistake! My mind rampaged. *What kind of mistake did that hospital make? How sterile were those needles at the railway clinic?* In an instant, India lost its allure. Rabid monkeys that attacked train passengers, germ-laden hospitals, dying young—it seemed like a bad dream. I wanted to wake up from the nightmare and find myself back in sterile America with wonder drugs that cured any ailment. Had I been given the tetanus shot in time? And what about rabies? The doctor at the clinic hadn't even mentioned that possibility.

The next day, a fever raged through my body. It broke by evening only to return the following morning. An elderly brother who cared for the sick in the house stopped by my room to console me. "Brother, today is Good Friday and, yes, you are suffering like Jesus. But, like him, you will rise from your illness on Easter Sunday if you have faith. Just pray."

The liturgical calendar was the furthest thing from my mind. Waves of fear, desperation and helplessness flooded over me, leaving me weak and incapable of thinking clearly. "Joe, I'm frightened," I admitted. "I know this is serious."

"And the infirmarian told you to just pray?" Joe raised his eyebrows. "Fine, pray. Meanwhile, you're going to the hospital."

———

"YOUR WOUND HAS become seriously infected. This is why you have a fever." The emergency room doctor stood over me and explained the situation bluntly. "I shall admit you immediately and begin a course of antibiotics. We don't want you to lose your leg."

Lose my leg? My heart pounded painfully in my chest. Was the infection that bad? Had gangrene set in? *I could die!* I looked at the doctor and lone nurse that attended him. If the infection was serious, shouldn't there be a whole *team* of physicians and nurses hovering nearby holding trays of bandages and clamps and antibiotics and narcotics? Where *was* everybody?

For the next several days I lay restlessly in my bed at St. John's, a teaching hospital reputed to be the best in town. In the mornings, a doctor led a group of interns on their daily rounds, discussing each patient's condition. The training was conducted in English, and since most patients didn't understand that language, doctors and interns felt free to make candid remarks in front of the patient. Each morning I was the nine o'clock lesson.

"I want everybody to touch the red area near Mr. James's wound," Dr. Gopal said to his interns. "You see how hard the tissue is? That means that the antibiotics are not working. Perhaps we shall try some other sulfa drug."

Perhaps? He's saying it *might* be a good idea to try something else?

The interns poked, without protective gloves, on the back of my thigh.

"Excuse me," I said, turning to look directly at Dr. Gopal. "From now on, I want to be informed personally about my progress. And I want to know your plan for treatment of possible rabies. Nobody has mentioned that yet."

"Rabies?" Dr. Gopal glanced toward me, surprised that a patient should have questions. "I doubt that will be a problem. We are not certain the monkey bit you. The wound may be from his claw." He turned away. "Now students, continue the rounds on your own and leave your reports in my office. Good day."

Three interns remained behind and plied me with questions, but not about my well-being.

"Is it true that doctors are the richest people in America?"

"Do you know a hospital that is needing more doctors?"

"I hear that only wealthy people can obtain hospital care in the United States. Is it correct?"

I responded to their questions in short sentences, trying not to tire myself out any more than the fever already had. My leg had begun throbbing again with an added feeling of sharp pain. I was convinced the monkey had left several teeth in my leg. And my anxiety was rising—I could not stop thinking about rabies.

"If you don't mind," said a young intern named Sanjay, "I shall return to speak with you this afternoon. We are completely bored because there is hardly anybody in the hospital." Sanjay explained why. The movie *Coma* had come to town two weeks earlier, and people were staying out of the hospital for fear that their organs might be stolen.

As promised, Sanjay returned later and sat on the edge of my bed to chat. "So very nice, you are having a private room. Most people do not."

A nun at the hospital named Sister Visitation had given me a private room after misunderstanding that I was willing to share one. Now, I was grateful for the mistake. In India, a shared room meant you gained not only a roommate but that person's extended family as well. In the rooms on either side of me, visitors came and went constantly, and one or two family members slept on the floor at night. A family member also cooked the patient's meals on the small balcony off each room. I was one of the few who ate hospital food. All through the day, juicy, greasy food smells mixed with the scent of rubbing alcohol floated through the halls. The banging of cooking pots filtered into my room and chatter continued late into the evening. I frequently blessed Sister Visitation for the partial insulation of my private room.

I had to ask Sanjay what had been on my mind since that morning. "Tell me, is rabies of concern in my case? What would happen if I had rabies?"

Sanjay described how a person died from rabies. "First," he said, "you are so thirsty you would vow your life to Shiva for a glass of water. But do you think you can drink, Mr. James? Not a single drop. The water, you choke on it instead. You will drown from it."

I silently tried to swallow.

"It attacks your nervous system so you cannot breathe. Sometimes you will twitch. Sometimes you will be paralyzed, and you will be having white foam at the corners of your mouth and begging for water. And that will be the end."

I was speechless, and did not even say good-bye to Sanjay as he left the room. It was the first time in my life I was convinced

I was going to die. The blood left my head and I thought I would pass out.

Fearing the worst, and wondering if every sip of water I took went down smoothly, I tossed in my bed. The evening wore on, though sleep would not come to me. Sanjay's words stalked me like a night predator. Even after the talking had ceased in the nearby rooms, I lay awake, listening to the fan drone overhead and watching black ants trail across the nightstand. The antibiotics were not working, the doctors were cavalier about rabies, insects infested my room. If only I could wake from this nightmare! A medical situation that would be handled in a forthright manner in America was taking on frightening overtones here. I should never have come to India. No project, no mission, was worth my life. I was not martyr material.

It was dawn before I fell asleep, exhausted from fear and frustration. Sister Visitation, who supervised my floor, had to call my name several times to awaken me for my breakfast tray. Seeing the distress on my face, she asked if I wanted to see the intern on duty. He heard my concerns and agreed that I should have ten rabies shots, starting the next day. I was relieved to have the medication prescribed, though I didn't look forward to having long needles stuck into my abdomen. The afternoon doctor, however, said only five shots were needed. And the next morning, just after Joe's daily visit, a new intern canceled the injections altogether after reviewing my chart but not examining my leg. I was falling away from all support. No doctor wanted to help me.

"Sister Visitation!" I called out from my bed. *She must be nearby.* I shouted again. Nurses and patients peered into my room. In India, no one shouted for hospital personnel. I didn't care. I would be the Ugly American. I kept calling out until she arrived, then insisted that I speak with the head doctor of the hospital.

Five minutes later he appeared. Through a clenched jaw I informed him, "I will accept your decision concerning the number of rabies shots I should have, but I want you to write that number on my chart, and sign your name next to it. I will not have it changed by anyone!" After a moment's thought, by some formula known only to him, he decided on seven shots and wrote it on the chart.

When he left, I turned to Sister Visitation. "I'm sorry for shouting. None of this is your fault. I'm just so...so worn out."

I lay my head back on the pillow and looked at the nun. A plump woman in a full white habit, she glided from room to room administering the balm of a pleasant smile and calm presence. As she put a cool washcloth on my forehead, I relaxed and began to feel sleepy. What a beautiful and perfect name she had.

When Sanjay came by later, I asked him about the injections. "No, no," he said. "They won't stick the needle all the way *into* your stomach." The serum, he said, would go into the superficial fatty tissue surrounding the navel. I grasped my navel area, wondering if my recent weight loss had left sufficient fat on my abdomen, but my findings were inconclusive. On his way out Sanjay added, "It's all set then. The head doctor has informed the government hospital that you'll be coming for rabies shots each morning for a week."

"The government hospital? Aren't the shots administered here?"

Apparently only the government hospital had the serum. With a growing sense of added frustration, I realized Joe would need to come to the hospital, take me downstairs in a wheelchair to an autorickshaw, and deliver me to a hospital on the other side of town.

The next morning we began the ordeal.

"Here's your wheelchair from World War I," Joe said brightly as he entered my room.

The chair had an enormously high wicker back, tall wheels with wooden spokes, and polished hardwood armrests which matched the wooden footrests.

"Oh God," I said. I had to laugh in spite of the throbbing pain in my leg.

After bumping across town in a careening rickshaw, my hands glued to the support bars, we arrived at the dilapidated state hospital. In a dark, brown room, I winced as a doctor pushed blunt needles into the fleshy area surrounding my navel while a nurse at his side rattled a tray of small bottles. The puncturing of my skin was a shock in itself, and my mind exacerbated the pain by imagining the serum—itself a poison—slowly oozing throughout my body. One day, a particularly dull needle refused to pierce the skin. My every impulse was to demand that the doctor stop, but I was afraid of even breathing deeply and making the procedure worse. I felt like a giant sausage slowly skewered by a dull fork and, just like a sausage, my skin at first resisted. Then, with a pop, the thick needle pushed through with an ugly hiss. The attending nurse abruptly left the room. I heard her vomiting in the bathroom.

The treatment continued for a week. During the daily rickshaw ride, in spite of my own pain I could not help but see the beggars in the street from a new perspective. As bad as my condition was, at least I was receiving treatment. These people were not. I felt sad for them and gratitude for the care I was receiving—imperfect though it was. Life was flawed and sometimes brutal, but it was still a gift. My attitude about the hospital stay began to change. I stopped resisting all the inconvenient details of daily life. I no longer tried to find better locations on my abdomen for the shots. I began to look at the bumpy ride in the autorickshaw, my leg propped up on the seat in front of me, as my daily outing into fresh air. I smiled when Sister Visitation asked how I had liked lunch that day, a lunch of rice and vegetables exactly the same as every other lunch. I said nothing on the occasions when the male nurse didn't show up to help me bathe. I hobbled to the bathroom and did the best I could by myself.

Did I no longer have any fight left in me? Surely I did, but the crisis had wrenched from me the conviction that I could control my life. Certainly I would always exert myself to protect life and limb. But I could, I would have to, live without trying to control so many aspects of daily living. Life's lessons seemed to be gleaned primarily from adversity, so I might as well learn, and accept what I couldn't change. No doubt I would sometimes continue to believe I could fix problems and avoid pain, but the crack in my habitual consciousness had begun. India, the Great Teacher, had ripped at my psyche as well as my body.

"I've rearranged everything," Joe announced one morning.

"What do you mean?"

"I've rescheduled our meeting with the bishops," he said, "and that gives us time for five days at lovely Kovalam Beach at the southern tip of India."

"Oh Joe, I don't know…" I hesitated.

"It's medicinal," he smiled. "They won't sew your leg back up for fear of infection, and the doctor told me salt water would be good for the wound. I wonder if the stores here have sun tan lotion…"

A week later, Joe and I headed for the beaches of South India. There, the sun and salt water of the Indian Ocean cleansed my still-open wound, and the air invigorated me enough to feel that I could now cope, at least mentally, with most challenges India might place in my path. True, I would never feel safe in quite the same way again and my honeymoon phase with India had come to an end. The country's harsh and violent side could reach out and touch me again. And yet my doubts about being there were gone. Joe, Steve, Gerry and I had pledged ourselves to the mission, and I would keep my side of the bargain.

THE PRINCES OF
THE CHURCH

THE CATHOLIC CHURCH in South India claimed that its roots went back as far as the Apostle Thomas. When I visited two bishops there before returning home to Delhi, I found out, to my dismay, just how traditional its customs were.

My gashed leg propped up on bus seats, I journeyed with Joe to visit Bishop Aloysius at the very tip of the Indian subcontinent, right after our time at the beach. We arrived mid-afternoon and, since my letter of introduction had arrived before us, our rooms were ready. Curious as to why there were bars on the windows, I poked my face out a bit. The two monkeys that immediately jumped up set me on edge, and I vowed to remain vigilant. Nevertheless, the rooms were pleasant, clean and welcoming. India still honored the traveler. Nowhere in America, to my knowledge, would the traveling brother be offered rooms at the home of a bishop. One would stay at the house of another religious order or in a hotel.

As we rested on the verandah, a late afternoon breeze rustled the palm trees—and the time slipped by quietly. I had just dozed off when an insistent car horn announced the arrival of Bishop Aloysius. Two servants, on vigil under shade trees, jumped up to pull back the compound gate. The bishop's car entered, stirring up the reddish dust of the driveway, and came to a halt as a small barefoot boy rushed forward to open the car door. By the time the bishop stepped out, two other houseguests—priests from outlying parishes—and three other servants had emerged to line the steps and greet the bishop. His Excellency's every homecoming, apparently, was a grand entrance.

Bishop Aloysius, a balding man with a tired-looking face, mounted the stairs slowly, his cassock trailing on the steps, and his right hand outstretched, palm down. The posture seemed strange until I realized that the others were kissing his ring and murmuring greetings. "Good afternoon, Your Grace." "Welcome back, Your Excellency." I knew I would not kiss his ring, a gesture which to me smacked more of subservience than respect. When the bishop reached me, I grabbed his hand, gave it a hearty shake and said, "Hi, I'm Brother Jim from America and I'm really pleased to meet you." Behind his thick glasses, the bishop's eyes either twinkled or narrowed, I couldn't tell which. "Please come to my parlor in an hour," was his reply.

Seated on a couch opposite him at the appointed time, I explained the situation and asked if there was any work in his diocese that we could do and thereby qualify for residency in the country.

"I have great need of you in my diocese," the bishop began, "perhaps work in my understaffed orphanage. But here is the situation..."

My spirits sagged as he explained that bishops didn't have the same power in this matter as they did even a few years earlier. The government had become quite strict, and he didn't think he could help. I had heard the whole discouraging story before, but I had hoped for a miracle. What good was all the pomp and circumstance that surrounded a bishop if he was powerless to influence people? To whom could I turn if these well-placed men couldn't help me?

After dinner, when the bishop announced that all would gather on the verandah, I begged off, saying I was tired, and returned to my room. An hour later, Joe knocked on my door. "Well, you got yourself out of that one!" he said.

"What are you talking about?"

"Gathering on the verandah wasn't for socializing over coffee. We had to follow behind 'His Grace' as he paced the floor, and recite Hail Mary's after him. He was always the leader, we the followers. Those two priests from the rural parishes seemed to love it. Not me! I didn't come to India to follow anyone around!"

As I climbed into bed that night I found myself sighing deeply. Tiredness, frustration, and leg pain were taking their toll, and I tossed and turned on the hard bed for another sleepless night.

A few days later, returning north through Bangalore, I visited the bishop there, who had been out of town earlier. Seated behind his desk and only half-turned toward me, he spoke with a hint of impatience in his voice. "It is a scandal, you must know, that so many religious orders want to work in this cool, lovely city. Why not have your brothers work in the villages first, then see me about coming to Bangalore?"

He's not listening to me, I thought. *We don't have anyone to send to the villages yet.* I explained it all again—that we were just getting started in India, that our Indian brothers were only in training at this point, that we foreigners needed visas to stay in India and complete their training—only to have him respond vaguely, "No, no, I don't think so. There are too many problems. Too much difficulty." After a short pause, he rang a bell on his desk, and a serious young priest opened the door and ushered me out of the office. I tried to maintain a calm face, but inwardly I was deflated—and seething.

I knew that many government officials used their clout to obtain coveted seats for their children in the high quality,

N THE LAND OF SHIVA

church-run schools. Why couldn't the bishop just "call in his cards"? After all, we weren't here for illegal purposes or to con- vert Hindus, we were here to render the service of education to those most in need of it. What was wrong with this country? What was I doing here?

Mountain Interlude

THE BRITISH DID at least one thing right in India. Along the crag-gy ridges of the Lower Himalayas, they created towns to which they could flee during the Hot Season. These were small enclaves where roses bloomed, fir trees scented the cool air, and preten-tious clubs served Scotch and soda.

The two hill stations closest to Delhi were Simla and Mussoorie. Simla, the largest and oldest of the hill stations, was the official summer headquarters of the British Government in India from 1864 until Independence in 1947. In those years, the British Viceroy would leave Delhi in his private white and gold train and head for Simla each April. He would be followed by his minions: secretaries, clerks, cooks, guards, ambassadors, tailors, hairdressers and others needed to run both the government and the social life of the British Raj.

Until 1903, the train from Delhi ended at the base of the Himalayas, some forty-two miles away from Simla. All luggage and supplies would then be brought up the mountain to Simla, at seven thousand feet, on lumbering horse carts or the bent backs of men. Many of the memsahibs were carried up the mountain on palanquins shouldered by four laboring coolies. Although more trains, new roads, buses and taxis had changed much of that in Simla and in all the hill stations, the weather in those high-perched towns remained the same—cool and invigorating.

Mussoorie was only a half-day bus ride from Delhi, and contained an added benefit for us—Hindi language school. And so Gerry, Steve, Joe and I met there for the months of May and June.

At 6500 feet, Mussoorie was a refreshing oasis and a welcome respite from the hot plains. The town was strewn out along a u-shaped ridge, and boasted many restaurants, hotels, a movie theater called Picture Palace, a skating rink, and even a small amusement park with a miniature Ferris wheel. The heart of the town was the Mall, where no cars were allowed but where hand-pulled rickshaws took Indian tourists past lamp-posts manufactured in Glasgow, and buildings with wrought iron grills marked with the insignia of Queen Victoria.

Away from the Mall, simpler shops—many of them literally large wooden boxes on stilts—clung to the edge of the roads carved from the mountainside. From their elevated seat, the proprietors of snack shops, tea stalls, and tailor shops greeted passersby with the promise of refreshment or renewal of ragged clothes.

One of those roads led eastward from the Mall, up another thousand feet to the town of Landour, and the Landour Language School. Though we would conduct our affairs in India in English, we wanted to have familiarity with India's national language. The Landour school was established in the late nineteenth century with the original purpose of teaching Hindi to Protestant missionaries, but now the student body was quite diverse, though all of us were foreigners.

We rented a small cottage outside of town and soon became accustomed to living in an area where almost no roads were level for more than twenty feet. Each morning, after prayers and breakfast, we hiked up another 1000 feet to the language school and arrived, panting, to be greeted by our instructors with the phrase, *"Dhum lijiey."* Take a breath, please.

Afternoons were for hiking the numerous trails or exploring the Mall, late afternoon found us gathered for Mass before dinner, and in the evening we studied our Hindi lessons, read, or played cards. A livable schedule, indeed.

With the help of the school headmaster, we had hired a cook for breakfast and dinner. He spoke not a word of English but somehow I managed to communicate with him in the basic Hindi I had learned in Delhi, and with the added knowledge of that language that each day at the Landour school provided. The dinner vegetables were always fresh, and the result of Steve's bargaining with the itinerant vegetable-seller who hawked his wares outside Steve's window each morning.

Language classes ended at noon, and we took our lunch nearby at Rokeby Guest House. A large, rambling house built by a British captain in 1840, Rokeby was now run by Methodists and catered to students at the language school as well as their own church members escaping summer in Delhi. The residents and other lunch guests at Rokeby provided us with lively conversation and additional companionship for our hikes and weekend visits to Library Bazaar, a bustling bundle of shops and restaurants at the opposite end of the ridge.

From Rokeby, if we took the Chukkar Road, the circular road, around to the other side of the peak, we could look directly into the 20,000-foot mountains of Tibet, a spectacular treat, especially at dusk when the setting sun glanced off the Abode of Snow.

One day I stopped at a small store in Landour Bazaar whose window sign said it had watches for sale. It turned out to be an antique shop and the only watches available were old silver pocket watches, most of them British, from the early part of the century.

"Does this one actually keep time?" I asked the shopkeeper, after finding a pocket watch whose weight felt good in the palm of my hand.

"Probably not, but it is good silver. You will be very happy with it," he replied.

I frowned, and he added, "You can always purchase a small clock in the Mall that will work. That will be practical. This will be beautiful."

I bought the silver pocket watch.

On weekends, Gerry, Steve, Joe and I often ate out, at the Whispering Winds restaurant in Library Bazaar or the Tavern restaurant near Kulri Bazaar, and leisurely walked the two miles back to our cottage.

Sometimes I hiked by myself to the Mall, which sat at the edge of a mountain precipice, and from which, on clear days and nights, I could look out across the vast, sweltering Doon Valley. As the dry summer wore on, I would sit on the lookout wall and see distant balls of dust swell to menacing size, roll like brown fog to the base of the mountain and occasionally have the temerity to reach up and slightly enter my citadel of cool air.

In this idyllic mountain refuge, we all relaxed, enjoyed each other's company, and almost forgot we were living in usually hectic India.

Then Steve collapsed. One weekend he and Gerry had gone out for a hike, but were back within a half hour.

"I'm so wiped out…" Steve mumbled, and lay down on his bed, his face ashen and his hands trembling.

"I don't like the looks of this," Gerry said. "Wasn't there a doctor staying at Rokeby this past week? Maybe he's still there."

Dr. Ernest Sundaram took one look at Steve, hospitalized him, and ran tests.

"He has amoebic dysentery," Ernest told me. "I have put him on the proper antibiotics, and when he leaves the hospital I want him to stay at Rokeby. He can't be climbing up the mountain every morning."

Dysentery! I'd never heard of dysentery cases in the U.S. Wasn't that a disease of the nineteenth century? Or maybe in the twentieth century during the First World War, but not these days.

Steve had had stomach problems ever since our trip to Dharamsala a few months earlier, but I thought he had been getting better. On that trip, he had drunk water from a stream because it looked clear and was high in the mountains, but became terribly sick for a few days. I had taken him to a local doctor at the time, Lady Doctor Dolma, and she had prescribed herbs which, at least at first, seemed to help. Though she was a famous doctor from Lhasa, her natural remedies clearly hadn't been sufficient.

The idea that Steve might have dysentery never crossed my mind. How foolish I had been not to take his stomach problems more seriously!

Steve slowly got better under Dr. Sundaram's care, but was still weak by the time Ernest and his wife, Sheila, left to return to Delhi. By some miraculous act of Providence, they lived a very short distance from our house in Delhi, and Dr. Sundaram said he would continue to care for Steve as needed.

Our last week in Mussoorie came to an end, and we faced the trip back down the mountain. Taxis were not permitted up the treacherous road to Rokeby, so I hired coolies to carry Steve in a palanquin down to the bus stand at Picture Palace.

Steve squirmed at the idea of looking like a pampered sahib of the Raj days, but knew he was too weak to navigate the steep hill.

Smiling wanly at me from the palanquin, he said, "Well at least now I'm able to say in Hindi, 'Quickly! Quickly! Where is the bathroom?'"

FEET OF CLAY

WITH EACH HAIRPIN turn that brought us down the mountain, the air got thicker and more oppressive. Happily the monsoons had arrived on time and had begun to cool down Delhi and the plains, but "cooler" meant 95 degrees and wretched humidity instead of 115 degrees and no humidity. Once at the apartment in Delhi, my clothes clung to me all day, and when the electricity failed at night and shut down the ceiling fan, it was a night without sleep.

During those sticky weeks bathing at least twice a day became a necessity. Each morning we filled large, plastic garbage cans in the bathroom with the relatively cool water collected in the rooftop tanks overnight. Throughout the day we refreshed ourselves by pouring cups of water over our bodies while squatting in the middle of the bathroom—the usual way to bathe in an Indian bathroom—and let the floor drain clear the water. Sometimes as I watched the water swirl down the drain, it seemed my energy was going with it. I was tired, not just from the heaviness of the monsoons, but from tension in our little community. For the first time, I found myself at odds with each of the others.

We were all on edge. Though we had to attend seminary classes, no one felt like studying in the heat and we had few other activities to occupy us. I told Joe, who was ready to expand our candidate base, not to give any recruitment talks in Delhi until we were certain we could remain in India. Joe understood, but looked discouraged. All of us planned to visit the novices again at the ashram on the next school break, but that was almost two months away. Steve had not yet fully regained his strength from the dysentery episode, but was restless. Like monks of old, we had little to do except study and pray. Unfortunately, none of us were monastic types.

To keep himself occupied, Steve searched for artistic outlets and discovered an art studio across town. For a small fee, he could use their clay, throwing-wheels, and kiln. "It's really quite a find," he explained excitedly.

I reminded him that the hour bus ride each way would be tiring and Dr. Sundaram had ordered rest. "I don't think you should go," I said.

"Jim, I need to do this," Steve said with a set jaw. I didn't press the point and so, after morning classes at the seminary, Steve worked at the art studio each day. A few weeks later it proved too much for him and he took to his bed exhausted. Dr. Sundaram made a house call and pronounced Steve dehydrated and still plagued by dysentery. "You must make Steve drink this mixture of sugar and salt throughout the day," Ernest said to me. "He doesn't have to go to the hospital, but be sure he takes his medication and keep him indoors during the heat of the afternoon. This is serious."

I can't *make* Steve do this, I thought. *I can't make him do any-thing—unless, of course, I invoke the vow of obedience.* But in my entire time as a brother, I had never heard of the vow of obedience formally invoked, though the vow was implicit in the assigning of a brother to a particular city. If I went through with it, Steve would have to comply or be in jeopardy of sin. But there would be a price. Invoking the vow would surely strain our relationship. I certainly would resent any Superior who resorted to wielding such power over me in the matter of my own health.

The day after Dr. Sundarman's visit, I stopped by Steve's room where he lay on his bed, ashen and thin, the hydration fluid in the pitcher barely touched. "Maybe I'll have to leave India," he said as I sat down, "though I wish I could stay."

I paused. I wanted to shout at him, *Just do what is needed, take your medication and rest! Then you can stay in India.* Suddenly, however, I felt a pang of guilt. Steve was the youngest, the least experienced in the group, and I had not been able to keep him healthy. I should have insisted on more medical care the very first time he complained of stomach cramps, or somehow have known about laboratory tests that can confirm dysentery in its earliest stages. I should have done *something* differently. I knew my feelings of guilt were irrational, but I partly blamed myself for Steve's condition even while I reproached him for not taking care of himself.

"Steve, stick with your medication and rest for now, and decide about staying or leaving when you feel a little better," I said, pouring him a glass of the hydration fluid. And, I said to myself, if he doesn't get better I'll put him in the hospital myself or send him home.

The monsoon season wore on, and our community moved listlessly from one day to the next, only gathering as a group for meals and prayers, those two times that traditionally fostered companionship and support. Joe, however, had begun to miss both. He spent his afternoons exploring Delhi and usually entertained us with his latest discoveries—the "lame" beggar who easily ran away when the police arrived, or the large cauldrons along the river in which the laundrymen boiled clothes before beating them on the rocks. "You won't believe what I found today," Joe began as he sat down late for dinner one evening in mid-August.

Steve interrupted him. "I don't understand this. You said the other day how reflective India has made you. All I see you doing is running around. How about coming to prayers and dinner? What about community life?"

"I like community life—you know that. But we have prayers and meals at all the wrong times."

"And just when *would* be a good time for you?" Steve asked icily.

When Joe hesitated, I jumped in, "Yes, you like community life. But you want the rest of us to sustain it so you can participate when *you* want to. We're all in this together, Joe. The rest of us aren't here just to provide a comfortable base for you." My voice sounded hard. Joe had plenty of time to visit the city without missing our group gatherings. And I wanted, needed, his upbeat energy those days. He had let us all down. We finished the meal in silence.

Gerry, on the other hand, was always present, but he upset me over something else. As Novice Master, he was responsible for planning classes for the novices, so, a few weeks before our upcoming visit to see them, I asked, "What classes are you planning to give the novices this time?"

"Hmmm, not sure yet," he replied, then returned to writing letters on the familiar blue international aerogrammes we all used. I asked again a week later, but got the same vague responses. After another week went by, I began to feel anxious, so I decided to offer a few suggestions, but got nowhere.

"That's *my* job! Don't try to take that over," Gerry said, his face an angry red. I was stunned.

Gerry continued. "You tell Joe to stay at home, you don't want Steve to go out, and now you're telling me what to teach the novices. I can handle my own job."

"Yes, it's your job, so *do* it! You sit around your room half the day writing letters back to the States. Well, you're here, in India. So *be* here. Gerry, we're leaving in just a few more days. We need a plan."

As I stalked back to my room, I wondered about Gerry. His response seemed so out of proportion, so unexpected. He should know that I want to hear his plans. That was my job, wasn't it? Was something else going on? Then again, maybe the heat was wearing him down like the rest of us.

At one time, I had been excited to be in charge of the India mission. Now, my enthusiasm was wearing thin. It seemed not just a burden but an impossible task, and so far I had accomplished practically nothing. I had very few leads on how to stay in India. I was managing only sporadic contact with the novices. The religious community I was in charge of was filled with tension. I couldn't make one brother take care of himself, I couldn't get another to support the house schedule, I couldn't force a third to do his job. And, besides all that, I was impatient, irritable, and resentful. Some Superior I made. Some *brother* I made. Suddenly the walls of my room seemed to close in on me. Even the house felt like a prison, reminding me of my failures. I hurried down the stairs and let myself out into the street, slamming the door behind me.

A few minutes later my walk brought me to the Kashmiri Gate, where the bazaar's swirl of scents—spiced tea, sliced mangoes, flower garlands—assaulted my nostrils and drew me into the market's narrow lanes. Down each alley, a variety of sounds also competed for my attention. A radio blared popular Hindi songs, a man called out "hot peanuts" while he shoveled his wares onto hot coals, and an old woman chanted as she strung flowers for temple offerings. I walked slowly past them, past the vegetable vendors and tea stalls, and finally came to the furthest edge of the bazaar where I spied a banana wallah loudly hawking his produce.

Bananas in India came in several varieties, from medium-sized yellow ones to small brown ones to the sweet, pudgy, red bananas of South India that always looked overripe. Because the bananas available in Delhi were on the small side, one always purchased a bunch, never a single banana, and since they had a protective skin they were safe to eat, no matter that they lay directly on a dusty sidewalk or were presented to the customer by a grimy hand.

The banana wallah, an elderly man squatting on the edge of a curb, caught my eye as I approached, then quickly surveyed his wares to offer me the largest bunch for three and a half rupees. I knew I couldn't eat the whole bunch, and I had no desire to carry the rest with me. "Half," I said in Hindi, and made a cutting motion with my hand through the middle of the bunch. Expressionless, he handed me exactly half the bunch, and change for the two rupees I had placed in front of him. The change was more than it should have been, and I attempted to return part of it.

"No, no," he said, his brow furrowed. For another minute we exchanged disjointed sentences and made useless hand gestures, his movements growing more and more defiant. I couldn't understand why he wouldn't be happy to receive money back.

"Jim...Jim," a familiar voice called out. Dr. Sundaram had pulled his car over to the curb and was getting out. "Is there a problem here?"

"Ernest, thanks so much for stopping," I said feeling relieved. I explained the situation and asked him to translate. He spoke briefly with the banana vendor, after which the coins I offered were accepted. The old man's demeanor had changed from belligerent to calm, and I was taken by surprise when he touched both of his hands to his head, then to my feet. Dr. Sundaram explained that the man had no idea I was returning extra change. He thought I was attempting some quick exchange of rupees where he would lose out.

"Jim, that is so like you. That man will never forget you." Ernest smiled, as he said goodbye and returned to his car.

Leaving the bazaar, I thought of Dr. Sundaram's words, *that is so like you*. I had done nothing special, for giving the change back was an automatic response. That indeed was the point. It reminded me that a million times in my life I'd done the right thing and still strove to do so. I was an ordinary, decent person who, under pressure, boiled over just like everyone else. I needed to let go of the idea that as a brother and a religious Superior I was supposed to act "correctly" all the time.

It was an important, if subtle, shift for me. For years I had thought that the true spiritual person was someone who was *always* good and calm and wise—that is, somebody *else*. As long as I held that view, I would always see spirituality as residing elsewhere and never claim it in myself.

THE GREAT DIVIDE

As so often happens in the brothers' houses, the tensions among the four of us silently softened through communal prayer and the genuine goodwill that underlay our sometimes prickly exteriors. Thus, several days later, when Joe, Gerry, and I visited the novices, we did so with a renewed sense of mission and mutual support. The summer heat still pressed on, however, so Steve stayed in Delhi to rest.

The rice paddies near the novitiate ashram displayed waving, willowy spears, made deep green by the September monsoons. In the ashram itself, fresh country air swirled around us as we fell in with the daily routine: early rising and prayer, classes for the novices under a shade tree after breakfast, chores in the afternoon, and evenings in a circle for conversation and games, or card tricks by Joe.

The novices—Barto, Juel, Johnny, Ben—had advanced in their knowledge of English, and Father Sevanand was justly proud of them. This improvement in communication was a welcome change from my first visit with the novices.

On our third morning as we sat under the arbor eating breakfast, the ashram cat rushed out of Joe's room and wailed mournfully. Juel, village-born and bred, understood exactly what had happened. "A snake!" he cried, and ran to pick up a shovel. I followed at a distance and watched Juel enter the room where the mother's kittens had slept. After several minutes of sickening thuds, Juel emerged with a limp snake draped over the shovel, a large lump in its body indicating the fate of a kitten.

"It's a cobra," Juel said excitedly. As the mother cat moaned and searched for her offspring, Juel carried the snake to a further section of the property for burial, a slight bounce in his step.

I left my breakfast untouched. Of course the snake needed to be disposed of, no question about that. But the gleam in Juel's eyes after he smashed the snake disturbed me.

"Cobras," Johnny said in a serious tone, "always travel in pairs. Probably the mate will come looking for its companion tonight."

"I am *not* sleeping in that room again!" Joe announced, setting his teacup down with a bang. Looking up, he saw the teasing smile on Johnny's face and realized he had been "taken," just as he had tried to fool Johnny with card tricks. Johnny had solved most of the tricks, and I had been pleased to see his mental quickness. He was certainly a solid candidate.

After breakfast, Joe and the novices sat on logs in a circle for English practice, and I joined in.

"First," Joe said, "I'll tell you about the city I grew up in—listen to the words I use—then you'll tell me about your village, okay?"

The novices smiled as Joe described his hometown, Detroit. "It's a really big city in the north of the U.S., and famous for making cars." He went on to say that the homes and buildings were made of brick, that there was snow there in the winter, and that unfortunately the city had a reputation for crime, especially murders.

"I've seen pictures of snow in books," Benedict said quietly, "and someday I hope to touch that white thing with my hand."

"Our homes," Barto added as he peered through his horn-rimmed glasses, "are made of mud walls like these here in the ashram. But we have tile on the roofs to protect against the monsoon, not like the straw roofs here."

"We have murders too," Johnny said, this time with no teasing smile, "and everyone knows who the bad men are, but we cannot tell that. The ghosts of the dead men visit the village at night."

"Ghosts!" Joe exclaimed. "Tell me more," he said as he leaned forward.

Barto, whose English was better than the others, explained that arguments over land was the usual cause of fights, which could end in someone's death. Since many of the villages were far away from cities and might be accessed only by foot, such crimes often went unreported.

"However," Barto said, "the ghosts come back to punish the murderers by frightening them in the middle of the night with shrieks and banging on pots in the kitchen."

The conversation continued in a lively manner, with all the novices except Juel joining in. Joe tried to coax him into talking about his village, but the most Juel would do was nod in agreement to the others' stories.

After English practice, it was my turn with the novices, though my topics were decidedly less interesting than murders and ghosts. I spoke about the historical founding of our religious congregation, what the brothers did for ministry in the U.S.—mainly teach in schools—what our brothers might do in India—avoid large schools in big cities, but focus on rural education, which had been neglected by the Church. The novices listened politely, but had no questions. Their faces also looked quite blank when I referred to our Brotherhood being founded in France shortly after the French Revolution.

"That's why we don't wear any special religious garb, I mean habit, or clothes. The French Revolution was about how all people should be seen as equal," I said.

More blank stares. They might not have ever heard of the French Revolution. Fair enough, I thought. What had I been taught about India during my high school days in America? I didn't even know the year of Indian Independence, 1947, until some months ago.

I sat in again later while Gerry spoke about Mary, the Mother of God.

"We are called the Society of Mary because Mary is a great example for us," Gerry began. "She completely trusted in God. She accepted her role as Mother of God, though she wasn't certain what that really meant. Similarly, we might not know where God is leading us, but if we trust, all will be well."

The novices listened politely, but did not take any notes on their writing pads. When Gerry asked them to speak about Mary, their faces lit up.

"We must say the rosary to her and sing songs every day in front of her statue," Johnny said.

"My heart feels good whenever I place flowers at her statue. She is my Mother," Benedict added with a smile.

"Because of prayers to Mother Mary, my little sister was cured of a terrible fever," Barto said.

"I like processions to Mary's shrine," Juel said. I was pleased to hear him add something, brief though it was.

Later that afternoon, Gerry and I walked along the dirt road near the ashram.

"The novices are very sincere," Gerry said, "but their devotional ways aren't that familiar to me anymore."

"Right! Sounds like what we had in America thirty years ago. I can go along with some devotional practices, but you're the one, Gerry, who'll speak to them about religious matters more than I. How do you feel about that?"

"Honestly, I'm not sure right now," Gerry said, his brow a bit furrowed. "It's been a long time since our brothers' communities had processions and saying the rosary in front of shrines. I had expected cultural differences, but now I see that the Church here is so different from the one we know."

"I agree. And there's also this chasm between us and them because of our city background, and their rural background. And we're not talking 'rural' as in rural America. We're talking villages with no roads leading to them, cobras slithering into one's bedroom, and then smashing it with a blunt tool! Ugh!" I said. "Do you think Juel seem a bit too pleased with himself on that one?"

"Well, it had to be done. We wouldn't want it coming back for more kittens, would we?" As Gerry looked out across the rice paddies, he added, "I suspect that in these outlying areas finishing off a predator is cause for celebration."

Gerry was right, no doubt. And if a change of pace and challenge is what I wanted in coming to India, I was getting my share. While Delhi was worlds away from St. Louis, at least it was a big city, something I was familiar with. The ashram and the villages the novices described were altogether another universe to me.

I was determined to understand and appreciate better what the rural life had to offer since our novices came from that background. So far, I had mainly liked the clean air of the countryside. Surely there was more to this bucolic setting than that.

THE PULL OF GRAVITY

I NEEDED A brief getaway, not only from the routine of the ashram itself, but from the crushing heat that built up each day by noon. A forest with a shaded pond, Barto said, was just a twenty-minute walk away. He showed me a path that would take me past a small village and eventually lead to that cool and pleasant place. It sounded like a good plan.

My umbrella helped ward off the afternoon sun, and I felt relatively comfortable in the *lungi* I had wrapped around my waist. Within a few minutes I came alongside the village where the men, resting during the heat of the day, sat on logs in front of their homes. Anticipating that as a foreigner I would receive silent stares, I waved to show I was friendly.

I suppose it was my quick movements that caused my *lungi* to come loose and fall off. The men stared. I froze. When I could move, I placed the umbrella on the ground and made furtive efforts to retie the *lungi* securely, a skill I thought I had mastered. A few children laughed as I hurried away to the jungle, where I had a pleasant dip in the cool pond.

I wondered what I would say to Barto when he asked about my walk, but surprisingly he didn't ask me anything. The following morning, however, he invited me to accompany him to purchase rice. Assuming we were going to the bazaar, I headed toward the main road outside the ashram gate, but Barto explained we were going the opposite direction. "We buy rice from the village just down the path, the one you passed yesterday on your walk."

I had already agreed to go, so I swallowed hard and followed Barto. As we wound our way to the center of the village, a group of chattering boys clustered around us. One of the boys feigned a tug at my *lungi*, an act for which he was scolded by Barto. I said nothing. Since it was Sunday, the men were not in the fields but had gathered near the village well, talking, while the women languidly sifted rice and chatted among themselves off to one side.

Barto approached two of the men and asked about rice. The men looked at him, then at me, and motioned us toward a hut where the transaction would be held. Several other men joined us, glanced at me, then spoke animatedly with Barto. I began to smile, guessing what was being said. Barto looked back at me, started to laugh, and soon the men joined in.

"Brother Jim," Barto said a few moments later, "they want us to take tea, and they have told me I must give you lessons on how to properly tie a *lungi*. And they said to be sure to tell you they are honored to have you visit their village. They even gave us extra rice because you came back."

Later, I sat reading under a tree at the ashram gate, a slight breeze seemingly my only companion, when a young man appeared. Not more than eighteen or nineteen, he carried a sickle in his rough hands and stopped directly in front of me to stare. I stood to acknowledge him, and took note of the gray string that crossed his chest diagonally and indicated that he had observed a "coming of age" ritual. A small patch of skin under the cord had lost pigmentation, and his hair was freshly wet and slicked back, making me imagine he had just cooled himself at a local well.

He eyed me steadily and smiled in response to my own hesitant smile. *Shall I speak to him? Or is it better to say nothing than have a frustrating half-conversation?*

"Namaste," I said, and he repeated the greeting. He unabashedly looked me up and down, staring intently wherever my light skin was exposed. No Westerners visited that remote region and

I must have been a curiosity to him. Uncomfortable with my body being an object of scrutiny, I decided to speak. "What is your name?" I asked in Hindi, and he replied with the name of the village down the road. Evidently my pronunciation left a lot to be desired. "What are you doing?" I asked and was pleased that I understood his response. "Cutting grass for the cows."

We stood silently for several minutes not saying anything else. He continued to stare at me and I found myself doing the same in return. In fact, I wanted to reach out and touch him and find out if his brown skin actually was softer—as I imagined—than my own pale covering. But I didn't. It would be presumptuous of me to touch him, maybe defiling his caste.

He gracefully shifted his weight to his other leg, then said something animatedly and laughed—so I laughed also. After another moment or two, he nodded in my direction and took off down the road. As I watched him walk away, his bare feet adjusting to the contours of the road, his arms swinging at his side and his whole body fluidly moving through space, I was simultaneously in awe of him and jealous of him.

That night I lay on my cot, tossing in the still, hot air inside the mosquito net. At midnight, sleep still had eluded me. Slowly, the moon slid out from behind clouds and its light seeped through the bamboo wall, creating jail-bar patterns on the mosquito net. I counted as many bars as I could, hoping to drift off to sleep, but it didn't work. Village sounds floated into the room from across the watery rice paddies—muffled conversation interrupted with laughter, a woman singing softly, the periodic tap-tap of pipes being cleaned of tobacco by banging them against a log. I had seen the men in the village do that. The villagers apparently weren't sleeping either.

A bath would help, so I pushed back the mosquito net and headed for the well. Someone had left a kerosene lamp by the door but lighting it would give off too much heat, so I counted on moonlight to illuminate the path. I headed down the dirt path, past the banana trees, and came upon the well in a small clearing. Frogs croaked in the well, but were momentarily silent when I dropped the bucket. I pulled up cool water, and took my time cascading it over my chest and each limb—slow-motion ablutions. I poured a second bucketful on my head, feeling the rivulets snake their way down my body. The water made my shorts cling to me, but I would change into a dry pair. On the way back to my room, a slight breeze that I didn't know was astir cooled me.

Sliding out of my wet shorts and fumbling in the dark for dry ones, for a fraction of a second I saw myself in suit and tie teaching mathematics. Not much more than a year ago that was the only life I knew, a very different one from the present. Then, I was someone not yet introduced to mosquito nets and bathing by moonlight, someone who didn't know the pleasure of an evening breeze against his chest, who knew of cobras and monkeys only from visits to the zoo. In short, someone out of touch with his body and removed from nature.

Trussed up in my white shirt and tie, I had had the security of knowing what my task was each day, but I hadn't been connected to the earth. I had solved quadratic equations in my mind but not felt my bare feet walking a dirt path to the well. India, however, was changing that. She was forcing me into my body more and more each day—and it felt good. Gravity, it seemed, pulled harder in India.

ALONG THE
SACRED RIVER

EACH SULTRY DAY of the monsoon season in Delhi continued to press in, as if a heavy weight lay on my chest making it harder and harder to breathe. I was certain there wasn't enough oxygen in the moisture-laden air. People on the streets moved more slowly, and even my thinking had slowed down. Then, just as night fell rapidly on the plains of northern India, so too, the cool weather appeared suddenly. We had gone to bed one muggy night at the end of September, only to arise the next morning to a crystalline sky, the heaviness completely evaporated. And with the cool weather, the remaining tension in our community also seemed to disappear.

Steve, stronger and more energetic, was planning a trip to see the novices and teach them the fundamentals of art. Art, he said, would be a perfect way for the novices to bypass language differences and express themselves. For his own leisure, he made pencil sketches of local people as well as a colorful drawing of Natarajan, the dancing form of Shiva.

Hindus said that Shiva Natarajan—with multiple arms, one leg raised in dance position, and a ring of fire surrounding him—both destroyed and created the universe. He danced on the demon of ignorance and destroyed all that was no longer useful, while simultaneously creating the new order in its place.

That a deity would be a god of destruction at first shocked me, but then I realized that that was the course of nature. The seed fell into the ground, was destroyed, and new life pushed its way up to sunlight. Hindus also said that if Shiva stopped dancing, the universe would cease to exist. That image appealed to me. It was dynamic, it held passion—quite unlike the cerebral theology of Thomas Aquinas I had had to study. Recent popular references to God had cast him more as a loving father than a stern judge, but underneath all those semantics lay the same old rigid rules and dogmas. A wild, dancing Shiva seemed anything but rigid. We all liked Steve's drawing, and hung it in the living room.

Gerry was enthusiastic about the novices' expected move to Delhi in January and was busy lining up classes for them. During August and September, Joe had lost weight and energy. "I have only one stripe on my pajamas," he had joked then, but had regained the weight and his usual upbeat spirit. My own energy was better than ever, no doubt buoyed by the fact that the others were doing well. I had fallen into the occupational hazard of the "in-charge" person: feeling bad and responsible when something went wrong, and feeling good and taking credit when things went well. Inwardly I laughed at myself for the amount of ego I invested in every turn of events.

The cooler weather of October also brought two weeks of Hindu holidays. Free concerts played in the parks, fireworks crackled in the night, and storefronts displayed mountainous quantities of sweets. On the darkest night of the month, the night preceding the new moon, Hindus celebrated Diwali, the Feast of Lights. Neighbors festooned their homes with colorful lights that pointed the way for the gods to visit the earth. Even the seminary acknowledged the importance of the holidays and canceled classes for four days. With the pleasant weather and a feeling of festivity in the air, I was drawn to explore the neighborhood more fully and I soon discovered the *ghats*, the temple-lined banks of the river.

The Jumuna, India's second sacred river, flowed just two blocks from our house and drew scores of devotees each morning to its banks. The worshippers filed past our apartment carrying plates of flowers and incense to be placed in front of their favorite deity or thrown directly into the muddy river. The faithful then entered the river, scooped up its sacred waters in a small pot, and prayed while slowly pouring it back into the river.

Once I had discovered them, the *ghats* often lured me to their special world. I would walk down our street past the white marble Krishna temple, cross the Ring Road, and follow a shaded walkway that led to the river. There, a dozen or more small temples crowded the river's edge, interspersed with resting pavilions for devotees. Upriver a short distance, the temples gave way to a flat, open space where wandering *sadhus*—India's holy men—might be found.

One *sadhu* lived there in a gunnysack. His loincloth and burlap bag seemed to be his only possessions other than a lone, tattered book. Matted, wild hair gave his thin body an aboriginal look, though his demeanor was gentle. His disciples sat quietly around him, hanging on his every word or honoring his silence by their own meditation. Once, this *sadhu* looked intently at me, and I tried not to stare back. I was unsuccessful. After a few moments, he went back to reading his book. I would have lingered to talk to his disciples, but mangy pariah dogs frightened me away. After my encounter with angry monkeys, I was still skittish around India's animals.

One afternoon in mid-October I came upon another *sadhu* who stood on one leg near the river's edge. As I squinted to see what strange objects he held in his hands, a small boy approached me and explained, in excellent English, that the man had been standing on the one leg for almost twenty years.

"And he hasn't cut his fingernails for longer than that. Do you see them?"

What I had thought were objects were his fingernails—yellowed and curled around many times, like rams' horns.

"Is he here all year? How does he eat?"

"Sometimes he goes further south in the cold weather, but wherever he goes, people bring him food and feed it to him. He cannot take food into his hands because of his fingernails. The people gain merit for feeding him. Now come, please greet my father."

The young boy took me by the hand and led me back downstream. His father was visiting the grandfather, who had appropriated a section of one of the guest pavilions for his own living space. Cooking utensils and a bedroll delineated his portion of the open-air structure, and clothes hung on a line between several of its pillars. Sparse was a generous word for his "home."

After introductions and pleasantries about how welcome the cooler weather was, Ashok, the boy's father, asked me what I was studying. I told him world religions. "Yes, organized religions may be useful for some of us, but not for my father. He seeks God directly." He pointed to the elderly man who had stayed in the background and had said nothing. "He has taken a vow of silence for twenty-five years now. My son has never heard his grandfather speak." The family seemed to take this behavior in stride.

After a few more minutes of casual conversation, I made namaste to the family and headed back home, after one more glance at the *sadhu* standing on one leg, silhouetted against the glare of the river. The *sadhu's* behavior was bizarre, but it was just another version of the grandfather's quest—seeking God directly. Neither of them needed a Brahmin, priest, rabbi, or lama to bridge heaven and earth. How different from my own Church which didn't trust such individual mysticism and lined up priests to show us the path. Even broad-minded Father Dave had not wanted Steve, Joe, and me to come to India without a priest, and so Gerry had been added to the group at the last moment. The *sadhu's* life stated there was no need for priestly mediation. That's why these Hindu holy men fascinated me. Why couldn't I fully connect with the Divine on my own? I could be like the *sadhu*, minus the extreme asceticism of course, and pursue God directly, individually.

Yet, the holy man's life did look lonely.

3 December 1980
Feast of St. Francis Xavier, Missionary to India

Dear Dave,

Our student status has renewed for another year! The approval came in a curious way, but no matter, we are all relieved.

It all began with the telegram that Joe's mother sent about his father's death. Joe can leave India easily, but in order to reenter India in January he needed his visa renewed immediately. The agent seemed quite sympathetic upon seeing the telegram, and granted approval on the spot. Joe then asked if the agent could track the renewal applications for his "study companions," and gave him our names. The following week all our visas were renewed.

We were trying to obtain renewal the American way—apply, wait for the system to work. We should have known it would take the Indian way, that is, make a heartfelt connection with the person in charge, and voila, it's all finished!

There is another way here, bribery, but I wouldn't dare attempt it—unless I was certain I could get away with it.

Shanti (peace)

Jim

GANDHI – THE MOVIE

THE SAUNA ROOM at New Delhi's Ashok Hotel was overly hot, but I would be leaving shortly for my massage appointment. Sauna and a massage were luxuries I had never experienced before. But pain in my neck—no doubt from bumpy bus rides—had persisted even after heavy medication prescribed by Dr. Sundaram who then recommended spa treatment at the plush hotel. When I told Santosh, at the end of our Social Justice class that morning, where I was going, he had chided me, "Could the poor go there? Didn't you get anything out of this class?" Fortunately I was at a five-star spa on the advice of my doctor, which meant I didn't have to evaluate whether the cushy situation fit with my vows.

The only other person in the sauna, a Westerner, had been there when I entered. His eyes were cast downward, half-closed, and his hands held tightly to the bench as perspiration streamed down his rather thin body. The door suddenly flung open and a short, stocky man entered. He looked Indian, but his speech soon pegged him as British. "Well, Ben," he said to the other man, "still trying to lose weight? I'm the one that needs to drop a kilo or two!" The man addressed as Ben gave a half smile though he said nothing as he left the room.

"Oh, my, I suppose I would lose more weight staying away from the hotel buffets than from coming in here," the stocky man said as he plopped himself down on the bench closest to the hot coals and looked directly at me. I smiled back.

"I say," he continued, "are you with the crew? I don't think I've seen you before."

"Crew? No. I'm a student here in Delhi. What crew are you talking about?"

"An American! Oh, I do love America. Why, the film crew for the movie *Gandhi*. I play Patel and that was Ben Kingsley who just left. He plays Gandhi you know."

I didn't know who "Patel" was, nor the man in front of me, and I had only vaguely heard of Ben Kingsley, but in spite of the rising heat I decided to stay. These men were film stars!

"I'm Saeed Jaffrey, but you probably didn't recognize me with my clothes off," he laughed.

I liked the good-natured man and was sorry I couldn't respond with recognition.

"They're looking for Europeans as extras, you know. Of course that includes you. Most Westerners here are tourists or government people with no spare time. But you're a student. You would be ideal."

I had to confess I was tantalized by the idea. As a kid, I had always imagined myself in movies after watching double features every Sunday in Milwaukee. Here, from a chance meeting, was my opportunity! Jaffrey happily advised me where to find the casting department and told me to ask for Penny. "Take along a photo and tell her I sent you."

I thanked Jaffrey and left for my massage appointment. "Discovered" in the sauna! The makings of another Hollywood legend, I humored myself, as a burly man dug into my tight shoulder and neck muscles. Exciting images filled my mind. Movie contracts, dinners with film dignitaries, an applauding public. I would be in great demand after my cameo appearance, that was certain. Those scenarios, I knew, were hardly the goals of a brother committed to founding a branch of his order in India.

The fantasies no doubt indicated my desire to escape the plodding realities of blistering hot days and long boring evenings. I wanted a little spice in my life.

The next day, Penny smiled when I introduced myself, saying she had heard my name just that morning and had the perfect role for me. Great, I thought. Perhaps the part was that of an ambassador, maybe a government official, or a military officer in a smart uniform.

"Let's see, a bystander in the South African train scene. Yes, you'd be perfect," Penny said. I hid my disappointment, but brightened when she explained that I was the only "extra" they were calling for that scene, and I might even get a speaking part if there was a need.

Back at the house that evening, Steve and Gerry seemed more amused than enthused about my new undertaking. "Well, at least we'll have that stipend of twenty-five dollars in the *community* coffers," Steve said.

As instructed, I reported to the Ashok Hotel at seven o'clock the following Monday to be outfitted and driven to the small village outside Delhi used for the South African scene. Penny greeted me brightly in the dressing room and explained that the scene was a very important one. "Gandhi gets literally thrown off a train in South Africa. It's quite dramatic." Gandhi had been enamored of the British until he presumed to ride in a first-class coach and met with opposition. "First class was not for 'coloreds' in South Africa, you see," Penny added. After that event, he returned to India determined to fight for civil rights and independence for his country.

Penny said I was to portray a European traveler who looks down at the ejected Gandhi. "Let your face show great disdain—think ugly thoughts." As she left the room she added, "The others have already left for the location, so I'll just send you out with Ben."

Ben Kingsley? "Gandhi"? What luck! On the way to the filming location, maybe he would tell me inside stories about making
the movie.

After being outfitted in an early 1900's suit, I waited in a
private car under the immense portico of the Ashok Hotel.
Several security guards hovered silently nearby, and the Sikh
driver stared straight ahead, his hands already on the car wheel.
Kingsley appeared, paused while a guard opened the car door,
then climbed into the back seat next to me. He wore a dark suit
and sported a black wig, effectively making him into the younger
man he was to be in the South African scene.

"Good morning. How are you?" I asked, as we sped away.
Kingsley half turned toward me, gave a weak smile and nodded
vaguely in my direction.

"I suppose you have a rather grueling schedule..." I ventured. Again, Kingsley sent a slight nod my way, then closed his
eyes. I reminded myself that the man was British, no doubt typi-
cally reserved. Maybe like their queen, British film stars were supposed to speak to *you* first, then only you could respond, though
Jaffrey hadn't fit that mold. But then, Jaffrey had Indian heritage,
maybe that explained his more outgoing personality. My mind
went through silly variations on those thoughts, only to come to
the obvious conclusion: the man was centering himself for his
performance, being "in character." Inwardly sighing, I turned to
look out my window and watched the Delhi suburbs slide by.

An hour later, the car pulled up at a train station in a small
dusty village. Crowds lined the streets and tried in vain to push
past police who wielded the bamboo sticks most Indian officers
carried. Two guards approached the car on Kingsley's side and
opened the door. When he stepped out, the crowd cheered and
clapped. Kingsley responded shyly by bowing his head and walking silently to the train platform, shielded by an officer on each
side.

Two more guards approached my side of the car. One man jerked the door open, then stood to the left, the other to the right. The crowd murmured. I stepped out hesitantly, slowly placing one foot after the other on the dry ground. Onlookers leaned forward over the police ropes. When I stood upright alongside the car, the crowd's interest increased. After only a brief moment's hesitation, the men, women, and children broke once more into cheers and applause, assuming that I, companion of "Gandhi," must also be a film star.

I smiled, waved, and said "Namaste" to those nearest me. A few children reached out to grasp my hand as I walked past them, though the officers quickly escorted me to the platform. Well, I had had my moment.

Disappointingly, the next several hours passed without event. Kingsley and the other actors boarded the train, which traveled back and forth on the tracks, while I sat quietly back on the train station platform, waiting. Finally, a friendly technician explained the situation to me. They were filming a night scene, though the interior train shots were being filmed by day. An illusion of darkness inside the train was created by gray translucent plastic that workmen placed over the train windows. The final part of the scene where Gandhi is thrown off the train onto the outside platform would be shot when darkness actually descended. Bored and disappointed, I realized I had nothing to do but wait the whole day for my part to be included in the filming.

To stretch my legs, I walked away from the platform and was surprised to find that the crowd, with absolutely nothing to watch, was still gathered behind the police lines. The children who had earlier tried to grab my hand waved me to come to them. They were of school age, and though I knew all children in India weren't necessarily in school, these eight or ten youths looked better dressed than the ragged youngsters who sold tea in the bazaars.

I walked toward the rope and asked them in Hindi if they had a holiday from school. They smiled brightly, said yes, and excitedly asked me my name and country. I told them, "Mr. James, America." "Amreeca, Amreeca," they repeated with wide smiles to each other. I asked them their names, and my attempts to repeat them caused more laughter. A few reached their hands over the rope to hold mine, almost as if physical contact would help me understand their names better. A policeman tried to push them back, but I assured him it was all right. I genuinely enjoyed talking with the children and continued the conversation in my limited Hindi. *What is your age? How many people are in your family?*

I told them the one joke I had learned to say in Hindi—about a passenger who thinks that the 2:30 train is on time because it pulls into the station exactly at 2:30, only to find out that the "punctual" train is really the previous day's train. The children laughed and clapped gleefully.

A few minutes later I was called back to the platform for filming, but it was a false alarm. When the technician finally informed me that lunch was ready, I walked past the children again on my way to the food tent. A small boy emerged from the group and presented me with a handful of long white radishes. "For your lunch," he said in Hindi. "They are from my father's garden." I gratefully knelt down to hug and thank him, then headed for the catered repast where, I was told, "The water is from England. Very nice clean water for you." I washed the radishes, which were deliciously sweet.

I spent the rest of the day making occasional forays back to the children behind the rope. When we ran out of things to say, they just held my hand. By five o'clock, darkness had come upon us, and for several "takes" I stood a short distance from the camera, mustering disdainful looks, while "Gandhi" was thrown from the train, landing on mattresses beyond the range of the camera. That part of the filming went quickly, and, after an offer to ride back to the hotel with the technical crew, I was ready to leave.

The day, I noted to myself, hadn't seemed quite as tedious as it might have been. As I walked toward the bus, I waved to the children, who beckoned me to come to them once again. This time they presented me with flowers as well as broad smiles and I finally got it. Forget the silver screen. I knew where my heart lay—connecting with the people of India.

NOTHING IS FOR CERTAIN

NEW YEAR'S DAY, 1981, arrived with the usual winter fog of Delhi, but the sun had broken through by late morning and promised a glorious day. Though not much of a religious holiday, New Year's was one of my favorite days, symbolizing as it did new beginnings. Though Joe was still in America because of his father's passing, in India, we were starting a new phase of our mission, for, in just another week, the novices would be living with us.

Steve, Gerry, and I gathered late that afternoon in our living room for prayer. Gerry lit a candle on the table between us, led us in the recitation of a psalm, then sat back and announced bluntly, "I'm leaving India and returning to the States."

I didn't know what to say. Once again, Gerry had taken me completely by surprise.

"Are you serious?" Steve asked.

"Yes."

Gerry hadn't given any indication of dissatisfaction recently and in fact had seemed more enthusiastic about the mission the previous month. What on earth was going on?

"I'll go back as soon as a replacement can be found," Gerry began, then continued to explain. Several reasons brought him to the decision: a recent kidney stone problem had shaken him, his counseling abilities seemed of little use in Indian culture, and though he had willingly come to India, he hadn't volunteered to do so. He had been requested to come.

"You know, I have to say my heart really isn't into this mission as much as the rest of you. I feel bad saying that, but it's the truth."

"Please, Gerry," Steve said. "Take more time with this decision. I've almost left too, but things change so quickly, especially around health. The worst thing I think we can do is make a decision when we're really feeling bad."

"That sounds like good advice, Gerry," I said softly.

I felt for him and the turmoil he had experienced the last several months. Gerry had been generous to join the mission, but that decision had taken its toll on him and on all of us. The spirit of the vow of obedience urged us to follow the directives of the Superiors, even when not formally "placed under the vow." We had all been assigned tasks we might not have tackled on our own, and we often grew from it. But just as often, a Superior who thought he knew best for someone else was sadly mistaken—and the result was heartache for everyone. I would respect any decision of Gerry's, to return or to stay, convinced that he knew best for himself.

Two days later, I was filling out forms to be sent to Rome and asked Gerry who should be listed as Novice Master. "Put my name down, I'm staying," he replied.

"Gerry, thank you, truly. And the novices will be happy to see you in a few days, I know that."

I was pleased that we were all back "on track," but I knew circumstances could change again, and they definitely would. I would have to just hang on to the roller coaster. If India was teaching me anything on a daily basis, it was the Law of Impermanence. One of the phrases our little community had coined over the past year said it simply: "In India, nothing is for certain."

EAST AND WEST

A HORSE-DRAWN CART PULLED up at our door and the novices, Barto, Juel, Johnny, and Benedict stepped off, each carrying a single small suitcase. It had not occurred to them to hire a taxi at the Delhi train station—something they had never done before. Their whole lives had been lived in villages where carts were the only transport.

The clamor and bustle of Delhi, on the other hand, was unlike anything they had ever experienced. Cars honked endlessly, dust and exhaust fumes filled the air, hundreds of people lived on the sidewalks, lights turned red and green to direct traffic—though no one really paid attention to the signals. In addition, the novices now lived in a house where the unfamiliar sounds of English constantly assailed their ears. Understandably, they looked slightly bewildered.

We rented the apartment below us for additional space, and since the apartments had an internal connection, the residence felt like one large home. Gradually we settled into a comfortable routine that consisted of classes in the morning, free time or sports in the afternoon, late afternoon Mass, and evening prayers. All of us Americans taught one of the classes—English, Church History, Spirituality, the Vows—and Gerry invited one of the seminary professors to teach a class in Scripture. Steve organized Sunday afternoon outings and took the novices to art galleries, the zoo, and several museums as part of their education. All the elements of a good community and training program seemed to be in place. There was only one more thing—find out what kind of people the novices really were.

The single most important factor in establishing the Brotherhood in India was, I believed, the caliber of the candidates we recruited. Training programs for the young brothers were only secondary factors. If a candidate was communicative, assertive, and dependable, he could apply that to the Brotherhood. If the person at age twenty or thirty didn't possess those skills and qualities, I doubted that any amount of training could make up for that lack.

One morning shortly after their arrival, I told the novices that I needed volunteers for three projects that afternoon—scrubbing down the kitchen, shopping with Steve, and purchasing fresh flowers for the chapel. "So, who wants to do the first job?" I asked. Silence. I waited a moment more, and repeated my question. More silence. The novices simply looked at each other, then Johnny said quietly, "The work will be done, Brother Jim." When I returned late afternoon from the bank, the projects had all been accomplished Indian style—by all of them simultaneously and without apparent organization.

At breakfast a few days later Gerry said, "We can fry up some more pancakes. How many does everyone want?" Steve, whose stomach was much better, said two would be great. Joe, now returned from the U.S., and I both declined more, but the novices said nothing. After a lengthy pause, Barto said, "We cannot answer. That is asking for more than we have been given. This is impolite for us." Gerry went to the kitchen and returned a few minutes later with a platter full of pancakes that he placed on the table. "Please take more," he urged the novices. The platter was cleaned in a matter of moments.

Though Barto ate well, his cheeks looked sunken and his arms thinner than ever. He seemed a shadow of the young man I had visited at the ashram. Benedict, quiet in general, had become physically listless by the third week and even skipped several days of playing field hockey with the seminarians. When I asked him one evening if he felt ill, he said no. I persisted. Was the noise and traffic of the city wearing him down? No. After more questions that received negative replies, I picked up the English newspaper and busied myself reading. Benedict picked up the Hindi paper and read. Ten minutes later, he said, "I never ate meat every day. I feel heavy." When I told Gerry, we decided to have meat only three times a week, a diet closer to Indian custom. Pancakes dripping with syrup, however, remained a popular Western breakfast with the novices.

I often came upon the novices speaking haltingly in English with each other and I encouraged their efforts. I need not have worried that English was an imposition, for they all were quite eager to develop their skills in that language. All except Juel, that is. Unless addressing us Americans, he spoke only in Hindi. Though I was concerned that he needed English proficiency for higher studies, it was the habitual look on his face that truly concerned me. Taciturn.

Each Monday night we gathered to discuss the running of the house and plan for the coming week as well as discuss the future. "How would you like the brothers' communities to look ten years from now?" I asked the novices one evening. I asked them to draw a picture of what that might look like. I was interested in an Indian perspective, I said, and even a rough sketch would be fine. Barto, Johnny, and Benedict readily took up the pencils and paper provided, and set to work. Juel only stared at his paper.

A few minutes later Johnny showed the group his drawing of a small compound that contained a mud building, two cows in the yard, and people streaming in and out of the house. "From this compound, we can teach reading and writing to the people, and some will come inside to join us in prayers." Johnny had captured the essentials—a community of brothers providing a needed service and bringing some people into a circle of prayer. Benedict and Barto had similar drawings, though Juel had none. When I invited Juel to add comments to the others' pictures, he said he had nothing to say.

The following day, however, I found out Juel was quite capable of expressing himself when he wanted to. On a street near the apartment, I came upon Juel and the other novices returning from a field-hockey game. Juel was speaking animatedly and forcefully, and to my surprise, smoking. When he saw me, he quickly put out the cigarette and his face darkened. We had no rule about smoking. I hadn't even thought to mention it, since nobody in any seminary I visited smoked. I was taken aback by Juel's presumption to smoke, but it was his demeanor and tone of voice I didn't like. I hadn't understood his words, but his gestures and tone were disdainful or overbearing, as if he were placing himself above the others. I knew that the "elder brother" in an Indian family often took on an authority role, but that attitude would not serve our community.

My next surprise came some weeks later from Johnny and Benedict. In English class I was stressing the need for good vocabulary for college studies. "I would like doing higher studies," Johnny said, "but I must first pass my exam from last year." I asked him to explain, and learned that neither he nor Benedict had passed what would be the equivalent of high school exams in America.

My eyebrows furrowed. The previous year I had been excited to meet the novices and I had enjoyed their company. But now I found that two of them had not even completed high school, a basic requirement. Another one had a rather sour disposition, perhaps even deep emotional problems. Only Barto seemed fairly solid, though he didn't look quite healthy. Maybe Juel would improve, maybe Johnny and Benedict could take their exams and pass. Maybe it would all work out. I kept that hope alive because I wanted them to be the candidates I was looking for. But my doubts remained, and occasionally I saw through that to my real feelings—deep disappointment.

FOR THE SAKE OF
THE KINGDOM

MIDWAY BETWEEN THE chill of winter and the upcoming hot weather, March was the perfect month for locals to carry garlands to the *ghats* and beseech the gods for favors. I often found myself, between my classes at the seminary and teaching the novices, sitting on our apartment doorstep watching devotees make their way to the river.

The raucous voices of the five women who advanced up the street one day could be heard from a block away. Tall and large-boned, they paused in front of the apartment and surveyed me inch by inch. They spoke in rapid Hindi and jangled their bracelets in my face as they gesticulated broadly, and one playfully tapped my arm. I was surprised at their directness since no other women, except beggars, had ever addressed me that forcefully—or touched me. While any number of men on the streets of Delhi had spoken to me or clasped my hand in theirs, such contact with women in India was simply not done.

They laughed coarsely and clapped their hands—as gypsies might to accompany their dancing—twirled in front of me and then moved on. Ramesh, the tailor whose shop was located across the street and who knew our every coming and going, called to me. "James, do you know who those people are? They are *hijra*, men with something missing between their legs." Ramesh made a slicing motion with his hand over his crotch.

Eunuchs. I should have guessed. The "women" had rough features and garish make-up as well as large hands, a tell-tale sign. An article a month earlier in the *Times of India* stated that a bill had been introduced in Parliament to officially recognize them as a third gender. Some *hijra*, the article said, were eunuchs because of a genital deformity at birth, and others had chosen castration to join the close-knit community. A few, the article claimed, had been forcibly castrated by other eunuchs. They roamed the city in groups, seeking out the birth of a child. At the child's home, they would sing and dance to drive bad luck away from the new-born, and, seen to possess special powers, would be paid for their services. Sometimes aggressive and rough, they might refuse to leave a birth celebration or wedding until enough rupees came their way. Though they lived outside of mainstream society, the *hijra* were quietly tolerated by most people.

"Just ignore them, like beggars, if they come again," Ramesh advised.

The description of the eunuchs strangely enough echoed words from the Gospels. In one passage, Jesus said that there were eunuchs who had been born that way, others made so by men, and still others who chose that path "for the sake of the Kingdom." Traditionally, being a "eunuch" for "the sake of the Kingdom" had been seen as a reference to celibacy. One chose celibacy in order to focus on spiritual growth and service to humanity.

I voluntarily chose the powerful image of a dedicated brother, where celibacy came with the territory. There was, however, another reality involved. Another truth existed under layers of confusion, shame, and fear.

From early youth, my sexual attractions were always to other men, but acting on such impulses I knew would send me to fiery hell for eternity. I, for one, had really believed that the Church had the right answers. Looking back now, it seems astonishing that I had abdicated so much of my judgment, but continual brain-washing from an early age is quite effective. General society in the 1950's, when I was a teenager, considered people like me aberrant. When word of "us" surfaced, it had to do with "perversion," beatings, and time in jail. I had no place in society, none as an active sexual being in Christianity, and so my overriding goal became *no one must ever know*. And in front of me at the time were my high school teachers, genuinely generous and devoted brothers, and I truly embraced that image and lifestyle. Had I been a perfectly celibate brother? No—there had been Hawaii.

One summer, I was sent to teach at the brothers' school in Honolulu. The balmy air, the smell of frangipani, the sun wrapping around my body at Waikiki, had begun to awaken my senses and prepare me for that day at Hanauma Bay. I had become friends with another teacher who liked to go snorkeling on the weekends and who periodically invited me and others along. He was married, so I was caught quite unaware by his actions the day it was just the two of us. As we swam out to the coral reef, our faces pushed into our masks underwater, he tapped me on the shoulder several times to point out colorful schools of fish darting off to the side. Then he tapped me on the chest to indicate other fish, then tapped my abdomen. By the time his hand was on my genitals, I knew what he wanted—and I wanted it too. In the blue waters off Hawaiian shores, I had my first, albeit clumsy, adult sexual encounter—at age twenty-eight.

By the end of the summer, however, guilt was the victor and I returned to my regular teaching job determined never to fail again against my vow and, double indemnity, against inherently sinful activity—though I was slowly but surely letting go of that latter belief. I resumed managing my vow of celibacy with a simple process—numbing my body.

The Indian eunuchs—some celibate, some not—at least looked at home in their bodies. I, on the other hand, struggling to be a "eunuch" for "the sake of the Kingdom," had been out of touch with my own body for many years. In high school I had walked with my arms swinging, won dance contests, and had been a passable tennis player, but by my twenties—repressing sexual and bodily sensations to remain celibate—I had anesthetized almost my entire physical being. My arms no longer swung easily at my side, as my sister had noticed on a visit home. A doctor once asked if I experienced pain in my tight shoulders. I had felt nothing. When I had played tennis with students at a boarding school where I taught, I learned from them my body no longer "followed through." I had always known that the vow of chastity proscribed sexual activity, but I hadn't expected to be robbed of my whole body.

But bodily sensations were once again pushing at me, and had ever since the first day I arrived in India. The swirl of people dancing in the streets of Old Delhi whose bodies had pressed close to mine, had pushed me into the pulse of India, and into my own flesh. I had often recalled that moment, the smell of sunny crisp air, the beat of the drums, the awareness of my feet planted firmly on the street.

The sense of my own physical body had increased since that day, with every massage received, with each blast of hot June weather that made me feel I had been hit broadside by a truck, with each article of damp clothing that stuck to me during the monsoons. Spicy food had delighted my palate, sickness had paid a periodic call, a cool breeze on a hot night felt heaven-sent. Because of India, I was slowly living more *in* my body, rather than, as in one writer's phrase, a "short distance" from it—and I was ready for that.

TWO RUPEES

I NEVER KNEW her name. She was simply "the old lady at the corner," and she appeared so timeless I thought she could never die.

Every day, on my way back from Hindi class or shopping, I would see her under the shade trees where the road in the neighborhood made a sharp bend. She spent her time beneath those trees on her *charpoi*, a rope cot. Her furrowed face and cloudy eyes always turned toward me as I passed, gazing at me more directly than would have been appropriate for a younger Indian woman. I often wondered how old she was. I guessed her age to be seventy or eighty, but I knew that her appearance could really be that of a fifty or sixty year-old woman in this harsh land.

Her cot stood in front of a low, one-story residence, the interior of which was dark yet full of chattering voices. The woman in the pale-green sari who brought her meals and tea was undoubtedly her daughter-in-law, dutifully serving the family matriarch. Two adolescent girls continually went in and out of the house, and sometimes sat near their grandmother. But for the most part, the old woman sat alone.

I can't recall ever seeing her stand or walk. Perhaps she couldn't by then. But she always had her hookah nearby and smoked frequently.

As I passed her she would greet me with a light touch to her forehead and a throaty "salaam" which I returned. A fleeting smile would cross her face, then fade. I didn't try to speak more with her.

There seemed to be too much distance. Yet, she looked steadily at me, and I sensed that she was comfortable with me—and also curious. I had come to know, from other neighbors' questions, that I as a foreigner living in their midst was as much a curiosity to them as they and India were to me. In the old woman's case though, the chasm of age, gender and culture seemed unbridge-able, and I chose to show my respect by a simple verbal greeting and a gentle nod of my head. During those times when our eyes met for more than a couple of seconds, I knew that we were a distant window for each other, a window to a world neither of us could expect to enter fully.

One day, a young man sat near the old woman, reading to her. She made her usual salaam to me, and I to her. The young man, in his early twenties and presumably a grandson, looked up and added his greeting in Hindi, "Hello sir, how are you today?" I replied with the usual, "Fine, thank you, and are you well today?" After his nod and smile, I walked on.

The grandson soon became a regular companion at the wom-an's bedside. As I would come upon them, he was either reading to her, massaging her feet or sitting quietly on a straw mat placed on the ground. He invariably wore a fresh, white *kurta*—a long-sleeved, hip-length, flowing shirt—and thin cotton pants whose cuffs dragged in the dust. Noticing his broad shoulders and quiet presence, I began to think of him as her anchor to this world. She seldom spoke to anyone else.

The old woman gradually greeted me only with her gesture of salaam, hand to her forehead, and direct eye contact, leav-ing verbal greetings to the grandson. The young man, whenever present, continued to ask me how I was each time, and I would reply with the usual pleasantries, occasionally adding a phrase I had learned in Hindi class that day. One day I ventured to ask him if he was a student. I had expected a simple yes or no response along with the usual pleasantries, but when he replied yes, he added, "*Sahib, baitiey aur chai lijiey.*" Please sir, have a seat and take tea. I squatted on the mat next to him while he clapped his hands and his sisters scurried to bring us tea and biscuits. What all he said that day, I am not sure, but from the corner of my eye I could see his grandmother smiling proudly and fondly on us. I felt I had had tea with both of them.

Her cough began slowly. More and more her hookah was at her mouth, and several people I hadn't seen before gathered around her cot. One afternoon she could barely touch her hand to her forehead to greet me, and she stared absently at the ground instead of looking at me. I asked those standing nearby if she needed medicine or anything at all. They said no. I persisted. Surely, I said, I could buy her some medicine, or get a doctor, for she was clearly very sick. But no, they told me, there was nothing to be done. I did not see the grandson.

The next day the grandson was again not there so I asked her directly if she needed anything—the first time I had said more than hello to her. Her face showed pain and she asked for two rupees for medicine. Two rupees! Of course I could give that, much more if needed. But somehow that was the one day I had not a single rupee in my pocket. "Tomorrow, tomorrow!" I cried. "I'll bring it tomorrow." She smiled and sank back onto the cot. The semicircle of onlookers said nothing. Standing a respectful distance from the cot, they only stared.

The following day I made certain I had money in my pocket, and headed down the road. At the shade tree on the corner, I looked expectantly for the old woman on her cot. The bed was now occupied by a middle-aged man whom I had not seen before. Those gathered near the cot looked at me with expressionless faces as the grandson came to me.

In a few Hindi words and gestures he let me know that the old woman was gone forever. He said it with little feeling, and the group did not appear to be in mourning.

I held the grandson's hand for a moment, mumbled something, and walked away with my own private sadness. The late morning sun felt hot on my neck as I headed for the riverbanks. Fewer people than usual milled near the temples, and the area was quiet. In the stillness of the morning, I felt deep disappointment in myself. I should have returned *immediately* the previous day with the rupees the woman had requested. Had I not accorded the situation its actual urgency, or the woman her importance? Was I *that* removed from life around me?

My rational mind told me that a few rupees for medicine would not have changed the course of the woman's life at that point. But my heart reminded me that I would have been responding to *her*!

The feeling of sadness in me increased, and I slowly wiped my eyes. The sadness was about the woman's passing, and it was also sadness for myself—a sadness evoked by seeing my own insensitivity.

The two rupees lay cold in my pocket, and I finally gave them to an insistent temple beggar, quite against my custom.

11 April 1981
Delhi

Dear Dave,

Barto has tuberculosis. He had become very thin and coughed frequently so I had Dr. Sundaram look at him. He is now on medication that can cure him, but we have decided to send him home. I hate to see Barto leave, but poor health has always been an impediment to accepting a candidate. Besides giving Barto enough money to return home, we are also giving him money for the six-month supply of the medication he needs.

We're also sending Juel home. He'd been very moody and incommunicative, so Gerry asked Father Mathias, a psychologist at the seminary, to interview and assess him. Father Mathias found Juel quite emotionally immature, and harboring much repressed anger. Our candidates must be healthier than that "lest we build on sand."

I have reread the information from Bill about all our novices, and I have to say that I find myself irritated. Both Barto and Juel had been with other religious orders that rejected them, presumably for good reason, but Bill recruited them to be part of our pioneer group! And Benedict and Johnny have not passed their high school exams. In the States we would never accept men in either of those conditions. What was Bill thinking?

And, Dave, what were you and your council thinking to accept these young men based on the recommendation of a man who saw them only a few times and who was not known for good judgment in the U.S.? He never lived with them more than a day, if that. There's been some rather unrealistic thinking going on here, and we in Delhi have to deal with the consequences. True, I myself was excited to meet them and glossed over the information I had read earlier, hoping things would work out.

Now, I'm more inclined to be stricter right from the beginning about whom we accept as candidates.

The decision to send Barto and Juel home has disturbed everyone. We Americans are discouraged about losing fifty-percent of our first group, though simultaneously we are relieved to have our intuitions about Juel confirmed by an outside source. We now know that our instincts are valid and that lack of communication is never simply a language issue. (Joe learned hardly one word of Hindi but he seems to have met half of Northern India. You know Joe!)

Since we announced our decision, Johnny and Benedict look a bit "lost" as they walk around the house, no doubt anticipating the loss of their "elder brothers" in a few days. I told them they can speak with me privately about the situation if they wanted to, but they haven't. Neither of them, however, appears surprised by the decision.

Since Easter is only a week away, Juel and Barto will stay until Easter Monday. Barto looks like he's taking the decision well. He is relieved to know the cause of his low energy and feels physically better already, just after two weeks of medication. Juel sulks, as was expected. It's a sad situation, because neither Gerry nor I know how we can help him understand. Of course, Juel seems incapable of understanding, and that's exactly the problem, isn't it?

During Holy Week we'll be singing the Lamentations of the prophet Jeremiah who mourns empty Jerusalem. We have our own losses, yet I know we are doing the right thing.

Sincerely,

Jim

GIN AND TONIC

THE SIGHT OF blood on my toothbrush opened my sleepy eyes. *Oh no, what now?* A serious bout of diarrhea the week right after Easter had left me weak, and now, bleeding gums!

"I can't believe it, Joe," I said later that evening as he and I walked on the rooftop before dinner. "My gums are bleeding. It's always something! I'll have to go see Dr. Sundaram again."

"It's stress. You worry too much."

The ice in Joe's gin and tonic clinked as he swirled the drink and savored its coolness. April was steadily heating up Delhi, though we would soon escape by moving south to the cooler city of Bangalore for the next two months. Bangalore, a center of summer school classes for religious orders, would provide educational opportunities for Johnny and Benedict, our remaining novices, as well as grant us all a reprieve from the deadening heat.

What Joe said about stress was true. Even my shoulders had cramped the previous day when I tried to adjust a curtain rod. I didn't need a psychotherapist to tell me that I was "shouldering" a lot of responsibility and that my body was rebelling. The recent tension involved in sending Juel and Barto home, and little response from bishops whom I hoped could sponsor us, had all weighed on me.

I rather envied Joe's easy approach to most situations. Somehow he had cultivated the attitude that things would work out, and if they didn't, well then they didn't. And that was that.

"What you need is a good stiff drink," Joe continued. "Let me fix you something. I found an excellent gin downtown the other day." He went downstairs and returned with a gin and tonic, assuring me that even the ice cubes were made with filtered water. "And the fresh lemon squeeze I added gives a nice fresh touch."

The following morning, there was indeed less blood on my toothbrush.

"You see, the gin helps," Joe said the next evening on the roof. "Just listen to 'Dr. Joe.' Do this for five days and you'll be better." He was right. By the fourth day, the bleeding had greatly decreased and I marveled at the curative powers of gin.

Dr. Sundaram was less impressed. "It was the lemon that helped. You have scurvy, a vitamin C deficiency." He explained that stress and my recent diarrhea had prevented me from absorbing food properly. "You need a rest, preferably in the mountains." Bangalore, he said, was just another hectic city. He suggested I return to Mussoorie, the mountain town where we had studied Hindi the previous year, and stay at a guesthouse there for the next two months. "The others can go to Bangalore. They can get along without you, you know. And mountain air will be a great tonic for you."

The thought of spending time in the mountains was appealing, but really not necessary. The bleeding had decreased, and ended within three more days. I could go with the others to Bangalore. A week later I woke up with a flu-like feeling and an outbreak of painful blisters on my face. Joe realized that neither lemons nor gin could handle the new situation and called a taxi to take me to Dr. Sundaram's once more.

"Shingles, you have shingles," Dr. Sundaram said. He explained that shingles came from the chicken pox virus that had lain dormant in nerve endings since childhood, and erupted when a person was under significant stress. "Rest at home for the remainder of April. The blisters will disappear soon. Then, a month or two in the mountains. Doctor's orders."

On the way home, I told Joe that I could study Hindi again at the language school while in the mountains. He stared at me. "Rest. Get it? Rest! And, a nightly gin and tonic during this God-awful heat."

ANGELS

THE BUS THAT left Delhi at six in the morning would reach the base of the Himalayas just as the noonday heat crushed down, and a second bus would then carry travelers up to Mussoorie, where at six thousand feet, cool and clean air awaited. Though it was "high season" for travel to the mountains, I had managed to obtain a reserved seat as far as the foot of the mountains. Hopefully I would have no problem getting a ticket for the shorter, last leg of the journey.

I left our house as dawn broke and headed toward Kudsia Garden, which lay between us and the bus terminal. By the time I reached the Garden, the tea stalls that lined its edge were already open for business, and the smell of coffee reminded me that there would be no other chance for breakfast for the next six hours. I surveyed the rickety tea stalls, each of them sporting an espresso machine on its front counter, and chose the cleanest looking one. At its shadowy back, a young man in a tattered tee shirt and hitched-up *lungi* leaned over a kerosene stove, boiling tea on one burner and frying eggs on another. Another man, apparently the owner, sat at the front, his face pushed into the *Times of India*. Only one other customer sat inside the stall, a young man in a bright red shirt and neatly pressed pants.

"Very good morning, sir," the owner said, peering over his newspaper. He asked what I would like, and I ordered an omelet.

"And you like chai, sahib?"

"Coffee, please." I was too American to substitute tea for coffee in the morning.

The coffee arrived quickly, but not the omelet. "Omelet is just coming, just coming," the owner said, and offered me his copy of the *Times of India*. Distracted by the news of the day—an increase in train robberies, police corruption, and bride burning, that tragic attempt to extort additional dowry—I had read almost half the paper by the time the owner placed the omelet in front of me. *Oh no, what time is it?* I hadn't worn a watch for years, trusting my usually good sense of time, and my travel alarm was packed away in my bag. The man in the red shirt was gone, and several other people had since entered the tea stall. When the owner informed me it was already six o'clock, I left a generous amount of rupees next to the uneaten omelet, grabbed my travel bag and left quickly.

I had all of Kudsia Garden to traverse, as well as to find the proper bus at the large terminal. Entering the park, I ran past large shady trees, flower gardens and the cool stone archways where I had often sat and read in more leisurely moments. Even in those pleasant times, however, there was often an eerie feel to the garden that I couldn't explain—a certain heaviness. Now, in the quiet of morning, the stone path crunched under my running feet.

At the other end of the park, I crossed the street, dodging cars, buses, and horse-drawn *tongas*, and entered the bus terminal. The terminal, a large and noisy concrete shell, housed dozens of buses besieged by early morning travelers. Black clouds of exhaust trailed departing buses, and the ever-present loudspeaker carried songs from popular Hindi films—but not information about bus departures. By the time I located my gate, it was nearly six-fifteen and the bus was not there.

How could I have been so careless about time? That wasn't like me, though I knew that recent illnesses had left me far from being my usual self. But to have missed a bus in the high travel season—what a mistake! No doubt it would be difficult, perhaps impossible, to get another ticket for weeks. Suddenly my legs felt shaky. The run through Kudsia Garden had exhausted my small reserve of energy. If only the omelet had been served on time. If only I had carried a watch. If only India had a good water supply, I wouldn't have had diarrhea last month, and I wouldn't be so exhausted now. And why did travel in India always have to be so difficult? I hated travel in India. I hated India. Why couldn't anything go right, just for once?

"Good morning, sir," a voice to my left spoke to me. I turned to see the young man in the red shirt from the tea stall. "Where are you going, may I ask? I saw you at the tea stall."

"I'm going to Dehradun, and then up to Mussoorie, but I missed my six o'clock bus."

"Oh, no problem. I am going on the same bus. It hasn't arrived here yet, and probably won't until after six-thirty."

Of course! I've been here for a year and a half and should know better than worrying about being ten or so minutes late.

"My name is Chacko, and your good name please?" he said as he extended his hand. I happily shook his hand, and replied that my name was James, having discovered that Indians seemed to hear that name better than "Jim."

"So, we shall be fellow-travelers then," Chacko smiled. "I am having tea here while we wait. May I present you with coffee? I think you like coffee, isn't it?"

"Yes," I replied, "that is very kind of you." And also observant, I thought to myself.

In a few minutes Chacko returned with coffee for me and tea for himself, as well as *samosas*, small triangular snacks of deep fried batter stuffed with curried potatoes.

"Please take," he insisted. "I think you didn't have time to finish the omelet you ordered." I thanked him, accepted the coffee and *samosas*, and took a better look at my benefactor. He looked to be in his late twenties, my height, wavy black hair, a solid build, and a slightly squared-off, handsome face. His complexion, darker than most North Indians, made his eyes look intense, and his bright red shirt, open at the chest, added to that vibrancy. With these features and his accent, I would have guessed he was from the southern state of Kerala. Upon my inquiry, he explained that he was, indeed, from Kerala and was a graduate student at Delhi University, on holiday. He would be going as far as Dehradun.

A demanding horn announced the arrival of our bus, traveling too fast for a crowded bus station. It had barely stopped and opened its doors when the orderly queue disintegrated as ticket holders pushed to board. Everyone knew that even reserved seats might be taken by another person. Chacko gently held my arm to keep me back from the crush. "It will be just fine, not to worry. If there is any problem, I will assist you for you are a guest in my country. It is my duty." We boarded last and, miraculously, our seats were still available though not together. Chacko placed my bag on an overhead rack and assured me it would be safe.

The bus crossed the Jumuna River, headed northeast and entered the industrial "trans-Jumuna" region. Outside the bus, people in autorickshaws and on bicycles wore handkerchiefs over their noses and mouths to protect themselves from pollution and dusty air, reminding me of how badly I wanted to get to the hills.

Within an hour, the flat scenery and rocking of the bus made me feel drowsy in spite of the coffee, though my relaxation wasn't due to those factors alone. It was because Chacko was nearby. I usually found it difficult to fall asleep on a bus while traveling alone, but knowing that Chacko was a few seats away provided me a sense of security I didn't often feel. For once, someone was looking out for me. Why I should have such trust in a perfect stranger, I didn't know, but the confidence was there. I could give up worrying about someone stealing my wallet or my luggage. Someone nearby knew where I was going, and would help me get there. It was like having a guardian angel.

I always loved the lore of the guardian angel. Besides prayers before meals, my earliest recollection of memorizing prayers was the plea to my guardian angel. "Angel of God, my guardian dear… ever this day be at my side." I was told, first by my mother and then by the nuns in school, that I had my own special angel. He knew my name, my destiny in life, and had nothing to do but guide me. He was my constant companion, the spirit-form that never left my side. No other church teaching commanded as much heart-felt allegiance from me as the belief that I was guided along my personal path by unseen forces.

Some time later, I heard Chacko's voice in my ear. "James, we have reached Meerut. Let us step out and stretch. The bus will be here for at least twenty minutes."

The heat of the day had started to build, and sharp lines delineated sun and shadow. Chacko guided me to a covered area and explained that Meerut was famous as the place where the Indian Mutiny of 1857 had started. The Indian infantry, he said, had rebelled against their British officers, killing many of them and their families that fateful May. Many of the British women had not yet taken to the hills to escape the heat, as was the custom, and found themselves trapped in the plains. There they were massacred along with their children. The uprising spread to several cities including Delhi, where a few British took refuge in Kudsia Garden. As they hid within the garden's thickets, they could hear the death screams of their countrymen.

"You must be knowing Kudsia Garden. It is across the street from the bus terminal where we departed this morning. They say that when the garden is quiet you can still hear weeping in the trees."

We stood quietly in the shade for a few more minutes, disturbed only by a constant flow of young boys carrying teapots and small clay cups, nasally chanting "*gurum chai, gurum chai,*" hot tea, hot tea.

The bus driver called for reboarding, and three hours later we entered the Doon Valley and arrived at the Dehradun bus stand. As I had feared, all buses going up the mountain were booked for the rest of the day. Group taxis, more expensive, were the only alternative and the few that remained were surrounded by desperate travelers. Somehow Chacko, carrying my bag, managed to find a place for me in a group taxi, at the very best rate. It was a welcome feeling, being taken care of. The healing that I was going to the hills for had already begun with the help of a guardian angel.

"Have a pleasant stay in Mussoorie, James. I have enjoyed your company." Chacko spoke from outside the taxi window, clasping my hand.

"Chacko, I cannot thank you enough for your help today. I would have been lost without you."

"Well, James, my brother, our meeting was meant to be. Did you know that 'Chacko' means 'James' in my language?" The taxi pulled away and I soon lost sight of Chacko's red shirt.

NIGHT TRAIN

By MID-JULY, WE American brothers and two Indian novices had gathered again in Delhi. I had been rejuvenated by my time in the mountains, as had the others while in South India, and we were ready to examine our situation with fresh eyes. During the previous weeks, Gerry had come to a clearer evaluation of Johnny and Benedict.

"They're both good young men, but they really need more peer interaction," he said, and the rest of us agreed.

I recalled that Father Ambrose in Patna—a sixteen-hour train ride southeast of Delhi—ran a training center for young Jesuits there, and had once told me he accepted "outside" candidates into the program. The classes, which concentrated on English and scripture studies, would be good for Johnny and Benedict, as would living with other men their own age.

I wrote Father Ambrose asking him to take Johnny and Benedict into his program, and letting him know I was on my way to discuss details. If by the end of the year, I told myself, I hadn't solved our residency status and we had to leave Asia, our novices might even be interested in joining the Jesuits.

The fastest train to Patna, the Tinsoukia Mail, was booked, so by necessity I had to take a slower train, one with more stops. As the train pulled out of Delhi in early evening, I sat on my berth along the aisle, pulled out a book to read, when someone spoke to me.

"Which country, please?" A middle-aged man with a large belly stood across the aisle from me at the doorway to his compartment. Behind him, two women sat on the seats and one squatted on the floor, arranging luggage, suggesting that the man was traveling with his wife, mother, and servant girl.

"America," I said. It was surely the hundredth time I had been asked that same question. Apparently it was an Indian's favorite way of starting a conversation.

"Yes, I like America. How very, very nice. I am reading in the papers about your new president. What do you think of him?"

Indians loved to talk politics. Usually I liked engaging in conversation with my fellow travelers, but I was distracted by the realities of the current situation. I was turning over our remaining two novices to the Jesuits for training. They had begun their training under a Jesuit priest, and after that we had only been with them a few months. Was this a portent that we were not meant to be in India after all? I had an uneasy feeling about our mission, and this trip.

Before I could give a response, the man continued. "Perhaps you support your president, and I'm sure he is a good man, but he speaks so stridently, that is the word isn't it, about the Soviet Union." He continued to give his views on the matter and praise Jarwahalal Nehru, "our first Prime Minister and architect of the Non-Aligned Movement, of course you must be knowing that," while I made perfunctory responses, nodded my head, and glanced several times at the book in my hands.

"Ah, then you must get back to your reading. I hope I have not disturbed you," he said in a disappointed voice.

"Oh, no problem. Have a pleasant trip."

"Yes, thank you. I am going to Patna. I heard you tell the conductor that you are going there also. Perhaps we shall talk in the morning." He returned to his compartment—and the train rumbled into the night.

After a vegetarian dinner served on gray metal trays, passengers began to arrange their sleeping areas. Those in compartments placed blankets over their open doorway, and the others, like myself, whose narrow berth ran along the aisle, put shawls and pillows on their beds, their suitcases underneath. I traveled with only a small shoulder bag but it was too large to keep in my sleeping area. I stuffed all my belongings, except for my sandals and the clothes I would sleep in, into the bag and placed it under my berth.

<hr />

"HALF-HOUR TO MUGHALSARAI! *Adha gunta* Mughalsarai!" A porter shouted in English and Hindi. It was already light. I had slept without stirring the whole night.

I reached under my berth to retrieve the shoulder bag and the morning toiletries it contained. Not feeling the bag where I had placed it, I lowered myself onto the floor to peer under the berth, thinking the bag must have shifted position in the night. No bag! The breath went out of me. In that instant I knew it had been stolen. I spent the next several minutes, however, combing the area wishing it hadn't happened, praying it hadn't really happened, while my stomach knotted ever more tightly.

It wasn't just a bag. It was "me"—my passport, my shoes, even my train ticket. I felt stripped and violated. And unprotected—the thin pants and loose shirt I was wearing would never guard me from the jostling and chaos of India. I slipped my feet into my sandals, though I knew I couldn't walk any distance in those flimsy thongs, and sat on the edge of my berth, staring blankly in front of myself.

"Mughalsarai just ahead," the conductor said as he passed me.

"Wait, wait! Excuse me, please, I must speak with you," I called after the conductor, and explained the situation. A kindly man, he nevertheless seemed uncertain what to do. I insisted that he must have forms I could fill out, official papers that would be useful when I applied for a new passport. He scratched his head, promised to look, and ambled away. Across the aisle, the man from that compartment stood looking at me, his wife by his side.

"I heard what you said to the conductor. I am so very sorry. There are some very bad fellows in this country. Please do not think poorly of all of us."

"No, I won't," I sighed, but I knew I said it without heart. All I could hear in my mind was, damn it, damn it!

"If you wish, please stay at my home in Patna while you contact your embassy and get your affairs in order. It will be my honor." He said his name was Subhash and offered me his hand.

I looked up, saw his wife nodding in agreement, and realized I was too choked up to reply immediately. At first I thought it was fatigue and the stress of being robbed, but then I realized what it really was. This good man, to whom I had been distant if not rude the night before, who really didn't know me, not even my name, was offering me his home. India had once again sliced with a two-edged sword. The treachery of the night visitor had elicited the kindness and hospitality of a traveling companion— another angel, ready to help. I thought I had come to India to give, but India was teaching me to receive.

I held out my hand and introduced myself. "You are very, very kind. You cannot imagine what your offer means to me." I said I had plans to stay with friends in Patna, but appreciated his offer very much. Subhash murmured, "Very good," and urged me to contact him if any need should arise. I would find his full name and address on the business card he pressed into my hand.

The conductor returned with the forms to fill out, then left. In another few minutes the train pulled to a stop. "Ticket, ticket," a younger man in a railway uniform said to me. I hadn't seen him before. He was either an assistant conductor or a local agent checking on tickets.

"My ticket was in my luggage that was stolen last night," I explained, holding the papers up for him to see.

"Ticket, no ticket?" He looked at me with hard eyes and said something rapidly in Hindi.

Oh no, he doesn't understand much English and I really don't speak enough Hindi to explain. Subhash had stepped off the train a minute earlier, and the women in his party had thrown up a shawl over the doorway to their compartment.

"No ticket? Go! Go!" the railway agent shouted and waved his hand in the direction of the platform.

"No, I'm not getting off. I'm going to Patna. Patna!"

The agent spat the word "police" at me, and headed for the outside platform. He returned with two local policemen who carried *lathis*, sturdy bamboo sticks the police used to beat wrongdoers. Pointing to me, the railway agent spoke rapidly to the police, who then advanced toward me holding their *lathis* in an upraised position. My depression and self-pity evaporated. Now I was angry. *I will not be thrown off a train penniless and shoeless in the middle of the Gangetic Plain!* The officers approached with clenched jaws, but their eyes belied slight surprise, probably at having to deal with a foreigner. They will not touch or intimidate me, I decided, and I rose slowly, ever so slowly and deliberately, to face them.

"Stop!" I said in Hindi when they were about five feet away. "Don't do anything. Don't do anything!" I couldn't think of anything else to say in Hindi. My body blocked the narrow aisle, a stance I assumed would portray strength, and they came to a halt. The police stared at me for a few seconds and I stared back, my face hard and determined. In the next few moments, all movement on the train, all noises from the vendors rapping on the windows, seemed to cease. The police glanced at each other, then lowered their *lathis*. I stepped aside, indicating for them to continue on to the next coach. They walked past. And it was over.

"Mr. James, please take chai," Subhash had returned, bringing a tea vendor with him. I thanked him for his thoughtfulness, and let the warm tea soothe my stomach, which had begun to unknot.

In Patna I made my farewells to Subhash and his wife, letting them know once again how touched I was by their offer. It was only after we parted on the platform that I realized I had not even one rupee to pay for a rickshaw to St. Xavier's School, my first stop. Well, I would just take a rickshaw and let the priests pay the driver.

At St. Xavier's, Father Jack, a tall American in charge of accounts, handled everything efficiently—the rickshaw driver, funds to tide me over, and a plane ticket for Delhi whenever I was ready to go. "Oh yes," he said, "there's a letter here for you from Father Ambrose down the street at the training center. He guessed you would stop here first."

The letter explained in courteous terms that he wouldn't be able to take Johnny and Benedict into his training program. Yes, he had once referred to taking candidates from "outside," but he had meant other *Jesuit* candidates from regions outside the Patna area. The mixing of two different religious orders, his staff thought, was not a good idea. He was certain I would find another solution, God bless.

THE HEART OF INDIA

WITH A NUMBED mind, I decided I had just received the final sign that the mission was doomed. All avenues towards visas, training for candidates, in fact, almost every venture I attempted had failed. I would have to accept that. It was terribly disheartening, but there was nothing left to do.

Although it was a hot afternoon, I decided to take a walk in hopes of throwing off my heaviness. Patna, situated squarely in India's heartland along the Ganges, was an ancient capital. It might offer diversion. Directly across from St. Xavier's lay a parade ground, a *maidan*, an immense grassy oval a good half-mile in length. Hardly anyone crossed its open space. My eyes searched for shaded areas, and came to rest on the tree-lined sidewalk that ran along the periphery. Even the shaded sidewalk was practically deserted. Most people were still resting after their noon meal. A few sidewalk vendors sat dispiritedly under the trees but said nothing as I passed—they only stared. No beggars or shoeshine boys bothered me and I set myself a leisurely pace. Summer birds shrilled from treetops, puffy white clouds hung motionless in the sky above, and tree branches dipped low over the sidewalk as if to welcome me. Even the moist heat felt welcoming, touching me everywhere, and, like a physical ether, it seemed to connect me to every other creature nearby. All of us experienced the same drowsy afternoon, the same silence in the park, the same push of weather against our bodies. I wasn't just seeing India, I was feeling her.

At the far end of the parade grounds, a movie theater commanded the space of an entire block facing the great oval, and next to the theater, a single road channeled all traffic from both sides of the parade grounds into Old Patna. Cars, autorickshaws, and buses pushed past each other, vying for the limited road space. Several fruit vendors hawked their wares above the din of traffic, but my attention was drawn to the clamor coming from a group of young men just beyond the theater. The six or seven youths looked about college age, though their casual attire—*lungis* and T-shirts—spoke more of cycle rickshaw drivers and errand boys than students, who would often be dressed in Western attire. Grouped in a semicircle, their heads leaning forward and arms clasped about each other's waists, they paid no heed to the tumult of traffic behind them.

I moved closer and peered over the shoulder of the shortest boy in the group. No one noticed my presence. They were focused on two other youngsters playing a game on a board that resembled a miniature billiards table. The players used a black checker to knock white checkers into the holes, and the game progressed until the winner sunk the last piece. The crowd cheered and jostled for position, apparently to determine who would challenge the winner next.

The winner, flashing a bright smile, looked up to accept congratulations from his companions and caught my eye. "Namaste. Hello." He pushed through the group and grasped my arm. "Caroms, caroms," he said, urging me toward the board. He spoke in rapid Hindi, waving the playing pieces in his hand and pointing to the board, his eyebrows raised in expectation. I didn't understand most of his words, but his desire to play the game with me was clear, so I smiled at him and sat down.

He handed me the black piece and let me begin the game. I didn't sink any chips, but my friendly opponent sank three in a row while I took a better look at him. The young man couldn't have been more than nineteen or twenty, though his forehead was already lined. I wondered if one of the cycle rickshaws standing idly by was his. His frame was slight, his arms bony. Long, thin fingers played with the black chip, placing it in several different positions behind the black line on the board before he shot.

On my next turn I sank four chips before missing. The bystanders who had been chatting during my first attempt now became silent. My opponent missed, and I sank two more on my turn. Warm bodies now leaned against my back and pushed against my legs as the observers drew in closer. This must be beginner's luck, I thought. I never was particularly good at these games.

My opponent sank several more chips before he missed. Now only one remained. We each missed again. Behind me voices called to others, and the crush of the bodies increased, though someone managed to struggle through the crowd and provide my opponent and me with cups of tea. As I lifted the cup to my mouth, I saw what was happening: there were no barriers here—none of language, nor of culture, nor of religion. There was nothing to explain or change, nothing to plan or do—except enjoy each other's company. This was the heart of India.

I put the cup down, took a shot—and missed again. My opponent paused, looked intently at the chip in his hand, then said something in Hindi and placed the chip to his forehead. Was he praying? I noticed the sweat on his brow. He took the shot—and sank the chip.

The crowd erupted in cheers, though the congratulations were evidently for both of us since as many people wanted to shake my hand as his. My opponent reached over the game board and firmly grasped my hand. "*Ek aur?*" he asked. One more?

"Thank you, no. I'm going. I am very happy," I said in Hindi. The gallant winner stood, parted the crowd with a wave of his hand, and escorted me toward the parade grounds. Saying nothing more, he bid me farewell with hands joined in the namaste position, and I mirrored him. As I left the crowd, a well-dressed man spoke to me in English, "Very good, sir. That boy is the neighborhood champion."

When I entered the residence at St. Xavier's, I saw that Father Ambrose had arrived from the training center nearby. A gray haired man of stout build and a kindly face, he greeted me and said he was so very sorry to hear I was robbed on the train. "We must assist you in your time of need. Come, let us talk about your candidates joining our program."

I shook his warm hand, wondering if it was Providence that I'd been robbed.

18 September 1981

Dear Dave,

How strange it is that one can put so much effort into finding a solution in one place, and then the answer comes from a totally different direction. By chance, or Providence, I discovered that Nepal—the small Himalayan kingdom squeezed in between India and Tibet—wants native-English speakers to teach in its schools. In its capital of Kathmandu, I visited St. Xavier's School (run by the Jesuits who have a "St. Xavier's" in practically every major city of South Asia) and the principal has assured us of resident status visas, even for teaching only halftime. This is what I've been looking for! The Nepal-India border is an open border for citizens of the two countries, so our Indian candidates will have no problem entering Nepal. I assume that you and your council will support our decision to relocate there. We really don't have any other choices right now.

Gerry and Steve leave shortly for the U.S. Both are in need of medical attention—Gerry for recurring kidney stones that have Dr. Sundaram concerned, and Steve for a lengthy period of recuperation that he so definitely needs. They both plan to rejoin Joe and me in Kathmandu in the coming year. Joe and I will close up our apartment here, visit potential candidates in both North and South India that have been referred to us, and move to Kathmandu in January. (January in the Himalayas? I guess I shouldn't have complained about the heat of Delhi.)

I'm looking forward to settling down in Kathmandu. Even though I will travel to India periodically for recruitment (Nepal has almost no Catholics, so we continue to focus on recruiting

Indians), at least there will be a solid base for me to return to. I need that.

Sincerely,

Jim

P.S. Mt. Everest is in Nepal though, contrary to several enthusiastic local guides, you cannot see it from the city of Kathmandu. A trip up the side of Kathmandu Valley, however, gave me a tiny glimpse of the world's highest peak, perhaps ninety miles away, but its dramatic height was softened by other high peaks near it and by the angle and distance I viewed it from. Perspective is everything.

22 October 1981

Dear Dave,

With crisp autumn in the air and my spirits buoyed by our new lease on life, I've decided to write you a more lengthy missive about the *real* India.

During the high Hindu holidays in October, students everywhere in India have a break from classes, even our novices studying with the Jesuits. I told Johnny and Benedict to visit their families and I would meet them at their homes—I really wanted to understand their background. I had been in rural areas before, but nothing quite prepared me for the nineteenth century way of life found in the tribal areas.

Johnny's home, several miles from the nearest bus stand, is accessed only along dirt paths. It was a pleasant walk through rolling hills, farmland, and rice paddies, but the idea that there was a village ahead with no road to the outside world was hard for me to grasp. India is the world's tenth most industrialized nation, but roads, even dirt roads, are a luxury in some places.

When Johnny said we'd take a boat across the river, I thought he meant, well, a boat. At the water's edge, a large canoe came dipping and bobbing toward shore, laden with a dozen people, bundles of firewood spilling over the edges. A man in a loincloth poled the craft while passengers inside sat quietly, bows and arrows leaning against the legs of some of the men. Our own crossing a few minutes later was pleasant enough, though I had to keep my feet propped up on the seat so the man with the bailing can could keep up with the leakage.

Along the way to Johnny's home, neighbors greeted us with "Jai Jesu," praise Jesus. The whole area is Christian. Missionaries a hundred years ago converted them by villages, sometimes by whole tribes. Johnny's parents, brother, sister-in-law, and their children were waiting in front of the small complex of three mud buildings that nestle on the treasured land they own, ready to receive us. A visitor to a tribal home is verbally greeted and then his feet are washed. Johnny's sister-in-law performed this touching and soothing ritual for me. Over the days, I conversed with her a bit since she speaks Hindi, having come from a village near a Hindi-speaking area. The rest of Johnny's family speak only the local languages, which do not include Hindi.

My room and the goat pen were in the same building, a mud structure with a pitched roof, though the walls separating the sections didn't go all the way up. A baby goat was born that first night and it bleated for hours. (I don't know *how* Jesus handled that manger thing.) In the morning I tried to look happy, but could scarcely keep my eyes open. Johnny saved me when he produced a jar of instant coffee he had purchased for me. He knows I like coffee in the morning rather than tea. Bless his soul.

Johnny's home is not directly in a village, but in an outlying area (it's *all* outlying to me) so I didn't meet many neighbors, though a few men from the area came to help Johnny's brother in the fields. They arrived early in the morning, harvested rice, and took a mid-morning break around ten. When the men beckoned me to join them near the kitchen, I assumed it would be for the ubiquitous tea and dry cookies. It was rice beer. A whitish fluid with the taste of a whiskey sour, it is potent. I drank mine slowly, though Johnny's brother and the workers consumed large amounts from metal bowls while grinning at me, then returned to work in the fields. For myself, I needed a quick nap after the alcohol.

Time in the countryside passes faster than one might think, and I can't even tell you what I did all day in Johnny's home, or in the others' homes. Sometimes now I can't imagine I ever led the packed life of a schoolteacher in an American city. Why *do* we, like Alice in Wonderland, run so fast but get nowhere?

Benedict's village sits on high ground overlooking a meandering river that is home not only to prized fish but occasionally land animals as well. Benedict showed me a good place in the river for my daily bath and told me not to be frightened if water buffalo came into the river next to me. They wouldn't harm me, he promised. They didn't, but you have no idea how intimidating their immense snouts are up close.

Benedict took me to visit his parish priest, one of the few remaining foreigners serving in the area. Belgian, I think. A gaunt and severe-looking man, Father Andre lamented the interest that the younger generation of tribals still has in the animist religion of their ancestors, "running off to the sacred groves and the like." He called animism the work of the devil and made sure that the worst offenders came to him, Christ's representative, for Confession. He also had the boys among them take turns carrying a large cross on their shoulders in Holy Week during the re-enactment of the Way of the Cross. Why doesn't he carry the cross himself if he's supposed to represent Christ? Of course I said nothing.

Father Andre reminded me how much sway the parish priest has over peoples' lives here. He tells them what is right and what is wrong and how to live. They didn't even know they were "sinning" by going to the sacred groves until missionaries told them so. The other day I mentioned to a Jesuit superior that I thought the Church had made two major contributions to India: education and guilt. He replied, (mind you, the Jesuits run scores of high schools and colleges) "Yes, but perhaps in the reverse order."

My third stop was in the village of a man named Sylverius, whom Bill had referred to us. Sylverius is a solid-looking, mid-thirties man who has long been interested in being a brother or a priest, though family obligations and work have prevented him from joining a religious order until now. (I have asked him to join us in Kathmandu next spring, so he can know us better, and we, him.) Sylverius met me at the bus stand with two bikes.

"The bikes will be useful since we have to go about six kilometers to my village." Six, maybe, as the crow flies. Our earthbound path, however, wound endlessly through low thickets and rice paddies. To travel over rice fields, you ride the bike on top of the foot-wide mud partition between the paddies. Because it's harvest time and the rice is high, you would hardly know that the path drops off a foot or two into the paddy. I did fairly well except when we had to turn a corner. After the third crash into the paddy, I walked the bike.

Sylverius' father is what I want to be like when I grow old. A serene, white-haired gentleman, he goes about his daily business with total presence and physical grace. Much of the time I was there, he sat in a small pit in front of his home, under a loom, and wove the dark red and ivory shawls that are particular to the tribals. He presented me with one that I treasure.

The village held a party on my last night. Platters of food, including generous portions of chicken, large pots of rice and lentils, curried vegetables, and rice beer were laid out. Everybody sat on the ground or on logs, except for me. "Here, Brother Jim, you must sit here." Sylverius pointed to a chair a young villager had brought forward. "It's the only chair in the village. Someone carried it in maybe thirty years ago and we use it for special guests. Please, sit."

We sat in a large circle, with a fire in the center, and ate leisurely for over an hour. "Now, they will perform our tribal dances for you," Sylverius said. Two men beat rhythmically on large drums hung from their necks while the villagers, men, women, and children, formed a line, their arms around each other's waists. (Tribals don't have quite as much separation of men and women as you see in mainstream Hindu society.) Dance steps, forward, back, and forward again, advanced the line around the fire, the dancers singing as they moved. When, perhaps twenty minutes later, they invited me to join in, I did—they loved that. I did too.

Dave, you've heard me say how hard it is sometimes for us to adjust to India. Now I believe it is more difficult for the young men from villages to adjust their whole way of being for us. They have to speak our language, experience cities with millions of people, live a style and pace of life unknown in the countryside. I'm not sure how they do it. Years from now when we look back, I suspect we Americans will be accorded the honors of "founders" and "pioneers," but it is these first Indians who deserve such accolades.

Sincerely,

Jim

THE FOUR STAGES

USED GOODS IN India sold for almost the full original price, though I didn't know that until halfway through our street sale. We became quite popular in our neighborhood by selling our furniture and kitchenware for a pittance, and I was glad we had made the "mistake" when I saw the happy faces of the neighborhood women as they carried away bargain frying pans and sharp scissors, and their sons dragged away extra mattresses. Steve and Gerry had left for America, and Joe and I were moving back to Light of Wisdom Seminary.

Father John welcomed us and gave us the same unused classroom we had when we first arrived in India. Entering that gray room sometimes made me sad, for it made me wonder how much progress we had made in almost two years. Half of the first novices had not worked out, and half of the pioneer group of Americans appeared unsure of their commitment to the mission. I was excited about the move to Nepal, but I was loathe to leave India. Even the seminary seemed boring with Santosh now gone and Joe off on a recruitment trip. It would be a few weeks before I would travel again, so with only a hard wooden chair and a creaky bed facing me in that dull room, I began to frequent the plush lobby of the Oberoi Maidens Hotel.

The Oberoi Maidens Hotel was a pleasant three-star hotel conveniently located a mere five-minute walk from the seminary. Though I occasionally visited the hotel's dining room for a snack and a glass of wine, it was the carpeted lobby and its oversized leather chairs that drew me there on a regular basis. I could often be found reading in my favorite chair just a short distance from the front desk, and over time I became acquainted with Kush, the evening desk clerk.

In his mid-twenties, about my height, with close-cropped hair and a smooth-complexioned oval face, Kush was a graduate student in English literature at the University of Delhi. He often asked my opinion about English authors, assuming I was conversant with them. Reaching back to my own college days working on a minor in English, I managed to make a few intelligent comments, though it soon became clear that he was vastly more familiar with the field than I was.

"I like so very much Chaucer's *Canterbury Tales,*" Kush said one evening, as I sat in my chair near a white pillar. "It is very Indian, you see. When we are on a long train journey, everybody in the compartment talks and tells stories. One is never bored, you never have to feel alone." I knew well what he referred to, and remembering the gentleman on the night train to Patna, I determined to be more gracious to my train companions in the future.

"And the Prioress's Tale is quite curious. I mean, the Prioress who tells the story. She is not what I thought a nun was supposed to be. I am told that 'nun' is like the Sisters who teach in the convent schools. To lead a simple life, isn't that the idea? Chaucer's nun doesn't seem so simple. And she's a woman, roaming about the country, wearing posh clothing, sipping wine I think, and speaking freely. Is that a proper nun? There is also a priest in the story. I believe they are called 'Fathers' in your religion, isn't it?"

"Yes, we have 'Fathers.' My religion also has brothers. I'm a brother." As soon as I said the words, I wondered how I would measure up in Kush's eyes. Surely the sisters teaching in the convent schools wouldn't be stopping at the Oberoi for wine or lounging in its comfortable lobby. I guess I was more like Chaucer's nun—more independent, more worldly.

"Brothers, Fathers, how beautiful!" Kush exclaimed with genuine admiration.

"It doesn't surprise you to find me, a brother, having drinks here at the hotel?"

"Oh, no problem. You're a man, and an American. But this means that you have a vow never to marry, am I correct?"

I nodded, and Kush continued, "Such a fine purpose, devoting yourself to God alone! We have what we call *bramacharya*." Kush explained that *bramacharya* often referred to one who had chosen a life-long spiritual quest and celibacy, but added that it also simply meant "student," the first of four stages of life in Hindu thought. I asked him to explain, and he continued. After the Student Stage when one learns a craft or skill, the person enters the Second Stage, raises a family, and sees to the well-being of his loved ones. This is the Householder Stage, and may last for many years. When the person's first grandchild is born, the person may choose the Third Stage, called Retire to the Forest. One secludes oneself in order to meditate and deepen the spiritual life.

"My father is in the Third Stage. He has spent several years in the Himalayas, fasting and meditating." After some time, his father would enter the Fourth Stage, or Return to the Market Place. After the spiritual deepening of the Third Stage, the person returns to the world, but in a different way. Knowing true spirituality, he can live anywhere, among any people. "In the Fourth Stage, the person is beyond religion."

Beyond religion. The phrase sounded both arrogant and intriguing.

Kush said his father was currently in Delhi at the free eye hospital, just five minutes from the hotel, because of a serious eye infection. "I shall visit my father tomorrow afternoon. May you join me?"

"I would love to," I said.

Mid-afternoon of the following day, Kush led me toward the Sant Baba Eye Hospital, located at the end of a tree-shaded lane in our neighborhood. Large homes lined the streets, remnants of the old British Civil Service enclave. The once beautiful residences had wide verandahs to shield the inner house from the summer heat and were surrounded by gardens. The gardens now were littered with trash that cows poked at, the homes themselves in disrepair and crowded with six or eight large families. One such large residence housed the eye hospital, though the walls and gardens looked in better shape than most. A few beds lined the outside verandahs, occupied by thin, elderly men, with patches or greasy salves on their eyes. No attendants were in sight.

Inside, a large, high-ceiling room contained half a dozen beds lined against each wall. Kush had been uncharacteristically quiet as we approached the hospital, and now walked quietly over to the bed of one man who looked to be in his sixties. The man's right eye stared straight ahead, glassy, red and smeared with ointment, though not as puffy as the eyes of some other patients. His good eye brightened, and a slow smile crept over his face as Kush drew nearer and touched his fingertips to the older man's feet.

Neither man spoke. For several minutes, father and son looked quietly at each other, then Kush lowered himself to squat on the floor next to the bed, while I remained several feet away. The two men's breathing appeared to synchronize, as if there were a physical cord connecting them. I found my own breath slowing down, and eventually matching theirs. Kush rose and stood closer to his father. His head leaned toward the old man, and he looked ready to speak, but remained silent. Nearby a few other patients coughed, an attendant walked past carrying a tray of medicine, and a dog barked in the yard. For a moment I, who had lost my father at age twelve, was envious of their relationship. A few minutes later, the older man spoke to Kush in a language I didn't recognize, and Kush responded, at one point gesturing toward me and saying my name.

"My father wanted to know who you are and I have told him you are my friend, and a Christian."

Kush's father spoke again, and Kush translated. "My father says, 'A Christian. How beautiful to love Jesus! Such a gentle man, this Jesus showed so much love. I pray to him also.'"

I made namaste to Kush's father, who smiled and pointed behind himself. On the wall above the bed hung an array of brightly-colored devotional pictures. I recognized Krishna, Ganesh the elephant god, Shiva in a meditation pose, Buddha, and Jesus. Rays of white and yellow light emanated from Jesus' face, a glorious Jesus. Dried flowers clung precariously to a single nail on the wall.

Had the old man always prayed to so many diverse religious figures, or was that a result of his spiritual deepening while in the Third Stage? It didn't matter, of course. What was important, and evident from his serene face, was that he was at peace. No doubt he already stood at the threshold of the Fourth Stage, the stage beyond adherence to one specific religion. He had found his own inner spiritual authority and had chosen what was right for himself.

I remembered Dave's assistant, Father George, admonishing us India pioneers on the eve of our departure from America to avoid being "pulled into the pantheons of other religions." Catholicism was the one true religion, he reminded us. There was no need to look further. Kush's father had evidently looked beyond his own religion, and found it good.

I couldn't get the phrase "beyond religion" out of my mind. It was at once fascinating and incomprehensible that there should be anything "beyond" what I considered an absolute. It was an easy matter to bypass customs like kissing a bishop's ring, but a leap such as going beyond religion triggered a more complex urge in me—my iconoclastic streak. Idols, it was said, needed to be smashed before a vibrant force could emerge.

The following week Kush told me that his father was being released from the hospital. "When he leaves Delhi, I'm not sure when I shall see him again, but he must do what he must do."

Murder And Mayhem

"THERE'S A PHONE call for you, Brother Jim, and it sounds urgent." Louis, the school registrar at Light of Wisdom Seminary, stood in the doorway of our classroom "home." It was the day after Christmas, and both Joe and I were sorting through mail that had accumulated during our recruitment travel the previous two weeks.

"Is this Brother Jim? This is Sister Gladys and I must speak with you today about Alberic and the murder. I leave for Bombay tomorrow, so we must meet today, this afternoon. I can come over shortly."

"Alberic? Murder?" What was she talking about?

"Father Dave told me he has written you everything. And even though the court has made Alberic your ward, I am still his aunt and family comes first here in India! We must talk."

"Who did you say you were?"

"Sister Gladys, Sister Gladys! It was my sister that they murdered! And shot her so many times and your American courts let him go free!"

"Brother Jim, Brother Jim?" Another woman's voice, calm and soothing, came on the line. "It's Sister Thelma. I can help explain but it would be best if we came over and talked in person. Are you free this afternoon?"

I trusted Thelma, whom I knew from classes at the seminary, so I agreed to meet them.

When I recounted the conversation to Joe he said, "This sounds just too bizarre, Jim. Are you sure there's no letter here from Dave?"

We both tore into the pile of mail, separating local letters from the blue international aerogrammes.

"Here's one from St. Louis addressed to you," Joe said.

A quick scan for "murder" and "Alberic" brought no results. But I paused to read more carefully two paragraphs which were upsetting, but for another reason.

"Dave says neither Steve nor Gerry is coming back." I felt as if the wind had been knocked out of me. I wasn't totally surprised at the decisions, but there had been no conversation about this possibility before each of them had left India. They had talked about returning, about us all moving to Nepal, about creating a home there.

"Steve really needs to get healthy," Joe said, "and India and Nepal are not the place for that!"

"Well, right. And Gerry's doctor advised him to stay in the U.S. because of those recurring kidney stone attacks he was having here. But, Joe, half of our pioneer group has dropped out. What's going on?"

"Jim, be honest," Joe said as he sat up straighter and looked at me with slightly narrowed eyes. "Weren't you frustrated with Gerry a lot of the time?" He paused. "And with Steve also? Are you really that upset they're not returning?"

"I am, and I'm not. Yes, they both caused me frustration, but they are good men, and I will miss them. And we don't know yet who will replace them, and we need to pack up everything and leave in a few days for a new country, and in a moment I have to deal with a frantic woman about something that sounds quite serious, and..." My voice trailed off.

"We'll manage," Joe said confidently, and I could almost hear those creative wheels of Joe's mind turning already. "I know we will. And tonight sounds like another occasion for a gin and tonic."

A few minutes later, a taxi pulled up at the seminary gate, and two nuns emerged. Sister Thelma, attired in her usual peach-colored sari, her braided hair pulled back in a bun, led the way. She smiled and greeted me as she entered the visitors' parlor. Her companion, Sister Gladys, had short hair, quite unusual for an Indian woman, especially a nun, Western style clothing and clenched fists.

"I've received no letter from Father Dave concerning you, Sister Gladys, so could you please tell me the whole story?" I asked after we were seated.

"It's a terrible, terrible story. I still can't believe it's happened. They should never, never have gone to the U.S." Gladys leaned forward, her eyes red and swollen, yet hard and angry.

"They? You really need to start at the beginning for me."

"Yes, Gladys," Thelma encouraged, "you must slow down and tell all the pieces."

Gladys began the story. In the spring of the current year, a farmer was looking over his fields in southern Illinois. He noticed an abandoned car on a side road, and went to inspect it. Inside was a dead and bloodied woman, shot multiple times. Her purse with money inside and personal jewelry were still with her. The woman was Sister Gladys's own sister.

"I'm so sorry," I said. "It sounds terrible. And clearly it wasn't a robbery gone bad…"

"Shot thirteen times!"

Gladys looked at me directly, and grief mixed with rage seemed to reside in her eyes. "This is anger, this is revenge."

I stared in disbelief as she took the story further back to the beginning, in India.

A short time after Gladys's sister, Marie, married a dentist in Bombay, the husband formed a connection with a colleague in a small town in Illinois, just east of St. Louis. The town needed another dentist—a good opportunity for him—so he left his wife in India while he went to set up his practice. She expected to join him soon, but their reunion was delayed for several years. Their son, Alberic, was about two when the father left Bombay, but was five when he arrived in America with his mother. His father was a stranger to him.

"The father and the son never hit it off and I think that's why they resented each other so much." Gladys's voice was starting to rise again, as were the tears in her eyes.

Thelma offered her a handkerchief and coached her. "So, tell what happened just a couple of years ago. Alberic is fourteen now, Jim."

The parents had started to quarrel often. Alberic would take his mother's side and the three younger children, born in the U.S., didn't know what to do. Things became so intense she divorced her husband, and received primary custody of the children.

"We're not sure why her husband became so belligerent. Most likely when the court granted her permission to take the children to India for a visit, he feared she would not return with them. He even told a couple of his patients he would kill her. Can you believe it?" Gladys said.

"One day, after dropping the children off at school, she didn't show up at work, so a co-worker called the police. A week later they found my sister shot dead in her car."

We sat in silence, Thelma with her hands folded calmly in her lap, Gladys staring blankly in front of herself, and I trying to absorb it all.

"What was the police conclusion about the crime?" I asked.

"The husband had a concrete alibi," Gladys said. "He was seeing patients in his office at the approximated time of the murder."

"And it's still unsolved!" Gladys continued. "After almost a year! These people are so stupid. Or else they are covering up for him. Obviously the husband hired somebody to do the job. Everybody knows it. I know it. Alberic knows it. That's why he threatened to kill his father."

"Kill his father!"

"Oh yes, and he could do it too. With a knife, I think. That's what he would do. The court had given the father custody of all four children, but Alberic hated living with his father."

"So the case is unsolved and the children are with the father. What's all this got to do with me?" I asked.

"Alberic is here in India. And he's your ward now!" Gladys sounded triumphant.

My *ward*? Could I be appointed guardian of a minor without my knowledge and consent?

Thelma offered more information. "Alberic really couldn't stay with his father, and the court was considering putting him in a foster home in Illinois."

"Foster home! What rubbish! For Indian people, family comes first and his uncle and grandmother are right there in Bombay," Gladys said. "That's why I went to the U.S."

"Alberic is Indian," Gladys continued. "He's Indian, I say. He was born here. Do you think for one minute I would leave that boy in the house of his mother's murderer? And who knows what the father would do to him since the boy knows he did it. Had her shot thirteen times!"

"So this is where you come in," Thelma said. "Your brothers were contacted since our sisters in St. Louis knew you had a mission here in India. The judge was willing to grant custody to the uncle in Bombay provided there was a reliable American citizen who would periodically visit the family and send reports to the court, letting them know how the boy is faring. Father Dave said you would do it."

How generous of Dave. "So, Alberic is not really my 'ward.' I'm to function more as a case worker in this situation, right?"

"Quite so," Thelma confirmed, and I felt relieved.

Finally I was beginning to see a picture that made sense. Though still a surprise, the role now being described was one I could handle, one that might have intrigued me had I not been in the middle of so many other changes and surprises.

"And how does Alberic feel about coming back here? He can't remember much of India, I'm sure." I asked.

"Well, I think he..." Thelma hesitated.

"He will get used to it," Gladys asserted. "He's an Indian at heart. I am sure everything is fine with him at my brother's house. It is a beautiful apartment overlooking the ocean in Bandra, a suburb of Bombay. And he's in the Jesuit school there and will receive a fine education. The point today is this, that you must go to Bombay at once and give a report, which I know will be favorable, to the Illinois court."

"I can't go right now. We're getting ready to leave India next week when our visas expire."

"There wouldn't be any rush had you been here last week when I arrived," Gladys said. "You must go now."

"Excuse me, I'm sorry about your great loss, but I don't appreciate your telling me just what I have to do and when I have to do it." I hoped my voice sounded even, though I doubted it.

"Oh, I'm so sorry, so sorry, I'm just so upset you see. You don't know how difficult this has been for me." Gladys dabbed her eyes again and rose to end the meeting. "Please, if only you can visit soon, thank you so much. Here is their name, address and phone number. I'm sure you'll find that the living situation is quite satisfactory. Please make that very clear in your report."

Thelma followed her out the door, glancing back with a half smile for me.

What a tragic story. I knew it must be terrible for Gladys, but I couldn't help but think of her as emotionally unstable. And my going to Bombay? I wouldn't make any move until I received more information from Dave. I wasn't sure how I felt about his saying "our man in India will do it" without consulting me. A bit presumptuous, but then, I had taken the vow of obedience.

The next day Joe and I turned our attention to tasks that needed to be done before leaving: closing bank accounts, getting a "permission to leave" document from the police department, saying goodbye to friends, and packing our belongings into trunks.

Finally, two days later, another letter from Dave and various court documents arrived. The facts of the case were pretty much as Gladys had described them. Dave had thanked me "ahead of time" for taking on the "social worker" role, and added cryptically that Alberic hadn't seemed very interested in coming to India.

There was no point in delaying a visit to the Bombay family. I called the number which Gladys had given me and found them at home. The uncle and his wife had heard of me from both the court and Gladys. Yes, they would be at home the next day, and three o'clock would suit them. I already knew they must be upper middle class since Gladys had said they lived in an oceanfront apartment in an area I knew to be upscale; their having a phone confirmed it.

Dave had also mentioned that Alberic resented Sister Gladys's taking him to Mass and making him say prayers when he was not used to it. Evidently little of Catholic practices had been part of his upbringing. And now here I was, a Catholic Brother, coming to investigate the situation.

For my trip the next day to Bombay, I put on clean jeans, tennis shoes and a long sleeved shirt. While the jeans might seem casual to the adults, it was primarily Alberic that I wanted to establish rapport with.

In Bombay, Gladys's brother answered the door wearing a business suit.

"Welcome, please come in, Brother Jim," Mr. DeMello said in crisp English.

He extended his hand and smiled warmly as he brought me into the living room. The grandmother sat quietly at one end of the room while I was introduced to Mr. DeMello's wife. No Alberic.

"Please have a seat over here. And how was your flight?"

"Quite fine. Luckily I was able to get a flight on short notice," I said. *Quite fine?* I'm beginning to speak Indian English, I thought.

"Yes, Bombay has good air service. I know because I fly quite frequently with my work."

"And what is your work?" And where is Alberic?

He explained his work with a company dealing with semi-precious gems, then drifted back to asking me how I liked India. We spent a few more minutes with such generalities that I knew were, in their own way appropriate, as we got a sense of each other. I liked his easy manner, his efforts at drawing out opinions from me, his overall graciousness. There was no indication that he or his wife saw me as an intruder in their home life, though the look on their faces was strained.

"Alberic is in his room reading. You can meet him shortly. I thought it would be good for us to speak first. Tell me, what kinds of things would you like to know?" Mr. DeMello spoke calmly though the tense look on his face remained.

"In simplest terms, I'm here to find out that Alberic is well taken care of. I'm sure there's no doubt that you can provide him with a comfortable home and a good education. Beyond that, how do you feel about his being here?"

"Well of course, we would do anything for our family, isn't it?" He looked toward the two women who nodded. "I should think things are fine. He gets along with our daughter, who is visiting friends right now, though he is slow making friends at St. Xavier's. But then, he had only a month there before they started the Christmas break."

"And how is he with yourselves, here at home?"

Mr. DeMello again exchanged a brief glance with his wife. "I really like the boy, but quite frankly, he seems so distant. I suppose it's the trauma he's been through. And, I am out of town quite a bit with work so my time with him is less."

"Mrs. DeMello, what about yourself?" I asked the younger Mrs. DeMello.

"I often accompany my husband on his trips, but even when I'm here, I get that sense of distance from him. *Mama-ji* says the same thing."

The grandmother offered no comment, though she sat upright in her chair, her eyes following the conversation.

"I think he's bewildered by Bombay and all this change moving to India," Mr. DeMello offered. He added that Alberic was not very religious—none of them were—and that he looked rather wary when told a Catholic Brother would be coming to visit. "Nevertheless, I'm sure he will be polite. Shall you meet him now?"

The younger Mrs. DeMello rose to bring Alberic in while the elder Mrs. DeMello left for a moment, speaking of bringing tea.

Alberic, a slender boy of average height, with thick black hair, wearing jeans, tennis shoes and a polo shirt, entered the room, his shoulders slumped slightly.

"Alberic, this is Brother Jim."

"It's nice to meet you, Alberic."

"Hullo." Alberic looked me directly in the eye for a moment, then quickly scanned me from head to toe. The priests at St.

Xavier's, I knew, would always be dressed in black cassocks around the boys in school. That garb served not only as a religious sign, but also helped keep a distance between teacher and student. I was hoping for the opposite effect, to help make a more personal connection with Alberic.

"Come, let us all take tea." The younger Mrs. DeMello spoke as she placed teacups on a dining room table, while the grandmother arranged biscuits on a platter.

We each pulled up a chair and busied ourselves with the pouring of tea and passing of biscuits. Alberic said little while his uncle again engaged me in conversation by asking me about my travels in India. I mentioned the trips to the tribal areas and tribal dancing, and entertained them with the monkey bite story. The women clucked and said "how terrible" periodically while Mr. DeMello bemoaned the poor state of Indian train stations. From the corner of my eye, I noticed Alberic constantly watching me, his faint frown gradually replaced with a hint of a smile. He eventually asked a few questions about my travels and wanted to know more about the hospital stay.

I was taken aback every time he spoke, for I would be lost in India for the moment, looking at their Indian faces, hearing the DeMello's Indian English intonation, and then jolted by hearing an American teenager speaking right next to me. India was not home for Alberic. I wondered how he really was doing here. There was only one way to find out.

"I'd like to walk along the ocean front here. Alberic, how about showing me the area?"

"Sure," Alberic replied. "There's a cool place nearby where the waves really crash hard on the rocks."

Outside, neither of us said much at first. I decided to let Alberic take the conversation somewhere. It was some minutes before he spoke.

"So what were you talking about with my aunt and uncle? What were they saying about me?" He didn't look at me directly but walked slowly with his hands in his pockets.

"Not much. They just hoped you were doing all right. They're not sure you like it here."

"I don't." He turned toward me. "I didn't want to come here. That was mainly Sister Gladys's doing. I knew I couldn't stay with my father, but this is too crazy over here. I don't fit in. And they're telling me I have to learn Hindi at school."

"Yes, that's a big item. And how do you like your uncle and aunt?"

"Oh, they're fine. It's not their fault. They try to make me feel at home. But, you know, they're really strangers to me."

"So would foster parents in Illinois be."

"Yes, but it would be America, my home," Alberic said.

We continued along the sea walk, and I asked Alberic about school.

"Well, it's a Catholic school for starters." He looked at me sideways. "Sorry, Brother, but I don't like Mass and prayers and all that. Also, it's huge, all boys, and it's madness getting there. Have you been on these commuter trains?"

I said I had, and told him I knew full well the frenzy of pushing onto already-jammed cars, with people hanging out of the doors, sitting on the roof of the train, and pickpockets grabbing for anything of value you might have. Alberic smiled at my descriptions.

"Alberic, my job here is fairly straightforward. The court in Illinois wants to be sure you're being taken care of properly. I'm supposed to write a report on how you are doing, in your uncle's home and at school, and how you like it here."

"I don't like it here. I want to go home."

"You've been here less than two months. What about giving it more time?"

He looked at me, then turned away, shoulders again slumping slightly. Was I his only possible ally so far from home and now he's not sure of that? Perhaps I had lost a connection I thought we had started.

"I will tell them you're not happy here," I promised. "I just want you to know that they probably won't bring you back right away, unless there is a serious problem. I think they want to have you give it a six month try at least."

"Six months? That's a long time."

"I know it seems that way. Maybe think of this as a time when, you know, you're just getting to know your family roots, its history. You're getting to experience another country, the country of your birth. Think of this as an adventure."

"Oh, Brother Jim," Alberic laughed, turning to me again. "Some adventure! But I really like hearing you talk. I mean your accent. Well, actually you don't have one, that's what I mean. At school, half the time I can't understand what they're saying even though it's in English."

We had walked a good distance along the ocean front and now simultaneously we both turned to head back. Our steps fell into an even pace and I wondered what it was that so intrigued me about Alberic, beyond his unusual circumstances.

Here he was, born in India, looking completely Indian, and not feeling at home. I, on the other hand, despite my complaining about the inconveniences of life here, was beginning to feel much more comfortable in India. I liked the thought of moving to Nepal in terms of the climate, and Kathmandu looked like a very livable city, but at some level I hated to leave passionate India, which felt more and more like home to me.

What really was home for Alberic? I felt for him, so young to be so adrift: mother dead, animosity to father, life now in a foreign country, the alternative being life with some other new family.

At the apartment I made my farewells to the DeMello's, and Alberic walked me back outside.

"Well, it was nice talking to you, Brother Jim."

"Alberic, I wish you all the best, and I think things will work out for you in some way. I'll visit again in six months." He looked at me. "If you're still here," I added. I put my arm around his shoulder as we walked the short distance to the commuter train station.

At St. Xavier's school, I heard a familiar story. Alberic felt out of place, the Jesuits had sympathy for him but were not sure they could get the Hindi requirement waived, and they too wondered if Alberic should really be in India.

The guidelines about what I was supposed to report to the Illinois court were vague. It was not clear if I was to make recommendations. I could still hear Alberic's young, sad American voice. I knew then that I would not only report the facts as I understood them, but also recommend he return to the States and be placed in a supportive environment there. The U.S. was his home.

And home for me was with the brothers, whether that be in St. Louis, Delhi, or Kathmandu. I had the luxury of taking my chosen family with me, and that made all the difference.

GOING OUT IN STYLE

OUR TAXI PULLED up in front of the large, pink, Ashok Hotel in New Delhi. White-turbaned men immediately opened the taxi doors, and Joe and I emerged to begin our last big celebration in India. We would ring in the New Year in grand style, and, a couple of days later, would move to Kathmandu, Nepal.

Everything was packed for the move. Several trunks had already been sent to Nepal. The government "permission to leave" papers had all been put in order without any problems. The only momentary confusion occurred when I had asked the woman at Royal Nepal Airlines if we could ship several trunks to Kathmandu with them.

"Ship? Ship? You cannot ship anything to Nepal! There are no ships whatsoever going there—it is a land-locked country."

Air freight was too costly anyway, so we had settled on overland transport. Everything was in order.

"Joe, we've got reservations for dinner and the New Year's Eve show in the Shalimar Room tonight," I said as we entered our rooms. I had reserved a small suite—two bedrooms and a sitting area. I wanted our "farewell to India" to be classy. "But that's not until nine. I think I'll just read in the hotel lobby for a while. They have a good health spa downstairs—steam, sauna, massage. You might want to take advantage of that. We're here to splurge."

After the previous hectic weeks of travel, the disappointment of Steve and Gerry not returning, packing, and knowing that for the moment the whole project rested squarely on just Joe's and my shoulders, I felt we deserved some pampering.

"Sounds great. Let's meet back here at eight," Joe said.

"Okay. I'll order hors d'oeuvres and we'll start off with a drink here before we go down for dinner."

I sat in the lobby until seven-thirty, watching the night's revelers arrive. Many had come early for drinks and window shopping in the hotel's arcade of boutiques. Women in all colors of saris—fuchsia, salmon, powder blue, peach, orchid—floated across the marbled floors. I loved watching their graceful movements, picking up the upper end of the sari that was beginning to slide, and casting it back over their shoulder.

Almost all the men wore Western business suits, though an occasional gentleman appeared in a brocaded, high-necked white coat that descended to the knees over matching pants. An occasional child entered the lobby with its parents, eyes wide to take in all the color of the evening.

Periodically a bellboy walked through the lobby carrying a placard with bells attached. At the tinkling of the bells, guests turned to see whose name was on the placard, who was being paged. At one end of the lobby, someone had begun to play "Don't Cry For Me Argentina" and other show tunes on the piano. The noise and tumult of the streets was far away—in this environment I could most deeply relax.

By eight-fifteen, room service had delivered a tray of cheeses and crisp-fried, twisted breads to our room, but Joe had not returned.

I set out the Scotch and ordered a bucket of ice cubes, after the man from room service had assured me, with only a touch of indignation in his voice, "All our ice is made from purified water."

At eight-thirty, loud, rapid knocking on the door startled me.

I smelled Joe almost before I saw him. Both pant legs and one side of his body were drenched in a foul liquid that still dripped onto the hall carpet.

"I can't believe it! I can't believe it!" Joe entered the room and quickly headed for the bathroom. I removed the snacks to one of the bedrooms.

"What happened? Are you okay?"

"I'll tell you in a minute. I'm okay but I think my shoes are ruined!"

The door to the hallway was still open, and two laughing young men from housekeeping stood there, proffering a box of detergent. "We have more if you need it," one said. I thanked them and closed the door.

What had Joe done *now*? Whatever it was, at least he was back safe, even if somehow this smelly event changed our evening plans. I recalled our community's phrase, "In India nothing is for certain."

The stench in the room assailed my nose again, so I propped the hallway door open, and waited for Joe.

Joe showered, then placed his clothes in the tub along with generous amounts of detergent. A few minutes later he emerged in a hotel bathrobe—I had a Scotch and water ready for him.

"So this is the conclusion to my stay in India! What does all this mean?" he asked philosophically, swirling his Scotch, before he told me what had happened.

"I decided to take a walk outside near the hotel," he began. It was dark as he neared an area of construction—a new hotel was being built next door. He had kept to the sidewalk, though he noticed from the reflection of street lights, that there was a small amount of water on the sidewalk in front of him. Assuming he could just walk through it, he placed one foot into the watery area, then fell into a deep pit.

"It was an open sewer! I don't know how far I would have slid down if I hadn't braced myself against the opposite side with one foot. And I had just opened all my pores in the sauna, as *you* suggested."

His return to the hotel and walk through the lobby toward the elevators hadn't gone unnoticed. Joe now leaned back, took a sip, waved his hand loosely in the air, and said, "Just like Moses, my very presence parted a sea of party-goers. Women in diaphanous gowns fled to the far corners of the lobby clutching their children."

"Pity the poor souls who try to use the elevator you were in!" I said.

"Won't they be surprised. But now I'll have to go to the party in old clothes. Well, such is life. This must be telling me something."

We both had another drink while Joe discoursed about the "incongruities of life," as he called them. "We're so fortunate, then something like this happens. But there's no point in feeling embarrassed anymore about it. It's over. I'm here. I guess I'm supposed to learn to live 'in the moment,' right?"

Joe nevertheless went back to multiple retellings of the story, and each time it seemed that the pit was deeper, there were more astonished partiers in the lobby, more muffled shrieks, and more swooning ladies. We laughed until it was time to leave for dinner, knowing that seeing the humor and absurdity in our lives was a key to surviving India.

And so at midnight, we clinked glasses in honor of the New Year, and "to the mission," and I told Joe he was the only person I knew who could fall into a sewer and come out smelling like a rose.

2 January 1982

Dear Dave,

Your several letters of the last few weeks have all arrived. I had really thought that Steve would return to the mission, that after a few months in America he would be healthy and fully recovered. I will miss him, but am glad that he has chosen what's best for him.

I'm not really surprised that Gerry's decided to stay in America too. At times he was completely committed to the work here, at other times unsure. As I've said before, the fluctuation in both his and Steve's commitment was stressful for me, as I'm sure it was for them. Your last letter said that their replacements are deeply desirous of coming here—great.

Your decision to send Father George to replace Gerry as Novice Master was a definite surprise. With his scriptural background and pastoral manner, George will have a lot to offer, though I have one concern. I think he sees himself as Defender of the Faith and the Keeper of Orthodoxy. He once told me that when he was appointed Rector of the seminary, he had a dream of himself as the Pope. Rather revealing, I would say. However, he has always been pleasant and cordial toward me. I just hope he can be flexible with life here in mission territory.

It will also be great to have Brother Del in the Kathmandu community, and I'm sure St. Xavier's school in Kathmandu will be thrilled to have a librarian of his caliber. Maybe Del can take over the house accounts. He has a good eye for detail.

Here is, perhaps, a little surprise for you. I have "canceled" whatever novitiate experience Johnny and Benedict had at the ashram. They weren't really ready to be novices so I'm looking upon the ashram time and their current training as "pre-novitiate" formation. Our own formal novitiate will begin in Kathmandu after George arrives, has spent time with Johnny,

Benedict, Sylverius, and three other candidates who have applied to join us, and decides to begin the novitiate training. I'm convinced this is the way to go, and I suspect George would rather start "at the beginning" with everyone.

Joe and I are both in good spirits, packed, and ready to leave for Nepal. I hate to leave India, Dave, but I know I will return here often. And I imagine I will come to love Nepal also.

Tomorrow we're off to Kathmandu!

Sincerely,

Jim

HIMALAYAN HOME

KATHMANDU LAY IN a bowl-shaped valley of the Middle Himalayas and, at 4500 feet, boasted a temperate climate in summer—but it was a January chill that greeted Joe's and my arrival. Since electricity was available on alternate nights only, we lit candles and threw blankets around ourselves in the evenings in our new home. The brick house, which I had found on my exploratory trip to Nepal four months earlier, was conveniently situated in the southwest area of the city, just a few blocks from St. Xavier's School. It would be a short walk to teach a few classes at the school, the arrangement that enabled us to stay in Nepal and run our own programs.

The house was spacious—five bedrooms as well as a large dormitory space, chapel room, study hall, kitchen, living room, and dining room. The landlord, a strict Hindu, held his nose when walking through our dining room, certain that we were eating beef in his residence, which we were. My room on the second floor, with windows on three sides, afforded views of the green hills to the south, as well as the northern rim of the valley, beyond which twenty-thousand foot peaks of the Himalayas showed their ever-snowy coats.

Closer in, the charm of Kathmandu's gentle people, its meandering alleys, colorful bazaars, and its neighborhood shrines—which contained images of Hindu gods and Buddha next to each other—took their place alongside other less welcome sights and sounds. Dogs barked all night, garbage littered every street, and naked children relieved themselves next to the bus stop. Nevertheless, I was happy to be living in a home that would provide stability in my life. For two years in India I had felt like a rat scurrying through the twists and turns of a maze, looking for the center. Now I had it.

Brother Del, four years older than me and with the logical mind of a librarian, joined us in our second week. Of short stature and blessed with a deep voice, he immediately threw himself into addressing the material needs of the community. He organized the house finances and opened a bank account for us. He waited in long lines to pay the electric bill, and ordered newspapers and magazines from the vendor under the peepul tree on New Road, next to a shrine of fat-bellied Ganesh the elephant god. Del exuded stability and I felt comforted by his presence.

"Maybe we don't need a chapel," Joe said as I measured the dimensions of the room allocated for prayer. He suggested we have Mass in the living room, and meditate in our rooms or outside. "Let's be more free about these things."

"We can all benefit from the support of praying in each others' presence," Del said quietly, and I agreed. Sometimes I could get enthusiastic about Joe's alternative ways of looking at things, but not in the matter of a designated prayer place. The chapel was the center of our common prayer life, a quiet refuge from the bustle of the rest of the house. Over time, a chapel or church absorbed into its very walls the peace and prayerfulness of its worshippers, so that entering that space was the beginning of contact with the Divine. I wanted a chapel.

Our cook, Maela, a man in his early forties, not only produced hearty food but also took on the role of translator with the neighbors and conduit to all other services we needed. He found us a laundryman and carpenter, both friends of his I later discovered, and hired boys of "the proper caste" to clean out the septic tank. As part of his duties, Maela recorded every purchase from the market in the "daily book," and handed it over for Del to scrutinize each week. With Del, the whereabouts of a single rupee didn't go unnoticed.

No furniture showrooms existed in Kathmandu, so I made detailed drawings of chairs and desks for the study hall, book-shelves for each room, and bunk beds for the dormitory. With Maela's help in translating, the carpenter made each item and carried them on his back from his workshop two blocks away—except for the beds, which he constructed in the front yard. Often I visited his workshop to see the progress of our latest order and to smell the sawdust and fresh wood shavings that lit-tered the floor. The carpenter would smile and continue working placidly. As a youngster I had loved carpentry class in the eighth grade, and had once envisioned myself working with my hands, crafting wood objects. Instead, I became a math teacher, and manual dexterity had become as foreign to me as the fly-infested, open-air butcher market at the end of our street.

By the time classes began at St. Xavier's, I made a risky deci-sion. One of us would have to travel to India several times a year to interview any new candidates that asked to join us. Such frequent travel wouldn't be compatible with a commitment to teaching, so I would forego resident status and spend time between the two countries on tourist visas. The three to six months allotted on each country's tourist visa would require planning and juggling, though I didn't realize at the time how complex that would be.

By mid-March, as winds began to blow dust up from the plains of India, George arrived from America. A dozen years older than me, with silver beard and gray hair atop his lanky six-foot frame, he was eager to assume his role as Novice Master. He immediately outlined several courses of studies, as well as training in prayer and religious ritual. I was confident the novices would be in good hands with George.

The following month, the six novice-candidates arrived. I greeted the smiling, familiar faces of Johnny, Benedict, and Sylverius, then eagerly turned to meet the new candidates. William, in his early thirties, articulate, self-confident, and equally fluent in Hindi and English, had been referred to us by a nun friend. Joe had interviewed him and deemed William a good potential candidate. Stephen, an energetic man from South India, had come to us in an unusual way. Joe, while on his travels, had paused briefly at a lakeside and chatted with several young men rowing boats for tourists. One of the men, Stephen, had lingered to ask Joe what he was doing in India. Stephen eventually decided to leave his boating job and join the Kathmandu community to become a brother. George had already woven a sermon around the event, referring to Jesus' disciples leaving their boats to become fishers of men.

Finally, John, a stalwart, self-composed young man from the tribal area of North India, completed the six. A friend of Johnny's, he had considered joining the Jesuits but felt drawn to join the group of which Johnny had spoken so highly. The Jesuits, whom John had already contacted, were not happy at the switch but I was. John looked like a solid addition to the group.

That first day our small community came together, I arrived early at the chapel for night prayers and sat on a floor cushion. One by one, all the brothers entered, bowed to the tabernacle, and took their places along the edges of the small room. I looked at each one carefully, amazed at our diversity. We represented two nationalities, five different mother tongues, a wide range of ages—and all of us living as foreigners in Nepal. What a witness to hope if we could truly grow into a cohesive community.

At the end of prayer, George announced that the novices' Day of Recollection, scheduled for the next day, would focus on adoration of the Blessed Sacrament. I was taken aback. Praying all day to the Communion host that the priest had changed into the Body and Blood of Christ had already fallen into disuse in America. The faithful apparently weren't interested in paying so much attention to that "miracle." I couldn't argue with the theology involved—it was a staple of Catholic thinking—but the sense of moving "backward" in spirituality was a feeling I could not shake. And my mood changed to one of unease.

Kathmandu, Nepal
21 May 1982

Dear Dave,

So, the Superiors in Rome were not pleased with my cancel-ing Johnny and Benedict's novitiate experience? I know the boys had been formally received as novices, but Rome's regulations would have required them to either take vows as brothers within a few months or leave the order, neither of which I felt was a good idea. Just tell those Superiors that all the rules can't apply in mission territory.

Our large home is a reddish-orange brick structure, and looks quite nice. Kathmandu Valley was once a vast lake until an earthquake cracked the valley walls and drained it. The resulting clay that lines the valley floor is used for brick dwellings every-where. The older buildings have a poorer quality of brick and seem to be crumbling, but our newer home has better-fired brick and is quite solid.

I bought us a Russian-made refrigerator. It seemed like a straightforward transaction until I realized there are no delivery trucks in Kathmandu. I had to hire four coolies to place it on a two-wheeled cart and push it to our house. The men, two pulling in front and two pushing in back, had to navigate narrow streets and a significant hill, as I walked beside them to show the way. Halfway up the hill they were out of breath and so paused—for a cigarette!

Lung problems are widespread here. The thinner air is highly polluted, and in outlying villages women hover over wood fires half the day for cooking. Modern medicine has lengthened the life span here, but I fear that chronic illness is the order of the day for many.

We all have our tasks here. George teaches theology and spirituality to the novices, Joe and Del spend a half-day at St.

Xavier's School, and I teach the boys English. Also, with the help of William and Stephen's translation skills, I'm composing brief articles about the brothers to be placed in the diocesan youth magazines, inviting young men to write to us if interested. I have been assured by other religious orders that within a few months I will receive many responses.

Now that so many things are in place, this is the perfect time for me to take my biannual home visit to America that was part of the original plan. The past two years of uncertainty, travel, and tension have taken their toll on me. I am ready for a break in the good ole U.S.A. I want to drink water without worrying if it contains parasites. I want to sleep in the summer without a mosquito net. I want to see the brothers, and my family in Milwaukee. India and Nepal have been exciting yet even I, a glutton for stimulation, want to be around the familiar for a while.

See you in a few weeks,

Jim

AMERICA THE FOREIGN LAND

PEOPLE UNDERSTOOD MY speech, planes flew on schedule, and no bribes were needed to buy basics like sugar. Cars whizzed by at crazy speeds, but pollution wasn't one-tenth of what it was in Asia. It did, however, take time to get used to seeing so many pallid American faces. Did I look like *that* to Indians and Nepalis?

In St. Louis, Father Dave welcomed me to the sprawling home in a residential area that served as both office and home for him and his staff. His observant eyes peeking from behind dark-rimmed glasses, he helped me get settled in one of the guest rooms, then led me on a stroll through the pleasant neighborhood. He mentioned that, though it was a nice area, one of the brothers was mugged there recently. "No place has a monopoly on crime or suffering." He paused, and said gently, "Now, how are you?"

"I'm weary." The words had just tumbled out of my mouth, and they said it all. I hadn't known how bone-tired I was until then. I assured Dave, however, that I was still enthusiastic about the Indian mission even with all its uncertainties. "I have to trust that we're moving in the right direction but, honestly, sometimes I just don't know."

"Trust in God's Providence is a key part of a brother's life. It can take us where we might not have chosen to go. Are you willing to go back to India and Nepal?"

When I said that indeed I was, Dave added, "Good, I want you to go back. You're doing fine. And, do you remember that old phrase 'grace of state'? It means that God gives you the grace to accomplish your duties even when you don't feel up to it. Count on that." Dave's words were reassuring and just what I needed.

The following day, Steve and Gerry, both living in St. Louis and finally healthy, paid me a visit. Any tension I thought might be present between us was not there. They were simply my brothers who supported the mission, and who had chosen other ways to live their lives. I enjoyed answering their questions about India since I knew they understood the situation. Several other brothers, however, couldn't quite understand that the "Indian brothers" weren't "helping leprosy patients, like Mother Teresa does." I explained that it required time for religious and academic training, but sensed only vague comprehension from them. One brother I encountered didn't even know I had been out of the country for several years. And although I thought I had missed the daily routine of teaching, I felt far removed from the actual talk I heard about running suburban high schools. America didn't seem to fit me now as much as I had expected it to.

After another week in St. Louis, I journeyed to Milwaukee to see my family. The streets of the city's Southside looked immaculately clean, but bereft of people. Where was everyone? In their homes, private cars, or enclosed shopping malls, no doubt. Much as I appreciated good sanitation, which Indian cities lacked, I remembered wistfully the pulse of life played out on Delhi's streets: the peanut vendor who served as my alarm clock each morning when he announced his wares, the turbaned Sikh taxi drivers who slept on string cots next to their vehicles, the woman who ironed clothes in her front yard with an ancient instrument that housed live coals which glowed in the twilight. In Kathmandu, small Hindu and Buddhist shrines adorned almost every street corner, and oil lamps burned before their statues. In Milwaukee, the only public sign of religion was a plain cross atop a cream-colored church. America had orderliness and hygiene—and also sterility. I was beginning to long for the vibrancy, and yes, the chaos of Asia.

My mother, a resourceful woman who had raised her four children alone after my father's death, brightened upon seeing me. We had always gotten along easily and, indeed, she was a source of inspiration for me. Her life had spanned much of the twentieth century, and she had resolutely moved through all its vast changes. Born on a farm in western Wisconsin when kerosene lamps lit the living room and a horse-drawn sleigh carried the family to church in winter, she had become a city dweller who was fond of jet planes to visit far-flung relatives. Though strong-minded, she did not impose her views on her offspring. When I, her only son, announced during high school that I wanted to join the brothers, she had murmured something about the "family name," but eventually said, "Of course, it's your life."

In her apartment living room we quickly fell into conversation that caught me up on family news. When I told her of my plan to return to Asia, she said, "So, this is what you *really* want to do, go back there?" When I assured her again, she gave a resigned smile. Though I knew she preferred I were closer to home, she also understood challenge and determination. I liked to think I took after her in that.

At a family barbecue with my three sisters, brothers-in-law, nephews and nieces, the younger generation sat wide-eyed as I gave details of the monkey bite story and described the holy man with curled fingernails. "Aren't the cows sacred and you can't eat them? Don't you miss hamburgers?" they wanted to know. I didn't miss hamburgers at all and, in fact, the American food that I had formerly enjoyed now seemed heavy and greasy. I longed for curry-flavored vegetables, chilies that cleared my sinuses, and refreshing drinks made from yogurt and water. I had expected to feel comfortable and at home in America, but to my surprise, I was quickly feeling homesick for Asia.

A few days before I was to leave Milwaukee, my mother and I went to a vast, two-storied shopping mall. "Maybe you'll see something you want to take back to Kathmandu," she said. In the mall I paused to look at the window of a kitchenware shop. One curious gadget claimed it could scramble an egg while it was still in the shell. *Are they kidding? It must be a joke.* But no, a poster claimed the item had been "one of last year's hottest Christmas gifts, saving the harried cook from unneeded hand labor." Hand *labor*? I thought of Maela humming away while he sat on the kitchen floor in Kathmandu, mortar and pestle at his feet, grinding fresh spices. I also thought of the millions in the world going hungry while technology and creativity was directed toward frivolous gadgets. I hurried away from the window in utter disbelief and dismay.

Before I could catch up to my mother, a perky woman in a polyester pantsuit approached and said, "Excuse me, I have some important questions I'd like to ask you." There was no escape. "So," she said as she clutched her clipboard, "which brand of diet colas has your family been purchasing this past year?"

My mind went blank except for one thought—it was time to return to Nepal and India.

BROOM BOSS

THE PLANE POKED down through the September cloud cover and came in low over Kathmandu Valley. The slopes of the valley, dotted with brick huts and terraced with narrow rice paddies, rushed under the plane and gave way to larger fields that hugged Kathmandu. It's really a small city, I thought, returning from my three-month visit to the U.S. One can easily pick out familiar landmarks, like the Ring Road that circled the town and had just passed under the plane, and the large distillery located a block from our house. As the plane banked and dipped lower, my eyes followed the street north from the distillery—and there it was. Our house! I had never seen my residence from a plane before, and the sight made me feel welcome. I was home.

The taxi from the Kathmandu airport swerved through narrow streets, honked madly at any pedestrian about to cross its path, and deposited me in front of our gate. George and the novices interrupted their class to greet me and we all chatted over mid-morning tea. When they resumed their study of the brothers' Rule of Life, I went upstairs, unpacked, and looked out the window. A small boy rode past on an elephant, and two goats grazed in the vacant lot next door. A vegetable vendor banged on a neighbor's gate, and a sari-clad woman rang the bell at the Vishnu shrine on the corner. It looked and felt wonderfully familiar.

Familiar, too, was our daily house schedule, which included meditation and vocal prayer in common each morning. Joe, however, usually didn't arrive in chapel until the recitation of psalms, but I knew his pattern. He would be walking on the flat roof, coffee cup in hand, breathing in the morning air and praying in his own fashion. "All this sitting motionless grates on me," he told me. When the novices asked me, "Why doesn't Brother Joe come to chapel for meditation?" I replied, "He prays best on the roof."

Besides prayer and classes, we placed emphasis on our daily "recreation" period. Enjoying each other's company was a powerful support to one's vocation, and our Kathmandu living room became as important a gathering place as the chapel. One of the highlights was Joe's dance lessons. One evening Joe said, "Jim, you won't believe this. I discovered today that the most popular music groups in Kathmandu are ABBA and Boney M! Let's all dance!" It took some coaxing to get the novices to experiment with disco steps, but they soon caught on and looked forward to learning new steps every week—their favorites were line dances.

"This reminds us of our tribal dances," Benedict said. "On special days in the village, we form a line and dance, sometimes the whole night." Though I had seen tribal dancing in Sylverius' village, the other Americans had not, so I encouraged Benedict, "Show us what that's like." Soon, a combination of tribal dancing and disco dancing became regular activities on feast days. Even a reluctant George and Del put their best foot forward on occasion, and were cheered on by the rest of us.

By late-September, the monsoons began to wind down as large splats of isolated raindrops landed on the brick driveway. Maela, always a storehouse of information, said they were called "elephants drops," which indicated that only two more weeks of rain was left. I enjoyed Maela's company, and because I knew he would inform me of any newsworthy gossip, I often sipped my afternoon tea in the kitchen.

"Maela, what was the *dhobi's* wife doing here this morning? It's not the day to pick up our laundry," I said one afternoon.

"Oh, just talking, talking," Maela replied. He sat on the floor to grind fresh ginger and attempted to look busy, while I wondered about our laundryman and his wife. City water was in short supply and prevented our household of ten from washing our own clothes, so Maela had procured the services of a *dhobi*, a laundryman, for us. Each Wednesday, one of the novices would count the pieces of clothing collected for the *dhobi*, who then shouldered the lot wrapped in a large sheet and trudged off to the *dhobi ghats*. With water collected from several small streams, the *dhobi* and his family washed clothes for a number of families. A few days later, the laundry would be returned, counted, and payment given.

"I walked through the *dhobi-ghat* yesterday," I said. "What do they put in those big pots they boil the clothes in?"

"They put ashes and something else in there, I don't know what it is."

"I saw the *dhobi's* wife and children working, but I didn't see the *dhobi*."

"*Dhobi's* family works very hard, Brother Jim, especially when they take wet clothes, swing them through the air and beat them on the rocks. Wet clothes are heavy, and bigger pieces, like tablecloths, are so very, very heavy."

"Of course, we'll give him extra payment this week," I said, remembering that the tablecloth we used on feast days had been sent for washing. I guessed that Maela received kickback for his various employment agency services, but I never questioned him on the matter.

"Did the *dhobi's* wife come to ask for more money?"

"No, Brother Jim." Maela stood up, walked over to the counter and picked small stones out of the rice that he would prepare for dinner. He was seldom reticent to talk about the stream of people who visited him at our kitchen door, so I suspected he had a sensitive topic on his mind and needed time to get to it.

I picked up the ledger in which Maela wrote his daily shopping expenses and took my time perusing it, a task I seldom did since Del handled the accounting. The usual items were present—rice, vegetables, meat, cooking oil. The most costly items were meat and cooking oil. It was understandable that meat would be expensive, but it perturbed me how costly cooking oil was. The peanut oil we bought came in a large, rectangular container adorned with an American flag and the words "Gift of the People of the United States of America. Not to be sold or exchanged." I didn't mind paying for it "twice," but it irked me that some government official was padding his pockets by putting the oil on the market. I placed the ledger back on the shelf and looked expectantly again at Maela.

"*Dhobi* likes *rukshi* very much," Maela began, referring to the local rice beer. "Sometimes he spends too much on *rukshi* for himself and his friends."

"Sometimes?"

"Every week. Then he is too drunk to help with the washing, and more work goes to wife and children. Because you pay him good money, he thinks he's a big boss and buys drink for all the men. He doesn't give his wife much for rice and she can't buy vegetables in the bazaar. You must pay him less," Maela concluded.

"Less? How would that help? We'll just pay his wife directly. Then she will have enough money for food."

"Oh, please, no, no, Brother Jim. That isn't the Nepali way. You must pay the man of the house, not the woman. That is a foreign idea you are having." From our first meeting, Maela had taken on the project of educating me in Nepali ways, even letting me know he should be given paid vacation and new clothes for the upcoming Hindu holidays. "*Dhobi* would have a very bad face in front of his friends."

"I don't care about his bad face. I care about the hungry faces of his wife and children. What can we do?" I asked.

"If you pay him less, he must drink alone, and then he will have more money to give to his wife," Maela insisted.

"No, definitely not, there must be another way. The work is being done, and it's hard work, you said so yourself. The family deserves the money, so we'll have to pay his wife."

Maela pulled out two cups and poured our tea. I waited again.

"Okay," Maela said finally. "The *dhobi* will collect the clothes, and *dhobi*'s wife returns them. At that time, Brother Del pays her. But please don't tell this to anybody."

"Don't worry. And Maela, tell the *dhobi* never to come here when he's been drinking. I don't want him in our house if he's drunk."

The arrangement appeared to work well. The clothes were delivered on time by the *dhobi's* wife and twelve-year-old son. If I was present when the wife delivered the clothes, she made a deep bow and namaste to me. I nodded, smiled, and said namaste in return. The son, an energetic and smiling youngster, helped deliver the heavy loads and seemed interested in lingering at the house after his mother had been paid and left. The novices liked him, and joked and laughed with him in the conversational Nepali they had picked up. Some days the boy appeared in the yard talking to the part-time gardener Maela had found, his face always beaming at any one of us who passed. We began to call him "Mr. Personality."

Several weeks later, I entered the house through the study hall and heard loud talking coming from the kitchen. Stephen looked up from his desk and said, "The *dhobi's* here. I think he's been drinking." The door to the kitchen was closed, unusual in itself, but through the glass panel I could see Maela and the *dhobi* in animated conversation. Maela stopped talking as I entered the kitchen, but the *dhobi* turned his glazed eyes toward me and said something in a slurred voice.

"*Dhobi's* just leaving, Brother Jim," Maela said, and snapped at the *dhobi* in Nepali. The *dhobi* made no move to go. He turned toward me and said something, broadcasting his *rukshi* breath across the small kitchen.

"Go now, too much *rukshi*," I said in a combination of Nepali and Hindi. The *dhobi* made no move but continued speaking and smiling in that "everything's-just-fine" manner that often accompanies too much alcohol. Both Maela and I again urged him to leave, to no avail. In some clear way I would have to show him his behavior was unacceptable. A *jharu*, a small broom consisting of yard-length reeds, leaned against the kitchen wall. I grabbed it and waved it at the *dhobi*, and again told him to go. He gave me a quizzical look but made no move. I hit the ground near his feet with the broom and when he failed to move I swatted his feet and ankles.

"Don't come here after drinking, now go!" I said, and he finally let himself out the kitchen door. I followed him and chased him down the driveway to the gate. Near the gate, he paused, laughed and looked like he wouldn't go further. I swatted his feet again, trying to keep a straight face as I realized we both must look ridiculous. The gardener, who had just arrived, smiled approvingly at the scene. I kept up the beating until the *dhobi* passed through the gate and headed down the street.

"Very good, Brother Jim-sahib," Maela said when I returned the broom to the kitchen. "Now, *dhobi* will remember." Maela had never called me sahib before, and I feared I had acted in too high-handed a manner. I was a brother, not a sahib. A few days later, John said he had heard me referred to as the "*jharu sahib*," broom boss, by the neighborhood youngsters. John said the tone was playful but also had the flavor of 'don't cross the sahib, he's a strict fellow.' "It's a compliment," John added. "Nepalis are like us Indians in this matter. We respect someone who is firm."

Still, it caused me concern. I hoped that the *dhobi's* son had not heard how I treated his father. When I asked Maela if he thought I'd been too harsh, he said that I shouldn't worry, and that everyone knew the *dhobi* drank too much, didn't take care of his family, and needed a lesson. Evidently Maela had become less concerned about the *dhobi's* reputation.

Two days later the *dhobi's* wife and son delivered the week's clean laundry. She made her customary namaste, with no different expression on her worn face, and the son gave me his usual wide grin. He lingered in the yard and, with the gardener's approval, picked a few flowers. I watched him skip down the driveway holding the flowers, a vibrant twelve-year-old, and a poem that I memorized long ago came to mind:

> Just a boy as you can see
> Always full of energy.
> Mischief and fun personified
> Every emotion at full tide.
> Such is the path that all men stride.

It was a cherished poem my own father had written for my twelfth birthday, just two weeks before he died in a factory accident. The first letter of each line spelled out my name.

The *dhobi* never returned drunk to the house again, and Maela, while shaking his head in disbelief, reported that the wife had taken a strong stand with her husband. She allotted him only a small part of the laundry revenue, so he was unable to drink as heavily as before. The *dhobi* averted his eyes from me when picking up the dirty laundry, but his son always smiled in my direction.

The boy's happy face gave me the satisfaction I needed to grow ever firmer in following my instincts. It didn't matter that the local culture proscribed paying the woman directly, there *was* another way to act and it had made a difference.

Kathmandu, Nepal
11 October 1982

Dear Dave,

On October 2, Feast of the Guardian Angels and our historical Foundation Day (and Gandhi's birthday if you recall), the Indian candidates took the Promises of the Novitiate. They should be ready to profess their First Vows in about a year. At times I feel that it has taken forever to reach this point, yet the priests at St. Xavier's are amazed at our progress. They reminded me that most foreign orders were in Asia many more years than three before getting to where we are now.

On Saturdays, the novices visit the Home for the Dying, tucked between the temples along the Bagmati River, to shave and bathe the men. Nuns from Mother Teresa's order attend to the women. I have been there several times and am in awe of the nuns who do that sacred work their whole lives. I don't think I could work with the dying every day, but then, we each have our calling and I suppose there is no point in comparisons.

The ads for joining the brothers I placed in diocesan newsletters in India have paid off. For several weeks we've averaged three inquiries a day. I write each young man and invite him to meet with me when I next travel to India. It won't be long before we have more candidates than we can handle.

I write this at my desk, looking out at our yard. The landlord's wife sits, knitting, in a chair below my window, making sure the men hired to dig a drain don't quit early. The drain is an open cement trough that carries kitchen garbage to the road, where stray dogs will fight each other for scraps. That means more howling at nighttime. As it is, those wretched dogs already awaken me constantly, so I keep a pail of stones on the verandah outside my room to throw at them. I have developed quite a pitcher's arm.

As always,

Jim

SACRIFICIAL BLOOD

THE CLATTER OF hundreds of hooves on Kathmandu's main streets was not unusual in October. Farmers, brandishing tree branches, herded goats down large thoroughfares and toward the parade grounds in the center of town. All week, they had delivered their goats to that temporary animal market where, along with duck and chicken sellers, they set up a brisk business supplying families an animal for religious sacrifice. It was once again the high festival season for Hindus.

Though I had seen these festivals in India, Nepal was different, at least in one major activity—animal sacrifice. The phrase sounded so primitive, so ancient. It was hard for me to grasp that the clerk who ran the photocopying service on New Road would most likely purchase a chicken or duck for sacrifice. The storeowner might be able to afford a goat, the errand boy would likely choose a dove. The thought of animal sacrifice disturbed me. All that blood. Watching the animal meet its death. Yet, the ritual was so ancient, I couldn't help but be fascinated by it. I surprised myself by my own dark interest.

When I returned from the market one day with boxes of sugar and coconut sweets, festival gifts for Maela and the neighbors, I found Maela in the kitchen although it was his day off. He had found several pumpkins in the market, "Just perfect for a pie for the brothers," and wanted them to ripen on our sunny porch.

"I can take the pumpkins upstairs and place them on the roof like the neighbors do. They'll get even more sun there," I offered.

"Oh no, Brother Jim, not up there. Pumpkins on the roof tell how many girls are in the house wanting to be married." Maela's eyes looked glazed from drinking and I couldn't tell if he was joking or saving us from embarrassment. He thanked me when I gave him the sweets, and said he and his family would enjoy them the next day. "Today I cannot eat, Brother Jim. We don't take food this day because tonight is *Kalratri.*"

Kalratri. Black Night. It was that very night that the slaughter of thousands of animals would begin and continue through the next morning. I made up my mind to visit the neighborhood temples to watch.

The following morning, while George taught theology to the novices, I made my way toward the temples. They were far enough from the house so I had heard no bells nor animal sounds during Black Night as I had feared I would. However, the morning air, I was certain, smelled sweet and humid—the scent of blood at once pulling me forward and slowing my pace.

In the main square children tossed balls near the Krishna temple, and women gossiped in twos or threes as they toyed with multicolored glass bangles available at one of the few open shops. Two small boys called to each other from rooftops for a kite-flying contest, in which they attempted to cut each other's kite string with the abrasives that coated their own. Men squatted in doorways, imbibed generous amounts of rice beer, and played cards or dice with their friends—and gambled away fistfuls of rupees. I wondered who had a head clear enough to keep tally.

Beyond the main square, men and women filed down a narrow alley that eventually became a dirt path and led to the edge of town. There, in a small field sat three temples whose metal roofs glistened in the sun. The worshippers stood in queues before each of the temples, most of them carrying ducks or chickens, though one portly man held tightly to a rope that encircled a goat's neck.

I knew how the ducks and chickens would be slaughtered, having seen my father and grandfather kill chickens. They had grabbed the animals by the legs, swung them through the air to disorient them, then laid their heads on the chopping block. The act hadn't seemed terribly macabre because the main purpose was to put food on the table. But a sacrificial goat was another matter. The whole point was to *spill blood*. Even though the Nepalis did indeed eat the sacrificial food, I was convinced that they actually relished the blood-letting itself.

The animals headed toward the red-stained steps of the temple, and I felt myself momentarily swept back to my image of ancient times—a populace lining up to appease bloodthirsty gods and goddesses with animal, or perhaps even human, sacrifices. Rumors still buzzed about a small town just outside of Kathmandu that supposedly had sacrificed a young child to insure fertility of the land. I shuddered every time I passed through the outwardly pleasant village.

Straw, sticky from blood and matted together, lined the ground in front of the temple. An attendant killed two chickens on the temple steps, then dripped their blood on small altars inside and rang the temple bell. It was the goat's turn. A young man emerged from the temple carrying a curved knife about two feet in length. The edge of the knife opposite the cutting side splayed outward, creating a thick and heavy piece of metal with which to follow through on the thrust. Two older temple attendants chanted prayers, the goat was sprinkled with water and red powder, and onlookers stepped back, though only a few feet. As if knowing its role, the goat stood still and bowed its head slightly while the young man raised his *kukri*, the sacred knife of battle and religion. I did not look away. I would watch.

Slish.

The temple attendant had severed the goat's head in one swipe. Smiles and murmurs of approval passed around the crowd, congratulations apparently for the attendant and the goat's owner, both of whom would attain merit for a deed well done. Once again, the attendant scattered the blood on the temple altar and rang the bell. I had seen enough for the morning, and followed the path further along the stream, away from the temples. I could not, however, get the sound of the goat's decapitation out of my head. Slish. Every time I heard the temple bells clang behind me, the sound came back.

Why had I felt the need to come to the temples in the first place? I was torn between repugnance and fascination for what I had just witnessed. Yet bloody sacrifice, as in biblical offerings or in the lives of martyrs, permeated all ancient religions. Blood was life, and death. That was it—the allure was the blood itself. I had needed to see sacrificial blood actually spilled because, while the shedding of blood for religious purposes was abhorrent to me, the core of my own religion centered on that very deed. A stern God had demanded the blood sacrifice of his own son to expiate the sins of mankind and save us all. Was that very different from believing in an Earth Goddess who expected blood sacrifice before she blessed the fields? Though Jesus had been a willing participant, and thereby a model for the best part of Christianity—helping others even at cost to oneself—his had nonetheless been a bloody sacrifice, and it was to a mangled and wounded body on a cross that we Christians prayed.

We not only prayed to Jesus, we Catholics said that we literally ate his body and drank his blood at Mass. How many Hindu hearts would gasp if I told them that I drank blood when I went "to temple"? Though they might envision a less hygienic version of what I was saying, Catholic theology would have been correctly reported. The temple bells clanged once again, and my mind's eye saw the blood spurt from the goat's neck. I quickened my pace away from the area.

My brain wanted to argue theology, but my gut went directly to the basic issue—a God demanding a torturous sacrifice of his son was an ugly and repulsive idea. How could I have accepted for so long that premise as a basis of my religion? I had not only accepted it, but had found it comforting that someone else had suffered for my failings. It was depressing to think I had led such an unexamined spiritual life—and the gulf between my religious views and official Church dictums once again widened.

I WANT TO BE A BROTHER

RESPONSE TO THE articles about the brothers in the Indian diocesan papers had been steady, and while an ad could hardly convey the spirit of a religious order, it was the only way to contact the many young Catholic men who lived, as most of India did, in the villages that dotted the subcontinent.

New Challenge

Young men with a strong trust in God and desire to help the poor improve their lives are invited to join a religious order new to India.

Composed of brothers and priests, we emphasize community life, team work in ministry, and the importance of education.

We hold our Blessed Mother as our special patron for these works and for our own spiritual growth.

If you are interested, please contact us at the address below.

Almost every bishop in India had spoken of a literacy program he wanted the brothers to undertake, or a boys' orphanage that needed administration, or ten villages that had no school whatsoever, or the poor living in the unsanitary conditions on city streets. "Send us your brothers as soon as possible, please," they had said. I wanted to somehow speed up the calendar and have numerous young men trained to do the work.

But India moved slowly, as slowly as the buses that carried Sylverius and me from one rural parish to another, or to the occasional bishop's house in an outlying area. Sylverius accompanied me not only as a translator, but also to become trained in recruitment work himself. The eldest of the novices, Sylverius possessed a quiet presence that had a calming effect on people around him. His physical build, short but muscular, had earned him the nickname "the mountain" when he played a defense position in field hockey. I myself felt comforted by his presence, as the buses careened down dusty roads, deposited us in forlorn bus stands, or broke down in between destinations, leaving us to fend for ourselves.

"Welcome, Brother Jim and Brother Sylverius," a smiling priest greeted us at the door of the bishop's house at one remote locale in northern India. "I have rooms ready for you, and here," he gestured to a small parlor near the front door, "is a good place for you to interview the young men coming to see you."

After the experience with Barto and Juel, I had frequently asked other religious orders in India for suggestions on how to screen candidates. I rarely met someone who didn't want to give advice.

"YOU MUST NOT take the oldest son," one priest stated emphatically. The eldest was needed to support the family since there was no welfare system in India. "Do not take a boy from a very poor family" said a brother in South India, for very much the same reasons. The advice made sense in a land where destitution was not far from anybody's door, but another piece of advice shocked me.

At a parish in northern India accustomed to power outages, candles flickered on the dinner table and a kerosene lamp hung on the wall. "Please don't quote me, but I wouldn't take any youths in this region from the scheduled castes," the priest said.

I knew that the term "scheduled caste" referred to the Untouchables. I stared at the priest. How could he say something like that? It was valid to know if the boy was needed at home, but social standing—how could that be a problem?

"Why do you say that?" I asked.

"Brother, do you know why they are called 'rice Christians'? It's the Church's own fault of course." In the old days, relief programs from churches in other countries often specified its rice donations for "the Christians of" such-and-such a place. Many non-Christians were equally in need and a good number converted to Christianity to be eligible not only for rice, but for other services like education and health care that the Church provided. The Untouchables, already at the bottom of the social and economic ladder, had nothing to lose and everything to gain by converting to Christianity. They had joined the Church expecting handouts and they still did. Well, of course, not every-body, the priest was quick to add. But many had an "entitled" attitude, and were quick to take offense if they thought they were being slighted. And they wouldn't stop at violence to get what they wanted.

"Look over here," the priest said, as he rose from his chair and walked to the wall where the kerosene lamp hung. He lifted the lamp from its hook and pointed to a large indentation on the wall that the lamp had covered.

"That dent was made by the previous pastor's head. A couple of men came late at night to rob the parish, men from the scheduled caste. Their gun blast threw Father against the wall. He died instantly. I'm his replacement."

THE BISHOP'S HOUSE, a solidly-built concrete structure, appeared similar to many religious houses in India—high ceilings, dark narrow hallways, a few religious pictures hung on otherwise plain walls, two or three hard benches or couches in a sitting room. Nuns' convents usually had brighter colors on the walls and curtains on the windows, but didn't always have a guest room for male visitors. Whatever the physical condition of the house, I nevertheless always felt welcomed. "Hospitality for the stranger and the traveler" was not an extinct virtue, but was alive and vibrant in India.

Five young men from outlying villages were to arrive sometime that afternoon, have their interview, and return to their homes by nightfall. No specific time had been set for their interview because distances, erratic bus schedules, and lack of telephones precluded such precise planning. So Sylverius and I read our books and waited.

By three o'clock, three young men—Vincent, Anthony, and Sudhir—had arrived, been offered refreshment, and each in turn joined us in the parlor. While Sylverius translated for me, I took notes on each candidate, and prompted Sylverius with questions to ask.

How is your family? Is everyone well at home? Tell me about your brothers and sisters. How are your studies going for you?

If a candidate had a brother or sister in another religious order, it was a sign of a solid family background, one very likely with no economic crisis. Educationally, each candidate was expected to have finished high school, and to be currently in the second year of the two-year "intermediate" studies that preceded college, preferably having passed his high school exam at the first or second "level."

How is your health? Did you bring a recommendation from your parish priest?

And finally, *Why do you want to join the brothers? Have you had this desire for a long time? What would you like to do as a brother?*

"I can serve God in whatever way the brothers and priests tell me. I am strong, and I wish to be a dear part of God's holy church," said Vincent, a robust young man with a pleasant smile.

"Mother Mary is mother of us all, and I love her so much. You love Mary. It is so beautiful. Please accept me." Anthony spoke softly, his eyes cast downward.

"The Father in my parish is very educated," Sudhir said. "He tells everyone God's word. I want to be like him and study at the seminary. There is no future for me in village life." Of medium height and on the thin side, Sudhir spoke in a strong voice and his eyes looked directly at Sylverius, then at me.

I invited Vincent and Anthony to visit us in Kathmandu the following spring, but hesitated to do so with Sudhir. Was getting an education an ulterior motive for him? Maybe he simply wished to escape a dull life in the village. I decided to get more information on him before proceeding.

As late afternoon darkness closed in on the parlor, I assumed that the other two candidates, for whatever reason, would not make their appointments. Sylverius and I prepared to return to our own rooms, when a sharp rap sounded on the outside door. "I am Rajesh. Sorry that I am reaching late to this place," a young man said in heavily-accented English.

"Please come in," I said, showing him a chair in the parlor. Tall and husky, with a thick head of hair, Rajesh was decidedly larger than the other candidates we had interviewed. His long legs extended under the small table between us, and the black sweater that he wore pulled tightly on his large frame. He looked too big for both his clothes and the room. He explained that he didn't live far away, but was detained when the bus suffered a flat tire. "I saw your statement in the paper, and now I am here to join you."

I asked him to tell me first about his family.

"Yes," he began slowly, "my family. There are three of us left."

Wind rattled the windows and distant rumblings blurred whatever else Rajesh was saying. A storm was brewing, sweeping over the rolling hills in the area, and when the sound of lightening crackled nearby, the lights went out. Sylverius and I rose to secure the shutters, and when we returned Rajesh had lit two candles on the small table.

He leaned forward in the semi-darkness and clutched the edge of the table. "This is like the night my father was murdered." His eyes gazed unblinkingly at the candles. "There was a big commotion at our house with people running in and threatening us. I went outside and hid in a ditch and covered my head. When I looked up, I saw my father dragged out of the house. Then, a few meters in front of me, my cousin stabbed my father."

The wind beat against the windows as we sat in silence. Rajesh spoke again, this time in Hindi and with a cold voice. Sylverius translated that Rajesh had apparently been only three or four at the time, and the violence had been over family inheritance. Rajesh concluded with, "I must settle this with my cousin," and continued to stare at the candles. I was at a loss for words, though Rajesh's trance-like demeanor suggested he hardly knew I was in the room.

The poor man is unstable, I thought to myself. If only we had a brothers' house *here, now*, we could assist him in some way. He came here with a good heart, but I cannot accept him.

"Sylverius, thank him for coming, but tell him he is not suited for the Brotherhood." Rajesh listened to Sylverius, no expression crossing his face. He rose slowly, shook our hands, and left. I watched him lean into the wind as he walked away, and wished I could have helped him.

The next morning, my heart clouded when I thought of Rajesh. He was one of hundreds who passed before me daily, in pain in some manner. Images of such suffering tore at the heart of every visitor to India, that was certain. Perhaps one day, young men like Vincent or Anthony or Sudhir would be living in the villages as brothers, more capable than I of responding to their fellow-countrymen's needs. That vision of the future would have to sustain me, and help me not feel guilty for letting Rajesh walk away alone into the storm.

2 November 1982
Patna, India

Dear Dave,

I'm writing this from a verandah at St. Xavier's School in Patna, India, where I am still gaining strength after a five-day stay at Holy Family Hospital—so this note will be short. While conducting interviews for new candidates (our work is growing, know that—details later) I managed to catch dengue fever, a viral infection borne by mosquitoes. One grows completely weak, suffers high fever and intense joint pain. I believe this is the disease they call "breakbone fever." Aptly named.

I hardly slept in the hospital. Hindus celebrate continual religious holidays this time of year, and a loudspeaker directly across from the hospital blasted devotional songs all night long. I'm afraid I cursed the pagans and their gods, though perhaps I may be forgiven because of my 104-degree fever.

In one area I visited, elephants roam the forests and sometimes venture close to the villages. When Sylverius and I went for a walk, we were admonished to be watchful. Just a month earlier, an elephant had crept up on a man walking along a road and killed him.

An elephant *creeping up* on you? Apparently elephants have padded feet and can move noiselessly as a cat. If the story weren't tragic, it would be funny. Sometimes I don't know whether to laugh or be sad, which sounds like much of my life here so far.

I should be home—Kathmandu—in a few more days.

Sincerely,

Jim

PASSIONS OF THE MIND

DEL APPEARED AT my door while I was unpacking from the trip to India. "Glad to see you're okay. We were all worried about you." Along with several hotel bills, the bill for my hospital stay had arrived several days before my own letter of explanation, and the hospital's financial statement, devoid of health information, had caused anxiety in the community. "You *are* okay, aren't you?" When I assured Del I was fine, he added, "There is one consolation, though. I see that your room at the hospital was cheaper than your stay in hotels."

"What a thing to say!" I feigned hurt feelings, though as an American, I had to laugh at the idea that a hospital stay was cheaper than an average hotel. On occasion, I had to stay in a hotel in India, having arrived at my destination in the middle of the night, or found myself in a city where I had no connections. Yes, the vow of poverty meant we were to avoid luxuries, but it didn't mean indigence. I liked Del, but his concern for frugality certainly didn't match mine.

"Well, we must set an example for the novices," Del said gravely in his barely audible deep voice.

"Yes, of course, so let's show them a cheerful attitude. Now, what's new around here?"

George had assigned the novices twenty-five pages to read on the theology of the Mass and was disappointed they had not completed it. "He wonders if they need more study time," Del said.

"I'll talk to him."

After exchanging pleasantries with George and asking about the novices, I broached the subject of academics. "You know, George, Indian spirituality is much more devotional than theological or academic. Theory isn't very appealing to them, and on top of that, the novices' English proficiency is pretty basic."

"Yes, but they need a solid background in theology."

I encouraged George to be creative in the matter, and was delighted later that week to find him teaching the novices songs about Mary, the Holy Spirit, and the Old Testament Prophets, after which they had a lively discussion on the topics. It was heartening to see George be adaptable, so I was slightly taken aback over the issue of a book I was reading.

One evening I asked if anybody had seen a book I left in the living room some days earlier. George motioned me aside, and explained that he had found the book and placed it on the top shelf in the pantry.

"Why there?" I asked.

"I wasn't sure whose it was and I wanted to get it out of the novices' sight. It's about Freud."

The book, *Passions of the Mind*, was a biography of Freud which included a brief explanation of his psychoanalytic theories. I had recently discovered several bookstores in Kathmandu that catered to English-speaking tourists and which had inexpensive, used paperbacks.

"I know it's about Freud. What's the problem?"

"His views on sex of course." George retrieved the book, handed it to me, and walked away with no further explanation.

The following week George was concerned once again. This time he questioned whether we should have a picture of the Hindu god, Shiva Natarajan, a "false god," in the study hall. He compared it to the "golden calf" and said it didn't belong on a wall opposite the Virgin Mary. I loved the drawing of the dancing god that Steve had sketched in Delhi and had dragged it, glass frame and all, up from India.

"Really, George. It's not a shrine we're worshipping," I said. "It's a piece of art work."

"Ask the novices what they think," he replied.

The next day at the end English class, I raised the question.

"We would never have such a picture in our home," Sylverius said. "You must remember that we feel oppressed by the Hindu majority." A Hindu fundamentalist movement sought to make India "Hindustan," the land of the Hindus, a country in which Christians conceivably would feel even more on the defensive than currently. A few years earlier, a right-wing Hindu group had tried to pass a law restricting Christians in the spread of their faith, a right Christians felt should be theirs. The issue was, at least, one of freedom of speech, a right supposedly guaranteed to all in the world's largest democracy.

"However," Sylverius added in his soft voice, "we must keep this picture. It was beautifully drawn by one of the first brothers to come to India."

It dawned on me how cavalier I could be about religious differences. The colorful Hindu pantheon was a source of fascination and expansion for me, a panoply of the many faces of the Divine. But I had not lived as a religious minority under the social oppression often wielded by a majority religion, as Sylverius and the other young men had. Yet Sylverius had enough heart to move beyond the social aspects the picture of Shiva might represent, and accept the drawing for its other significance—a beautiful picture, created by one of our own brothers.

I was moved by Sylverius' comments, but not George's objections. Sylverius spoke from a lived, vulnerable experience. George came from a theoretical and righteous position. George's thinking, however, was closer to the Catholic norm than mine, and I realized I was fast losing patience with the Church's claim of spiritual hegemony, the position that "*We* have the one, true faith, and *they* don't." Living in my Catholic community was comfortable, but the price was beginning to look like my integrity, and it disturbed me deeply.

When I walked through the study hall the next day and saw the picture of Shiva, I realized I wanted it all—dancing Shiva, self-sacrificing Jesus, playful Krishna, and ascetic Buddha. If I had any "passion of the mind," it was to bring all those images into an integrated spiritual view.

STAR OF BETHLEHEM

As WINTER APPROACHED, the skies over Kathmandu Valley gradually changed. The crisp, clear morning air was replaced by misty fog that, if we were lucky, burned off before noon. On those days when the fog lingered or dissipated only to reveal an overcast sky, the house remained cold all day. With no central heating and nights cold enough to form paper-thin ice on water patches in the driveway, the chill settled into the brick walls, and into my bones.

My bedroom, which jutted onto the second-floor verandah and had windows on three sides, had seemed ideal in autumn for viewing the beauty of the valley and the pulse of the neighborhood. In winter, the room became an icebox. I padded the windows with newspaper and at bedtime wore a knit cap that eventually caused my scalp to itch. Down the hall, a space heater slightly warmed the chapel in the morning, an added motivation for me to move quickly out of my room and get to prayers on time.

The novices suffered more from the cold than I, and discarded their shawls for full blankets that they wore in the house all day. Happily, afternoon tea at four o'clock warmed our stomachs just as the winter sun slipped behind the valley's ridges and the temperature dropped abruptly. The added chill seemed to signal the end of the day even though the sky was not yet completely dark. In the downtown area, people headed for buses and rickshaws, pulling their clothes tightly about themselves. Beneath their jackets or shawls, both men and women wrapped a wide scarf around their stomach to ward off the cold. I had learned to carry an extra sweater for that moment of sudden cold.

One afternoon, I stepped into a favorite bookstore that carried a wide array of books in English. A shelf in the back carried several volumes on mythology, and the cover of one book, *Krishna, The Divine Child*, caught my attention. A man and woman leaned over a small boy. The blue-skinned, shining child was surrounded by blazing light, and was apparently secure from the demons and soldiers in the background who were slaughtering other children the boy's age. The book recounted the legends surrounding Krishna's birth. In those days, the story went, an evil king ruled the land, causing much suffering to the people. After many years, the gods decided it was time to send a savior—Krishna, an incarnation of Vishnu—who would destroy the king and restore the balance of good and evil on the earth.

The wicked king, however, heard a voice saying that a young boy would usurp his authority, and set out to protect his throne. First, he slaughtered all the sons of the mother in question, then later, fearing he still had not destroyed his adversary, ordered the systematic killing of all boys Krishna's age. But the boy's birth, accompanied by inexplicable events—manacles dropping from his imprisoned mother and father, guards sleeping through their watch, bolted doors swinging open, river waters subsiding—proceeded successfully, and divine powers protected him from further danger. During the celebration held for his birth, the high priests announced that the boy would slay demons and bring a new age of prosperity to the land.

Why were both Hindus and Christians disposed to believe that a divine child was born on earth? Some clue to basic spiritual yearning must lie in the answer to that question. A deep-seated chord in our souls must be struck by the image of god in child form. This Christmas, my first in an officially-Hindu nation, I would let Krishna dance in my mind alongside Jesus in the manger, and see if I attained any insight about the question. There was no need, of course, to muse out loud to my brothers about contemplating the two religious figures. Christianity was interested in only one divine child.

I placed the book back on the shelf and hurried outside to find a bus. Men and women queued for half a block to push onto the bus I wanted, so I paid the extra fare for an autorickshaw to reach home in time for Mass. As the small vehicle snaked through the streets, the cool winter air blew on my face, carrying both exhaust fumes and the sweet smell of incense. The rickshaw driver had placed incense sticks at the base of a plastic flute-playing Krishna who perched on his dashboard.

"What shall our Christmas look like?" I asked one evening at a community meeting. "What are your Christmas traditions in the villages?"

"We walk to midnight Mass, maybe one hour away, then after Mass, dance until morning. Of course we have special food, chicken curry and rice," John said.

I responded that we wouldn't be dancing till dawn. Our neighbors would surely not appreciate that. By the end of the meeting, we had decided that the house must be decorated with pine branches, and colorful garlands from the bazaar. We would join all the local Catholics at the parish midnight Mass, then host a "high tea" for our friends the afternoon of Christmas Day. For high tea, Maela could bake sugar cookies, lemon bars, and nut breads, in addition to traditional Nepali sweets—milk and sugar squares, caramelized banana slices, and salty nuts mixed with peppered rice crisps. The day after Christmas would be a good day to hike up Pulchowk Mountain at the edge of the valley, perhaps even see snow there.

Johnny volunteered to build a manger scene, and Sylverius said he would make a Star of Bethlehem. For a Christmas tree,

an American woman working in Kathmandu came to our res-
cue. One Sunday after Mass at the parish, she had informed
me her landlord usually "topped" the pine trees at her home
in December, and we would be welcome to have one of the
castoffs.

The next afternoon, as Sylverius laid out long bamboo poles,
colored paper and thin strips of wood on the rooftop, Stephen
accompanied me to pick up the pine tree. As so often happened
in Kathmandu, neighbors and acquaintances along the way
waved at us to stop and chat, and by the time we headed back
with the tree, the winter sky was already darkening.

Stephen held the front end of the tree and I cautioned him
to go slowly. With the base of the tree on my shoulder, the pine
branches obscured the view directly ahead and I turned my gaze
upward. Stars had begun to appear in the western sky, beginning
with the Evening Star, the planet Venus. Like the Morning Star,
the Evening Star was one of the many names given to Mary, a
bright light among Christians. Mary had always been presented
as the perfect "model of faith," for she had fully believed the
angel Gabriel's message. I felt a small tug in my stomach, for
blind faith was becoming more and more alien to me.

"Jim, do you see the star? It's so bright and clear." Stephen
called back to me.

"Yes. Did you know it's actually a planet?"

"No, our star. Put the tree down."

I lowered the tree to the ground and looked up.

A five-pointed, multicolored star shone above the rooftops
two blocks away, over our house. Sylverius' large, three-dimen-
sional star with a light bulb in its interior cast a warm glow in the
evening sky, causing several Nepalis on the street to stop and
point in the star's direction. One small boy ran excitedly toward
the luminary.

For a moment it seemed audacious to have the star on our own rooftop, for tradition said the Star of Bethlehem announced the presence of the Divine. Could that be us? Were *we* divine? Perhaps that was really the message of the divine child whose image captivated both Hindus and Christians. There was something about a divine child born of a very human mother that told us we all had divinity in ourselves, waiting to be brought forth. We were drawn to an image that somehow said *we* were divine.

What an almost frightening thought—it is *we* who are divine! Too much responsibility went with that idea. Certainly it was easier to believe that we were *like* God, but not the *same* as the deity—that was blasphemy. But the idea that each of us was truly divine, that together we constituted the complete Divine, settled warmly in my soul. Such a concept was contradictory to the beliefs I had been taught. But I was becoming less and less enamored of beliefs. I felt as if I were *remembering* something from deep within.

TIRED SOLDIER

ALTHOUGH THE TRAIN leaving Bombay's Victoria Terminus would be my first overnight train ride since I had been robbed, I felt safe. I was in a semi-private compartment with three others and we had a door that could be locked from within. No thief could enter. It would be a relaxing trip.

I had traveled to India to follow up on recruitment leads and had just interviewed several young men for the Brotherhood. Now I was headed to Bangalore on the fast night train for the same purpose. Three other men were already seated when I entered the compartment, two of them dressed in business suits, the third in the traditional *pyjama* and *kurta*—the loose-fitting pants and baggy shirt many Indians wore. One of the men with a business suit looked up and greeted me.

"Good evening, please have a seat," he waved his hand to the empty place next to him. "My name is Subramanian. And your good name please?"

"My name is James, thank you. This is cabin eighteen, isn't it?" I inquired as I sat next to him, my ticket in my hand.

"Quite so," he replied as he glanced at my ticket. "I see you are assigned a lower berth for sleeping. But if you wish to retire early you may take my upper berth. It would be no problem," he offered. I thanked him, saying the lower berth was fine. We chatted briefly about the benefits of our destination, Bangalore—its temperate climate and its growing electronics industry—while the two other men in the car, having nodded a greeting, returned to their newspapers.

As the train advanced along its slow path, winding behind warehouses, shanties, and crowded brick dwellings, our conversation died off and Subramanian returned to his reading material while I stared out the window. It was soon dark as the train began its ascent of the Western Ghats, the coastal mountain range that separated the lowlands around Bombay from the Deccan plateau rising to the east. The guidebook said that the mountains slopes were green, harboring numerous waterfalls, and providing "wondrous" views of the lowlands, but I didn't mind missing the sights in the fading light. The night train was the fastest train, and I looked forward to its gentle rocking to put me to sleep. I expected more rest on the train than in my Bombay hotel. Constant noise day and night were an integral part of that city's character, and I had not slept well the previous three nights. A first-class compartment on the fast night train would be an oasis before arriving in another noisy city, and I looked forward to a good night's sleep.

The express train rattled quickly through smaller stations where passengers waited for local trains. Many squatted on their haunches dangerously close to the tracks. Others, no doubt expecting a long wait, had already bedded themselves down, forming long rows of white, bundled figures, laid out as if in a morgue. A few hours later, it was time to retire, so I stretched out on the seat cushion, and sleep came quickly.

———✥———

MURMURING VOICES. *WHAT were they saying? Perhaps they'll go away.* Banging on the door. Louder voices. *Am I dreaming? No, someone's speaking Hindi. I can't be dreaming.* A door opening. Many voices. *People have entered the compartment!*

I bolted upright. Four men in khaki uniforms stood near my berth. Voices from the hallway barked orders into the compartment, and other uniformed men stood in the aisle. "Subramanian, what's happening? Who are these men?" I hoped my voice sounded calm, though I didn't feel that way. Surely we were safe if this was the military, but what if it's the police? The police in many areas were noted for their practices of extortion and cruelty.

"Oh, James," Subramanian called down from his berth, "there is some small problem, but not to worry. They haven't placed sufficient coaches on this train, and the military that boarded at this junction must have berths. We shall all double up. Each soldier will join one of us. It will be just fine."

Three soldiers climbed onto the other bunks, while a fourth soldier stood quietly next to my berth. He was no doubt as surprised to find a foreigner as his potential sleeping companion as I was to discover that I was to have a bed partner. He looked to be in his mid-twenties and of a slightly more solid build than many young men his age. The military was considered a good career in India and could select from the fittest men India had to offer. After a few seconds, the soldier cautiously sat on the edge of the berth but kept a polite distance. He made no move to lie down, and would make none, I knew, without an invitation from me.

I looked at my sleeping area, less than three feet wide. If the soldier shared this space, I would be so conscious of him, for many reasons, I'd not sleep at all in spite of being tired. Indians were accustomed to sleeping close to others, I was not. In my entire adult life, I had slept in the same bed with another person at most three or four times, while traveling. And those had been double beds, not narrow cushions. No, this would not work, but what should I do about it?

I pulled myself up close to the wall to test my theory that there wasn't enough room. There wasn't. I needed this night's sleep after the madness of Bombay. That city's noise, pollution, fast-moving double-decker buses, clanging rickshaw bells, and humidity had drained energy from me, and I just wanted to rest. But the soldier needed sleep too. I had thought that compassion was becoming an ever deeper part of me. If that were true, I wouldn't be hesitating.

The soldier made no move, though he looked expectantly in my direction. Then I knew that what really bothered me more than losing sleep was the intrusion. I was expected to share the cramped space like Indians. But I wasn't Indian. I had tried to adapt to Indian culture but I had my limits.

The soldier sighed and leaned his body against the side wall. He still said nothing. He took off his cap, held it in his hands, and turned to look at me once more. I remained silent, making no gesture to invite him to lie down. He turned back, and rested his head against the wall. I stared at him for a few more seconds, then realized that he was giving me exactly what I needed— my own space, with no pressure from him to share it. While the other soldiers had automatically climbed into a berth with another Indian, he had not done so with me. At some level he had understood. I watched him a few more minutes as his eyes closed and his breathing turned to light snoring. Then in spite of all my internal churning, my mind had grown as weary as my body, and I fell asleep in a few minutes.

Hours later, the train slowed, the change in movement awoke me, and the brightness in the compartment told me it was morning. The other members of the compartment began stirring, though no one spoke. Silently, three of the soldiers gathered up their belongings and prepared to leave the compartment. The young man at the end of my bunk still slept, slumped against the wall. One of his companions roused him, and he too stood up. He turned toward me, his eyes soft, and gave a gentle nod as if to acknowledge the small amount of space I had given him. Then he picked up his knapsack, and left the compartment.

I watched him leave, remembering how graciously he had responded to the previous night's situation. And I, quite deservedly, felt ashamed.

12 March 1983
Kathmandu, Nepal

Dear Dave,

Last week the novices were presented to the King and Queen of Nepal! The boys had joined a field hockey team sponsored by St. Xavier's School, and the team took second place in a citywide tournament held at the national stadium. With field hockey in their bones, the novices constituted the core of the team, and Sylverius was named Most Valuable Player in the tournament. The trophies for both first and second place team members were awarded to each player by King Birendra and Queen Aishwarya themselves.

Their Majesties sat on chairs draped with gold cloth, with a few attendants hovering nearby as the players were presented. Each young man received his trophy, made namaste to the King and Queen, then returned to the playing field. Naturally, our novices were excited. The King didn't appear to be closely guarded. Most say that his rule, practically an absolute monarchy, is secure, but I know there are rumblings from university students about wanting more democracy. For now, things appear stable.

As you know, Brother Alfred from Austria was here recently for a visit. I met him in Delhi, and in my enthusiasm to show him the "real" India, I fear I dragged him through the labyrinthine bazaars and backstreets too soon. By the time we emerged from that chaos into downtown Delhi, he was desperate for a drink. Wouldn't you know it, that was one of Delhi's "dry" days. He looked so disappointed that I told the waiter that Alfred was "German" and that he *had* to have beer everyday.

Moments later, the waiter appeared with a tray containing a delicate teapot and two tiny cups. "We must keep this hidden," he whispered to me as he glanced around the room.

Again, this is India—rules, rules, rules, but let's make an exception.

Joe plans to return to the U.S this summer. He's not particularly unhappy or ill. He just feels it's time for him to move on. You know Joe, it's hard for him to stay in one place for any length of time. I will miss him. Beneath his excitable manner, he's really a practical person. He has a good sense of what will really work, whether it's teaching Hindus at St. Xavier's Moral Science (the students love him and hang on his every word), recruitment, or bringing the community together with singing and dancing. Our evening get-togethers just won't be the same without him.

You asked about our overall plan for recruitment and training, so here it is:

a) advertise for the Brotherhood in Indian diocesan papers

b) visit and interview the young men who write us

c) invite qualified candidates to live several weeks with us in Kathmandu—we call this the "Come and See Program"

d) place those accepted from the "Come and See Program" in Indian seminaries for a year of basic training in English, community living, and liturgy

e) have the candidates return from the seminaries to Kathmandu for more time with us, pre-novitiate, followed by their novitiate year after which they will take vows as brothers

Several diocesan seminaries in India have graciously agreed to accept our candidates for basic training, knowing that they are not geared primarily to the priesthood. However, the initial training in English and community living is the same whether the goal is to become a brother or a priest. I have made arrangements with the diocese of Patna, and two other places you may not have heard of, Bhagalpur and Bhopal.

The city of Bhagalpur gained notoriety recently because of its treatment of prisoners. The jail was overcrowded with unruly men waiting for trial, so the guards blinded many of them to keep them in line. India is a violent country.

Bhopal is a more prosperous, pleasant city. Situated on a plateau it will be cooler in summer, and the bishop there personally took me around his diocese to meet people and visit the seminary.

I'm now in my fourth year here in Asia! America seems so distant, in so many ways.

Shanti (peace),

Jim

COME AND SEE

A LETTER LAY ON my desk from a young man who had seen our ad and who had taken the effort to write in English.

> Respectful Brother and Father. My name is Prakash Lakra. My village is one hour bus ride from Ranchi. My father is well, thank you. So is mother. Eldest brother sits at St. Xavier College in Ranchi, and younger brother is finishing intermediate school. My sister is married two years. Now you know all about me. I have great respect for the Brothers and Fathers. Last year I finished intermediate.

Though the letter said little about Prakash himself, it contained much valuable information. His last name indicated he was a tribal like several of the current novices. Also, he was not the eldest son, and therefore not required to head the family in an emergency. His parents must have at least modest means or his older brother wouldn't be attending St. Xavier's College. Since Prakash had completed intermediate studies, he himself was ready for college. He appeared to fulfill all the basic qualifications, but there was no time to interview him before the "Come and See Program" starting in just a month. I would send Prakash a letter of invitation and evaluate him during the program itself.

The "Come and See Program" was a chance for young men interested in the Brotherhood to get to know us, and we them. We would maintain the usual house schedule—classes in the morning, sports and study in the afternoon, community gatherings and study in the evening. And, of course, the regular prayer schedule—morning prayers, afternoon Mass, and evening prayers. At the end of three weeks, we staff members would assess the candidates, aided by impressions the current novices had of the candidates and by insight from Father Mathias, the psychologist we had invited from Delhi. With all that information, we could make a reasonable decision about whom to accept.

May arrived and twelve young men, most of them nineteen or twenty years old, appeared at our gate. As the newcomers settled in, a babble of conversation swirled through the house—English, Hindi, Tamil, Marathi, and several tribal languages. The novices, each of whom spoke two or three languages, took charge of all practical matters—sleeping arrangements, dish crews, sports teams, and personal needs such as extra towels for showering. I concentrated on memorizing the names of the newcomers, some of whom I had interviewed almost six months previously, and several last-minute applicants I had invited sight unseen.

At the end of the day, I motioned John, the novice in charge of dorm assignments, to step into my room. "I'm confused," I said. "I don't remember inviting Anil Lakra, only a Prakash Lakra. Is that the same person?"

"Oh no, Anil is Prakash's younger brother. He explained it to me."

"Explained what?" I asked. Of all the novices, John conveyed the most practical sense. I always felt I could obtain accurate information and sound advice from him.

"At the last minute, the parents didn't give permission for Prakash to come. He is still needed at home since his eldest brother must stay longer in college. Prakash sent Anil, the youngest son, in his place."

"In his place? John, one can't just take someone's 'place' in the Brotherhood. This is a vocation we're talking about, a life choice like marriage. That would be like substituting a brother as the groom in a wedding!"

"That happened once in my village. The sister of the bride, too. These things are all arranged, you know."

I told John I knew about arranged marriages, but joining the Brotherhood wasn't like a brokered wedding, or a career choice, or an economic consideration. It certainly wasn't a decision a parent or older brother made for a young man. It was a free choice made from deep inside. The moment I stopped speaking, I wondered how sure I was about what I'd said. How free had I been when, at age sixteen, I first decided I wanted to become a brother? I hadn't felt free in the area of sexuality, that was for sure. And perhaps, on top of that, I was simply an idealistic adolescent, caught up in stories of saints and missionaries, or a teenager just eager to leave home. One thing, however, was clear—the decision to join the brothers was my own.

"Does Anil himself want to be here?" I asked.

"Oh, I think so. I have a good impression of him. We must give him a chance," John concluded.

Since Anil was already in Kathmandu, we certainly would give him a chance, but I had my doubts about a young man sent to us on the directives of his older brother and his parents.

One afternoon several days into the program, I walked to St. Xavier's playing field to watch the boys play soccer. Basant, a new candidate, bigger than the others, caught my eye. He was aggressive on the playing field, using his bulk to intimidate others when he rushed recklessly for the ball. Most other players stepped out of his way to avoid being hit, but Anil stood his ground. He and Basant collided several times. Each time Anil maintained a calm face, while Basant scowled and flashed his dark eyes. I knew, however, that Basant could be warm and friendly, for I had seen him coach another boy on passing the ball and even seen him reward the boy with a congratulatory smile and pat on the back. I wondered if Basant was another friendly "diamond in the rough" like Juel had been. But then, Juel had not worked out.

On the way back home, I conversed as best I could with the boys in a smattering of Hindi and English. At one point, Basant and John walked near me. "How are you, Basant?" I asked in Hindi. He gave me a smile and said, "Very fine, thank you. It was a good game. I am strong, you can see."

"John, tell Basant that I can see he is strong. He could be my bodyguard and protect me from robbers when I travel near Ranchi." As John translated, I saw a strange look steal over Basant's face. He didn't laugh or respond. He only touched my shoulder and moved on.

As the days progressed, Anil began to look as steady as the nearby mountains. Of medium height, he didn't stand out physically, but mixed well with everyone, a good sign that he was fit for community life. He danced with the other tribals in the evenings, and was conscientious in his kitchen duty, scrubbing pots. Maela said, "Brother Jim, I want more boys like Anil. He works like a water-buffalo and laughs at my jokes." That was the closest Maela ever came to commenting on the candidates. I happily concluded that Providence had sent us a real treasure in the "replacement brother." Well, I would no longer think of him as a replacement, only as Anil.

Over the next two weeks, I formed impressions of each young man, but Basant remained an enigma. He was always ready to volunteer for any project—carrying mattresses to the roof to be aired out, or helping Maela bring back groceries from the store. He apparently had a good heart, but he could become sullen and withdrawn for no apparent reason. His moodiness didn't augur well for him, but I liked him anyway. There was a certain charm in the transparency of his feelings, and he was certainly always pleasant with me. I hoped he would work out.

A few days before the conclusion of the program, John came to my room. "I have a little story for you," he said with a half

---

smile on his face. "It's about Basant and Anil. Sometimes Basant gets in a mood and orders the other boys around, telling them to pick up things or let him use the bathroom first. He's older to them, you see. Anil is polite, but doesn't let Basant bully him. They had an argument last night in the dormitory, and it came out that Basant is a *dacoit*."

"What!" A *dacoit*—a highway robber. The area around Ranchi where Basant lived was famous for thugs who stopped buses and even trains to rob the occupants. Youthful *dacoits* seldom hurt people, though older, more ruthless men slashed faces or maimed anyone who resisted.

"Are you sure? Maybe he's just trying to impress the others."

"I think it's true. He told us some robbery stories that sounded real."

"I can't believe it. Why is he here? Does he want to give up that life?" The information caught me off guard, though it could explain some of Basant's erratic behavior.

"I think he still plans to be a *dacoit*. But he said that he would never rob the brothers when he returns home. He says he likes the brothers. He likes you. He said that you show him respect. But I don't think he wants you to know he's a *dacoit*. Maybe don't mention it."

Not mention it! John sounded much too casual about the information. Basant was an unabashed outlaw, and I couldn't pretend that was okay. I should talk to him, convince him to change his ways. Since he planned to return home but never "rob the brothers," apparently he had already decided to stay with his old life of crime. How strange that he had come to us in the first place.

"I'm not sure what I'll do," I said, "and don't forget, I need a brief translation of the letters that are due today." The previous day I had asked all candidates to write a letter stating their intent with regards to the brothers. They could request to join the brothers, or if they had changed their mind and chose not to join, that was fine too. That evening John brought me the stack of letters, at the bottom of which was Basant's. He had requested admittance to the brothers.

The following day, the staff—George, Del, Joe, and myself—discussed all the feedback on the new candidates. We included Father Mathias in our deliberations, and reviewed our own perceptions, Father Mathias' psychological evaluations, and the novices' opinions. Joe had analyzed each young man in terms of assertiveness and cooperation, not only through games, but also by the way he danced. "You can learn a lot just by the way a person moves," he said.

To our satisfaction, we found that all methods had reached very much the same conclusions. All twelve had requested to join, and we decided that eight of them were good candidates. Four would be refused for reasons as varying as poor health or emotional immaturity. The four that were rejected included Basant. Regardless of his supposed illegal behaviors, his mood swings were considered a detriment to team effort and community life.

In my interview with each young man, I would tell him our decision. "What about Basant and this *dacoit* business?" I asked the staff.

Father Mathias offered his advice. "Even if it's true, you can't really counsel or admonish much through translators. There's little point in bringing it up," he said.

With John and Stephen's help in translating, all the interviews had gone well, but I had yet to face Basant. When he sat opposite me, his mouth was drawn in a tight line and his brow was furrowed.

"Basant," I began, "we don't think you're suited for religious life. Perhaps family life would be more satisfying for you."

Basant's face lit up.

"Yes, thank you. Can you put your refusal of me in a letter?"

"Why do you want it in writing?" I asked.

"It is for my mother and the parish priest. They sent me here because of their devotion to Blessed Mother Mary. I must show them your word that this life is not for me."

John asked more questions and the story unfolded. Basant's parents had had no children in the first several years of marriage. To gain divine help in the matter, his mother made a pilgrimage to a local shrine of Mary. There she promised that if she became fertile, her first-born would be given back to the Mother of God. Basant was born the next year.

The mother had recently confided the story to the parish priest, who in turn promised to look for a religious group devoted to Mary. Our ad had appeared the following month, a clear answer from God. With family ties running deep among the tribals, Basant—though a bandit—felt he must satisfy his mother. So he had reluctantly come to Kathmandu.

"But the brothers are fine people. Thank you for the very good time spent here," Basant finished.

I shook his hand and wished him a healthy and happy life. "And, Basant," I looked him steadily in the eye fervently hoping my words would stick, "be kind and honest."

Following John's translation, Basant said slowly, in English, "Yes, Brother Jim."

That night, as I walked the veranda, I pondered the ups and downs of the last several weeks. I had doubted Anil's potential, but he had come through. I thought Basant had promise, but he didn't work out. Several other candidates from India hadn't even shown up, yet we now had eight new candidates. It wasn't how I had planned it all, but I couldn't deny we had good results. In Delhi, Santosh had once said, "Are you here to organize India? Do what you will, then just accept what happens."

A TASTE OF THE OCEAN

TRAVEL GUIDEBOOKS STILL referred to Kathmandu as Shangri La, and during the slow months after the "Come and See Program," I settled into an easy schedule that included exploration of that Himalayan city. Though I taught the novices English in the morning, most of my afternoons were free that first full summer in Nepal, and I determined to know the city better. One afternoon Del and I visited Sleeping Vishnu, a large statue of the god resting in supine position, which the king of Nepal wasn't permitted to view. The king was an incarnation of Vishnu and mustn't see himself in repose or he would die.

"Such superstition in Hinduism!" Del exclaimed as we returned for afternoon Mass. When Father George held up the communion host and announced, "This is the Body of Christ," I recalled the lesson that the previous October's animal sacrifice had taught me. One person's religion was indeed another man's superstition. But Christianity, its practices burned deeply in my psyche, was still home.

Though the days were pleasant with mild weather, a relaxed schedule, and the delight of marigolds and jasmine and sweet basil blooming in our front yard, an old complaint returned to haunt me—neck pain. Neck pain and accompanying headaches had plagued me periodically over the previous three years, and most remedies—medicine, chiropractic, stretching—had brought only temporary relief. One afternoon, a small wooden

sign in a Kathmandu side street caught my attention—*Massage*—
and I remembered that massage in India had provided more
relief than most other treatments. With a dull pain in my neck at
that moment, I decided to give massage a try once again.

A man in his late-twenties, wearing orange sweat pants and
an orange *kurta*, answered my knock on the door. "Namaste. My
name is Sudip. How can I help you?"

I explained my problem and Sudip felt confident he could
help. As I lay on a low table in the sparse room, he massaged only
my feet and never touched my tight shoulder and neck muscles.

"Sudip, it's my neck where I hurt."

"Yes, yes, James," he replied and continued to work on my feet.

In spite of feeling I had made a big mistake, I nevertheless
drifted off into a half-asleep state, and when Sudip later asked
me to sit up, my neck pain and headache were almost gone. He
showed me charts that indicated neck pain was related to a particular place on the feet, and, impressed with the results, I made
another appointment with him.

At dinner that night I told everyone about Sudip and his
miraculous work. Del raised one eyebrow, commented on how
expensive the sessions were, and asked how many more did I
think I needed.

"Quite a few, I'm sure," I said, and Del harrumphed something into his soup.

During my following sessions, I grew curious about the
orange clothing Sudip wore and asked him about it. He explained
that saffron was the color of a *sannyasin*, a disciple dedicated to
the spiritual path, and that his guru, the Bhagwan, required it of
all his followers. The word *sannyasin* was new for me, but I was
familiar with *Bhagwan*. A Sanskrit and Hindi word that meant
"Lord," it often appeared in the Hindi hymns we sang in chapel.
How strange it sounded to refer to a living person as Bhagwan,
since my ear was attuned to the word pertaining only to God.

"Bhagwan teaches true spiritual attainment," Sudip explained. "Are you interested in the spiritual path? We have a large collection of Bhagwan's teachings where I live. You could borrow books on his lectures if you wish. Many foreigners admire Bhagwan's words."

"I'm a Christian monk and I'm not really looking for another religion."

"Bhagwan does not teach a religion, but goes beyond religion."

Beyond religion? That concept, once again, intrigued me. "Maybe someday I'll visit, but if I do, I don't want any pressure to follow the Bhagwan. That would irritate me."

"Not to worry, James, not to worry. We shall merely place the rose on the table for you. You may pick it up if you like."

That evening when I related the conversation to Joe, he said, "The Bhagwan? Oh yes, that's what they call a guru named Rajneesh. A lot of Americans and Europeans flock to him, but he's too radical for most Indians and Nepalis. In fact, he's moved to America now. America..." Joe's voice trailed off.

I knew from the wistfulness and anticipation in Joe's voice that he was already thinking of America and home, for which he was leaving in just a few days. I hated to see him go. I would miss his upbeat energy and creativity, but, as he had told me earlier, "I've done my work here. My contribution was to help get things started, then move on." Even as he had said those words, however, there was a mistiness in his eyes. One's home country might beckon, but there was sadness in leaving. India and Nepal could do that to one.

Unlike Joe, I had no idea when my time in India and Nepal would be finished. I had no desire to return to the U.S. except for visits. If I stayed for another three years, I would have spent seven years in the mission—seven years, a mystical number, and the number of years it took to replace every cell in the body and become almost a different person. Well, no need for me to decide now how much longer I would stay. When the moment arrived, I would recognize it.

A few days after Joe's farewell party and departure for America, I saw Sudip again and told him my visits would become less frequent because, happily, I had very little neck pain remaining. "Even if you don't come for sessions," he said, "remember that you are most welcome to come to Ananda Ashram and look at our library."

After a ten- minute walk from our house the next day, I knocked on the door at Ananda Ashram. The door opened and a chubby man in a saffron robe asked how he might help me. I introduced myself and asked to see Sudip, but he was not there. The man, however, opened the door and waved me in. "My name is Divendra and I assist Swami Jyoti, our overall in-charge, in the running of the house. You may sign out books with me. Sudip said you would come," he smiled knowingly.

The three-story brick building was a large house where devotees of the Bhagwan lived, studied, and meditated together—a "commune" not totally unlike my own. In the upstairs library, Divendra settled himself on the floor behind a small platform that served as a desk, and busied himself with paperwork while I surveyed the room. The longest wall was lined with books by the Bhagwan, apparently a prolific writer. Topics ranged from Zen to Taoism, from ancient Hindu sutras to Greek philosophical writings, from Zarathustra to Jesus. It seemed there wasn't a religious or philosophical tradition the Bhagwan wasn't familiar with. "Divendra, is there a particular book I ought to start with?"

"You may begin anywhere. Dip your finger anyplace in the ocean, the taste will be the same," he replied. "On the other hand, if you are Christian, you please begin with *The Mustard Seed*. It is Bhagwan's teachings about Jesus." Divendra found two cassettes and handed them to me. "Please listen to Bhagwan first, before reading him. It is like sitting at the feet of the Master himself. Even the sound of his voice will be beneficial to you."

That evening I settled into the reading chair in my bedroom, pulled out a small tape recorder, and let the rather monotonic, but soothing, voice of the Bhagwan speak to me.

"I don't lecture about this fellow Jesus very much, you must have noticed," the Bhagwan said. "He was a great man with many beautiful teachings. But he is so sad. Where is the joy? Such a serious fellow. I cannot connect much with him. And he has influenced so much of the world, especially the West. Is it any wonder that Westerners who come to me must be freed of this gravity? That is one reason I tell jokes. Many of you have come here as serious about enlightenment as you were about following the rules of your churches. Forget enlightenment! Forget it, I say. Just laugh, dance, love."

A Master telling his disciples to forget about enlightenment! I tried to imagine my own Novice Master of many years earlier suggesting we forget about holiness and striving for perfection, but to laugh and dance instead. I smiled to myself as I tried to picture Father Willis, the hem of his black cassock sweeping up sanctuary dust, telling funny stories instead of giving a serious sermon. Striving for perfection was sober business in the Church. Its saints were known for their long-suffering, not their jokes. The problem was, I liked to laugh. Father Willis had once punished me for laughing too loudly at the dinner table by having me remain silent during the next three meals. I was beginning to like this Bhagwan.

The Bhagwan addressed the disciple whose parents feared he was brainwashing their son. "Yes, I am brainwashing you. You need it badly. Do you understand? I am washing your brain, scrubbing it clean of all the conditioning you have been subjected to. Whatsoever you have been taught in religion as a child is conditioning. You don't realize that *that* was real brainwashing. A fish doesn't know it's in water. You were soaking up whatever your parents told to you, thinking it was reality. Do you believe Jesus is an incarnation of the Godhead? Why do you believe that? Because you were told that many times. Do you think Krishna is an avatar, a form of the Divine come to earth? And why do you believe that? Because you were told that many times as a child. This is true brainwashing. And people say I am brainwashing you! What rubbish! These religions have been your prisons, keeping you inside their narrow thinking. The priests and rabbis and imams and ayatollahs have been your prison guards—and you have been cooperating with them! Wake up! Get out of the prison!"

The Bhagwan continued to criticize priests and other ministers who "insist you must find God through them." His words struck an all too familiar chord. During the "Come and See Program" George and I had taught a class in which we were to describe the different roles of the brothers and priests in our order. I had explained that brothers could engage in a wide variety of works—teaching, health care, running orphanages, sacred art—almost any need that presented itself.

When I asked George to speak about the role of the priest, he had used the chalkboard to draw a picture of God high in heaven, people on earth and, in the conspicuous distance between the two, wrote the word *priest*. Turning to the group, he announced formally, "Just like Jesus, the priest is the channel of grace between heaven and earth."

Oh, no, what old theology! I had reacted instinctively. "Don't translate that. Translate what I say," I said to Stephen and William. I redrew the figures in a circle, and described the priest's role as one of many offices in the religious community. My voice shook from anger but I tried to sound casual. I couldn't tell from the faces of the translators what they thought about the intervention, and the new candidates merely smiled and nodded their heads.

To my surprise, George didn't seem perturbed when we talked together later. "Oh, fine. That was a nice little addition you made," he merely said, even though I had somewhat "corrected" him in front of the novices who translated. George liked to maintain a sage, unruffled visage, and preferred not to enter into debate or argument.

My relegating George's comment to "old" theology was correct in terms of vocabulary, but not in terms of Church thinking. The drop in priestly vocations in the U.S. was lamented mainly because so many Catholics would be "without the sacraments." Without the priests and Mass, how could the faithful connect with God?

I was weary of being told spiritual authority was always somewhere else, never within me.

That evening I put on a sweater and stepped onto the verandah outside my bedroom. The evening air was crisp, and my cheeks tingled. Stars sprinkled in every direction, winking at each other and at me, and chill Himalayan air made me aware of every breath I inhaled.

I gulped in the oxygen as if I were coming up from a near drowning—and I knew why. While the Bhagwan's words had resonated with me and made me feel I was "coming home" to important truths, the experience was also an unnerving one. If I questioned ingrained religious beliefs and claimed my own spiritual authority, my life would turn upside down. I would be alone, outside the religious culture of a lifetime, prey to my own lack of vision, uncertain about everything. Where would all this soul-searching lead? Would it all be okay in the end? As if in answer, from somewhere deep inside me, there arose my favorite scripture passage from St. Paul: "For those who love God, all things work together unto good."

Shifting Ground

"Del, I won't be going to St. Xavier's for Mass with you this week," I announced one evening. I was alone in the house with Del because George and the novices had left Nepal for India. George was giving a nuns' retreat and the novices were teaching catechism in Christian villages and working in literacy projects during a break in their classes.

"No? Where will you go to Mass?"

"I'm not going to Mass. I'm going to the Bhagwan's ashram for their morning meditation."

"Meditation at that ashram? But no Mass?"

I told Del I wanted to experience the ashram's style of meditation, which involved moving the body and special breathing techniques.

"Hmmm," Del responded in a guttural tone.

At six the next morning I walked briskly past the farmers entering the city with their carts of fresh produce, and hoped the morning walk would help wake me up. I didn't want to miss any of the meditation instruction. Near the ashram, two Nepali men and one Indian woman approached the building in silence. We exchanged no greetings, as in a monastery where monks pass each other quietly in the cloisters, each focused on his current duty and the need for recollection.

"Welcome to all for today's meditation," Swami Jyoti, the ashram director, announced promptly at six-thirty. He sat in front of the large meeting room where we all squatted on the floor. In his mid-forties, with a full dark beard, he wore an orange sweatshirt and sweatpants, and spoke in a deep resonant voice. Sudip sat near the front of the room, and Divendra leaned against a wall next to me wearing a tee shirt and sweat pants, his belly lapping over the drawstring. The two Nepali men and the Indian woman sat in the middle of the room, their eyes cast down toward the floor.

"Since we have a new meditator today," the swami continued as he glanced in my direction, "I will give a brief explanation of the process. A woodcutter or field worker need not do our style of prayer, called Dynamic Meditation. All day long they are using their bodies actively, and are throwing off tension and negative energy. But it is different for us modern city people with our desk jobs and mental pursuits. We must do cathartic meditation or we will remain in our own negative energy. Bhagwan has seen this and has created the Dynamic Meditation for us.

"For the first ten minutes we shall breathe chaotically in through the nose and out the mouth, concentrating on the inhalation." We were not to concern ourselves with exhalation, it would take care of itself. We were to breathe as hard as we could, then do it even harder until we became "one" with the breathing. "You must *be* the breathing. Permit your body to move, this will assist you. Let us stand now and begin."

Taking my cue from those around me, I began the rapid breathing, and within a few minutes my nasal passages and the rear of my throat had become dry. Rather than feeling calm, my mind raced. *I'm already feeling light-headed, and hardly five minutes have passed. I wonder how healthy this intense breathing really is. If there are any cold viruses in the room I'll be sure to get them. But breathwork is a time-honored prelude to meditation. I must continue.*

"Now, do catharsis," Swami Jyoti shouted over a tape of drum music. "Shout, scream, cry, go totally mad. Begin by acting, if you wish. Eventually your real emotions will take over."

A loud, piercing shout came from Divendra as he flailed his arms in the crowded room. Sudip lay cowering on the ground, sobbing. Cries of "No! No!" burst forth from the Indian woman as she punched the air in front of her. One Nepali man laughed in a high-pitched voice, as if on the verge of hysteria. *O Mother Mary, what have I gotten myself into? These people look unstable, and I'm supposed to imitate them. How can I begin? Should I begin?* I contorted my face every way imaginable, and prayed that such activity would trigger genuine responses in me. I wasn't successful, I didn't feel anything. *What had possessed me to come here? Why didn't I go to Mass with sensible Del?*

The second Nepali man shrieked at the ceiling. His eyes rolled back into his sockets showing almost complete whiteness, then he lay catatonic on the ground. *This is definitely unhealthy. These are fragile people, ripe for joining cults. I wonder if I can slip out the side door unnoticed? It was a mistake to come here.* I walked slowly about the room, my eyes cast down to block out the madness around me, and groaned from the sheer discomfort of the moment. *But, I must stay with the process a little longer, give it a chance.* Within a few minutes, deep, sad sighs assailed my ears, as if someone had pulled up grief from a hidden place and was letting it flow out ever so gently. A few seconds lapsed before I realized whose sighs they were—my own. The sighing continued, as tears wound a shaky path down my cheeks. I made no move to wipe my face.

"Be totally in your experience. Completely feel it!" The swami's voice shouted from across the room.

I felt like a large watery reservoir, with streams and currents coursing inside me, picking up debris from sadness and pain and discharging it through my eyes. I had no control over it. It was a feeling of nakedness, and I knew I looked childish and stupid. But at the same time, each tear felt cleansing. Something held inside for a long time was flowing away. I could not remember when I had last cried. Later, I found myself seated against a wall, my hands relaxed in my lap, my breathing gentle. Sitar music played in the background, its unmetered, flowing melodies as fluid as my insides. I sat quietly and peacefully.

At dinner that night, Del asked, "So, did you get enlightened?"

"Not sure. It was different, but I liked it." Liked it when it was over, I added to myself. I was not used to emoting in public and I liked to name my experiences, which I was unable to do concerning the tears. In the version I gave Del I played down the wild, cathartic expressions of my fellow meditators and omitted my own crying. I wasn't prepared to be open and vulnerable with someone who wouldn't be receptive. Yet, the experience had felt worthwhile.

"They all asked about you this morning at St. Xavier's," he said in a higher tone, and let the sentence hang.

"Give them my regards and tell them I'll drop in for tea one afternoon this week."

"So, you're going to that thing again tomorrow morning?"

"Probably the whole week."

"Hmmm," Del said in his usual way, then added, as we cleared the dinner dishes, "orange is not your color, I'd say."

By the end of the week and a few more tears, I had had enough of the ashram's style of meditation. The experience convinced me that, appealing though the Bhagwan's theories were, the actual living out of his spiritual path was not for me. I couldn't let group hysteria be the catalyst for my spiritual growth. Swami Jyoti said that I looked "changed," and offered to speak with me "about anything, anytime." But I was not in a talking mood. I didn't say more to Del either, but if he was worried, I could have assured him that I had no intention of donning orange robes and becoming a *sannyasin*. When George and the novices returned the following week, I was content to pray in our own chapel.

A few weeks later toward the end of August, an event happened that made me rethink those conclusions, and it happened on my birthday. The whole house shook and the windows rattled. It was an earthquake, a sign of the Himalayas' growing pains. The incessant push northward of the Indian subcontinent, which had formed the planet's highest mountain range, was continuing with creaks and groans. What seemed like the most solid and permanent landmass in the world was changing, sometimes traumatically.

The tremor caused me to leave my bed and rush outside at four-thirty in the morning. Though the shaking of the house and the fear of aftershocks were disorienting, the movement had felt somehow *familiar*. Strangely and deeply familiar.

It's A Scandal

As SEPTEMBER CAME to a close and the monsoons ended, church-goers at our local parish tended to gather early and socialize on the church steps before Mass. As I climbed the steps one Sunday evening, a young woman separated herself from a small group and approached me.

"I'm Mary, a new English teacher at St. Xavier's," she said in an enthusiastic American voice. In her late twenties, shoulder-length blond hair, rosy-cheeked, and a quick smile on her face, she offered her hand and continued. "I'm told you're in charge of the brothers' house and you people have a phone. And you live just a few houses away from me. We've got to talk! After Mass?" I smiled at her directness. She had sniffed out one of the few homes on our street with a phone and was forthright about why she was interested in us. I liked this new teacher immediately and invited her over after Mass.

"This house is wonderful!" Mary exclaimed after a quick tour. "I love those verandahs upstairs and those cute little desks in the study hall and these Nepali rugs in this huge living room. And wherever did you get those portraits of Nepali hill people? They look so indigenous. I could go on and on. But, let me sit down."

Seating herself in a wicker chair, Mary informed us that she wanted to see the whole world, and had just completed a year as an English tutor in Cairo. "Egypt was so passionate! And Mohammed, yes, he wanted me to stay, but… Well, I'm here now in fabulous Kathmandu and I love it, I just love it. Of course it's only been a week."

The novices' eyes followed Mary's every move as if watching a performer. She somehow managed to emphasize almost every word in her sentences and she gesticulated constantly.

"Jim, this floor! It's wood parquet! What a treat compared to the cold cement floor where I live," Mary said.

"Yes, we're lucky. And it's really great on special days when we have tribal dancing and disco dancing. We'll invite you and some of your co-teachers next time."

"Great. Now, the phone. I would so-o-o love to talk to my friends in the U.S. on some of these long evenings. Is there a chance I could...?"

I showed Mary the phone, which had come with the house. A new home in Kathmandu would be on a two-year waiting list for a phone, so we were happy to share ours. I explained that it could only receive international calls, not make them, so she should arrange specific times with her friends to receive their calls. To make an international call, she would have to go to a phone service center near the city stadium. Over the next month, Mary became a regular visitor to the house, stopping in for after-noon Mass and occasionally staying for dinner. She enjoyed being a "big sister" to the novices, joined them and me in volunteer work at a local health clinic, and squealed with delight when summoned at night for a phone call from America. "This phone," she said one night after her weekly Wednesday night call, "is a godsend. There doesn't seem to be much to do in Kathmandu at night."

The following week, as I sat at my desk and read letters from Indian candidates, the gate opened and shut rather loudly, so I knew someone other than the novices had entered.

"Jim, Jim, are you there? Can I come up?" Mary had already started to ascend the stairs.

"Can you get away tomorrow night?" She had reached the verandah and was slinging her backpack down while addressing me. "Three Americans I know are visiting Kathmandu. We're all going for dinner at the Everest Sheraton tomorrow. Why don't you join us?"

I paused only a moment before accepting. A night away from the usual card playing at home would be a treat, not to mention a change of pace in food. The Sheraton was known for its excellent cooks.

The following night Mary's three friends, two men and a woman, greeted us at the hotel and led us to the dining room. Mary glanced over the extensive menu, and asked the waiter if he had any recommendations.

"All continental dishes are very good. Our chef, Mr. Gomes, is excellent. He worked at a large hotel in Calcutta before coming here. You will not be disappointed."

During dinner, the questions turned to the usual ones for tourists. For souvenirs, I suggested they patronize the local woodcarvers, whose art was available at a reasonable price, and for an unusual place to visit, I mentioned the small, ancient hillock kingdom of Kirtipur just a few miles from Kathmandu. In the eighteenth century, I told my companions, when a Gorkha warrior invaded Kathmandu Valley, Kirtipur put up an extended resistance. After the small city-state finally fell, the conqueror exacted a grisly punishment from the men who had opposed him. All males over twelve years of age had their lips and noses sliced off, except for the flute player who had endeared himself to the victors.

"Ugh. Thanks for the dinner table story!" Mary said, as the waiter arrived with coffee and dessert. By the time we had finished our chocolate mousse, the house specialty, a band at the other end of the dining room burst forth into seventies' disco music. Only a few diners ventured onto the dance floor, and

Mary's friends Bob and Jack appeared content to order another beer and stay at the table. "C'mon you guys. Let's dance," Mary urged them, but they only shook their heads and raised their glasses to their lips. "Okay then," she said to Susan and me, "let's the three of us go out there. This is disco, no need for partners."

I hesitated a moment. A brother or nun dancing in public in America might seem avant-garde, but could be shocking to the Indian and Nepali mentality. I tried to weigh the matter rationally but my body was already swaying to the music. I stood up and followed Mary and Susan to the dance floor.

As the music increased in volume, several more dancers ventured forth, and Mary, Susan, and I joined the rhythm of the disco beat. The deep bass tones reverberated in my chest and I twisted and turned, the beat itself moving me. Ten minutes later, the music's pace picked up, but rather than tiring me, the fast dancing gave me energy. Blood pounded in my temples, my arms flew into the air, my feet moved me effortlessly around our dance area. Usually my arms were stiff and my legs sluggish, but that night my body let loose, undulating and flowing, and I felt like Shiva Nataraj creating the world through his incessant dance.

The following week, George knocked at my door and asked to speak with me. His speech was halting and he seemed self-conscious, but the corners of his mouth turned up in a slight smile. "Jim, I, uh, thought you'd like to read this letter," he said, and handed me a pale blue envelope. Inside was a sheet of paper covered with small handwriting that slanted backwards and left no margin on the page.

Dear Reverend Father George.

It is my duty to bring this to your attention, the improper behavior of Brother Jim. He has been seen roaming the hotels of Kathmandu with Miss Mary, the new English teacher at St. Xavier's, and also dancing and drinking where everyone can see. This is a great shock to Christians that a Brother is behaving in this manner. It must be a terrible example for the young men in your seminary.

Also, last Sunday at Mass, it was like this. I was standing at the entrance to the church. Brother Jim came up the steps and when he reached my place he had no greeting for me, only he looked at Miss Mary next to me and gave her an embrace with everyone seeing this.

I hope you will correct this scandal and have Brother Jim to live properly by the vows he has taken before God and the Blessed Mother.

The note was unsigned. I laughed to myself and looked up to see George chuckling too. Evidently there was no need to explain to him that the events had been exaggerated.

"So, who wrote this?" I asked. "And why was the letter sent to you?" Of course I knew the answer to the latter question. Undoubtedly this was another case of someone assuming George was the Superior because he was a priest and I "only" a brother. That irritated me, but, realistically, who else would they send the letter to? Not to me surely, for confronting the offender was much too direct for Nepali culture. George said the letter was stuck on the front gate, but that Maela, on his way back from the store, had seen Miss Gomes scurry away from the gate just before he noticed the letter.

Miss Gomes, of course. Miss Gomes was a young woman in the neighborhood who often attended Mass at the parish. Her father was the cook at the Sheraton, and recently her brother had taken a job as a busboy there. The brother, constantly entering and leaving the dining room, would easily have seen me. George gave me the letter, and we said no more about the matter.

The next afternoon I walked past St. Xavier's just as Mary was leaving class, and called to her. Over cinnamon rolls and strong coffee at the German bakery, I showed Mary the letter and my guess about its author. "Oh God, give me strength!" Mary groaned. "Can't you just imagine the Gomes boy staring bug-eyed from the kitchen and running home to tell his gossipy sister? Don't they have anything else to talk about? At least we gave them their thrill for the week."

"Evidently I rudely ignored Miss Gomes at church but gave you a hug. Do you remember that?" I asked.

"Sure. I told you that I had finally received a letter from Mohammed—Jesus, I thought he'd never write—and I was so excited I gave *you* a hug."

After coffee, we headed down our road and had almost reached Mary's house. From a side street, a young woman, clutching the sari wrapped modestly about herself, had turned the corner and was staring at us. It was Miss Gomes.

When I returned home, Del looked up from the books covering his desk. "Maela was asking for you. He made the spiced tea you like and wanted you to have some."

"Oh, I just had coffee."

"So now he's making that deep-fried, bitter squash for dinner that you told him was so good last week. Have you noticed how he caters to you? He even makes special dinners when you return from a trip to India." Del's tone sounded accusing.

"Del, I don't ask him to do those things."

"Right, but you don't discourage him," Del said, and added, "All brothers should receive equal treatment, including the Superior."

"That's right, but really Del, don't be such a grouch. Lighten up a bit." I left him with a surprised look on his face, walked upstairs, and sat on the concrete verandah ledge that overlooked the front yard.

Dancing at hotels. Accepting special treatment from the cook. I was a worldly brother and no doubt had been for a long time. What, I wondered, did the novices think of my going out, or Maela's treatment of me, or my listening to the Bhagwan's tapes at night? I didn't care what the Gomes family thought of me, but the novices would soon take vows. They were my brothers.

Later, I pulled Sylverius aside. "Right now I am the Superior," I said, "but eventually, you Indians will be the Superiors. Maybe you yourself. What would you do differently if you were the Superior? You know, different from how I run the community, how I spend my free time, things like that."

Sylverius knit his eyebrows ever so slightly, then replied, "Of course each person will do things differently. You have your own ways, others have theirs. But the main thing is to take time to know each brother. And, Jim, of all the foreigners who have come here, you have understood us and India the best."

FIRST VOWS

DECEMBER 8, THE Feast of the Immaculate Conception of Mary, and the date chosen for the first Indians to profess vows as brothers, lay just one week ahead. All of the six novices—Sylverius, John, Stephen, Johnny, William, and Benedict—had asked to be admitted to vows, and Father Dave and his council, upon our staff's recommendation, had approved each one. A ten-day vow preparation retreat had just concluded, invitations for the ceremony had been sent out, and arrangements had been made to hold the Vow Mass at the parish church.

As plans moved forward, I noticed myself responding sensitively to seemingly small things. A song I chose to play at the Mass, "Here I Am, Lord," brought tears to my eyes. When I practiced the words to call forth each novice to profess his vows, my voice choked. I hadn't realized how emotionally laden the profession of the First Vows would be for me, and I wasn't exactly sure why. Of course the event was a symbol of all I had worked for over the years, but something else was afoot.

The Vow Day began with congratulatory phone calls from both Joe and Dave, which helped brighten the overcast day. By four in the afternoon, as December cold settled on Kathmandu Valley, friends and neighbors bundled themselves in shawls and overcoats and gathered in the parish church. William's mother and brother had made the trip up from India, as had Johnny's brother, though the families of the other novices were not able to make the event. The church was a large, carpeted room capable of holding sixty or seventy people, spacious enough for the celebration, yet small enough to feel comfortable. I sat on the floor near the front and faced the congregation, ready to begin the music when the novices entered from the back of the church.

The novices soon came down the center aisle, followed by George and two other priests. Watching the novices approach the sanctuary, with John and Stephen smiling in my direction, it finally hit me why I had been feeling so emotional recently. Establishing the brothers in India was not simply a "project" that I had been engaged in, it was a furthering of my family. These young men were my sons.

I had often looked wistfully upon the youngsters I taught in school knowing that their fathers were only slightly older than me. That instinctual urge to perpetuate one's self had not been rubbed out of me by taking vows. I was flesh and blood and I wanted to make my mark on the earth with offspring who would remember me. Though the men in front of me might some day leave the Brotherhood, that moment in that chapel completed a deep evolutionary yearning in my life—and I was deeply content.

The novices took their places on the floor and the priests intoned the familiar ritual of the Mass. After the Gospel reading, I stepped forward to call each novice's name and, one by one, they approached the altar, professed their vows of poverty, chastity, and obedience, and returned to their places. Later in the Mass, in the silence that followed the reception of Communion, I took a moment to observe each novice individually—no, not novice, *brother*.

Stephen, closest to me, wore an impish grin. What energy he had, what wonderful assertiveness. John, so strong—his jaw line, his character, everything about him exuded stability. He would be a "pillar" of the community. Sylverius, the eldest, sat with his eyes cast down. Another strong, solid man. He might be the first

Superior. Benedict, next to him, young but of a good heart and with abundant musical talent. Johnny, gentle, kind Johnny, never uttering a cross word. And, William, bright, filled with boundless energy and a storehouse of talent. I immediately realized that, like a doting father, I saw only their positive sides and ignored the other. That's what one does at a celebration.

It was intoxicating to know that a whole new foundation in India would issue from these young men. And so, here I was, drifting away from the Church, when I was stopped in my tracks. I thought I was becoming less committed to being a Catholic brother, but the great rush of energy and satisfaction that flowed through me when I looked at my Indian brothers put an end to my previous concerns about faith and spiritual authority.

Fathers Know Best?

ONE SUNNY FEBRUARY afternoon I sat reading the paper when George entered the room and told me of his problem. The novice retreat day was the following week and he could not be there since he was scheduled to teach at St. Xavier's. "None of the other priests at St. Xavier's are free either so I wonder if I should cancel the retreat," he said.

"George, what about me? I'm free. I could do it."

"Well, I, uh, wanted someone to give them talks about Scripture, and then say Mass for them at the retreat house up in the hills."

"You could come out at the end of the day for Mass. You're finished with classes by three in the afternoon."

"But what about preaching the theme of the day?"

"What are you talking about? I can do that. I've done it dozens of times for high school students, and I've been on many retreat teams for the brothers." My jaw tightened. "So, why didn't you ask me to help out?" I finally asked.

"I guess I just didn't think of it, of you."

"That's the point! You didn't think of it!" Blood rushed to my face. Being discounted was infinitely harder for me than being challenged or even directly insulted. Such an omission was true condescension. "Here's the problem, George. You have a mind-set where you don't think that anybody but a priest can take a significant role in the area of spirituality. What kind of message does that send to the young men about the place of a brother? Or is it just *me*? Do you think *I* couldn't give a good retreat?"

"Yes, yes, of course you can do it. I'm sorry I didn't think of it before. Let's have you do the retreat then. I'm sure you'll do well and it will be a good example for our young men," George replied. He said nothing about my challenge to his attitude, and left the room. I didn't follow him and thrash the issue out because a part of me knew it was useless.

At the retreat the following week, I chose the Gospel story of the apostles sent out to speak to the villages, comparing that event to the day when they, the Indian brothers, would leave the training houses and venture forth to help others. It didn't matter if they felt fully prepared or not for the important tasks in life. No one ever is, I said, thinking of my coming to India. Later, during my private talks with each of them, they said they understood my comments but hoped that the American brothers would be around for a long time to guide them. "We just don't know about these things," was all I said.

The following month, I headed once again for India, where winter's chill was fading from the northern plains. I spent two weeks interviewing young men who had written us after seeing our newspaper ad, and I had invited six candidates to visit Kathmandu in May for our next "Come and See Program." My last stop was the parish that Anil belonged to. Anil had come to Kathmandu as the "replacement brother" and had shown great promise, but his parents later refused to let him leave home for more training. His recent letter to me, in halting English, had stated only that fact with no further explanation. Nevertheless, he wished to see me on my next visit to northern India.

The parish priest, Father Sebastian, was expecting me and welcomed me into the rectory. A kindly man with graying hair, he said he knew Anil's family well and had persuaded Anil's mother to come with her son that day to speak with me. Father Sebastian would be happy to translate anything I didn't understand.

In mid-afternoon, Anil arrived with his mother. He beamed and shook my hand. "Brother Jim, this is a blessing that you visit my area. I am honored." I smiled back, made namaste to his mother, then sat down while Anil asked for news of his companions from the "Come and See Program." We chatted for a few minutes before I asked the question that hung mid-air in the room. "So, what happened to your plans to join the brothers?"

Anil's face clouded and he turned to say something to his mother. She leaned toward me and spoke in a soft but determined voice. Though I didn't understand her words, her face indicated that a decision had been made concerning her son and that decision would not be changed. Father Sebastian translated.

"She says that her son must become a priest. She will give up a son 'only if he can celebrate Holy Mass and give Communion.' She had not properly understood that most members of your order are only brothers and that priesthood is not guaranteed, or she wouldn't have permitted Anil to travel to Kathmandu in the first place."

All of us in the room fell silent, though the phrase *only brothers* clanged in my brain. I turned to Anil and asked him, "What do you wish for yourself?"

"I want to be a brother, but I must obey my mother," he said in a quiet voice. "That is what I wanted to tell you in person."

"May God bless you, Anil. You will be good at whatever path you choose in life."

There was nothing more to be said. I gave Anil a warm handshake and a hug as sadness settled on me for the fine young man who was not permitted to follow his own yearnings. Irritation and disappointment also arose in me and came from several sources—the short-sighted mother, the caste system that pervaded the Church and meshed so well with the Indian psyche,

even Father Sebastian who no doubt had instructed all his parish-
ioners about the primacy of Mass, and hence, of the priesthood.

When Anil and his mother left, Father Sebastian said, "I'm
sorry. People just don't understand the role of the brother very
well. I hope you understand."

"Oh, yes, I understand," I said. I understood very well.

X-RAYS OF THE PERSONALITY

SPRING IN KATHMANDU breathed fresh air into the Valley, asters and snap-dragons blossomed in every front yard, and magnolia trees sprouted their short-lived blossoms. Amid this beauty, I had settled into my usual routines of teaching English to the novices, and in writing letters to aspiring candidates.

Another job had come my way by the request of the priest at Kathmandu's one Catholic parish. At the English Mass on Sunday attended by our brothers and novices, as well as the community of expatriates in Nepal, I led the congregation in songs I had rehearsed with the novices. When George said the Mass and gave one of his heartfelt homilies, both locals and foreigners expressed their gratitude for what our group brought to the liturgical service. I was pleased that we were an integral part of the local Church.

"Jim! Wait for me!" Mary called to me as I passed her leaving Mass one Sunday evening at the end of April. Catching up to me, she gushed about a palm reading she'd had just the previous day that told her everything about her life, both past and future. "If this reader, Lalji, is right, I won't be in Kathmandu for too much longer. How about that! Now, you *must* go see this guy as soon as possible. He's amazing," she concluded.

Mary had piqued my interest, though it sounded unrealistic that a palm reader could be a source of guidance. Nevertheless... "How do I get an appointment?" I asked.

Mary handed me a map to Lalji's house. "I knew you'd be interested," she said, and smiled.

After lunch the next day, I followed Mary's map to a two-story brick home. A small sign next to the door announced "Palm Readings. In English Only." A Nepali woman appeared before I had a chance to wonder about knocking or searching for a doorbell that may or may not work. In a business-like tone, she invited me in and explained the procedure. "Today, I will take an ink print of your palms and then we shall choose an afternoon for your reading. In the meantime, Lalji will be studying your hand prints."

The woman picked up a padded roller, wet it on a large ink pad, and rolled it several times over my right palm. She then pressed my hand onto a large glossy sheet of paper that announced: "Hand Prints: They are Life's Map. They are the X-Rays of the Personality." The print looked larger than my actual hand. I wondered how that could be. She repeated the process with my left hand and concluded by offering me an appointment at two o'clock the following day. After scrubbing my hands with the coarse brush provided at the sink, I thanked the woman and left. My hands tingled on the way back home. I knew they were saying something important.

The following afternoon, Lalji was already seated at his desk looking over my handprints when I arrived. A round-faced, plump Nepali man in his forties, he peered over his glasses at me, and beckoned me to sit opposite him.

"Welcome, Mr. James. May I see your right hand, please?" He held my hand under a bright desk lamp and examined it carefully with a magnifying glass, saying nothing. After holding my arm upright for five minutes, I realized Lalji was not given to cursory examinations, so I relaxed my arm and laid the back of my hand directly on the desk. Lalji readjusted his light and magnifying glass, and continued his inspection.

My eyes drifted from Lalji to my surroundings. His brick home, like the brothers' house, had plastered walls painted off-white. Electrical wiring was not hidden as in American homes but stapled along the base of the wall, occasionally shooting upwards to a wall light. Polished cement floors, small rooms, and protective iron grillwork on the windows completed the picture, as in most Kathmandu homes. This seer lived in a quite ordinary house.

Lalji not only peered closely at my hands, but began to stretch the skin, as if examining the depths of the lines. I knew nothing about palm reading, and wondered if his conscientiousness was, in reality, theatrics designed to impress me. Still, he said nothing. When he finally spoke, the clock on the wall indicated that forty-five minutes had passed.

"There are so many things to tell you," he sighed as he looked up at me and released my hand. "Let me begin with the greatest impression. The overall most significant thing to note is the need, at this time in your life, for a more independent lifestyle."

Independent lifestyle? Where did he get that from and what did it mean? I loved community life, the companionship of my brothers. And yes, I loved the freedom I had when traveling in India, but I didn't want to *live* alone. Yet the phrase he had used rang true in some way. I pulled out my pen and pad to take notes on what was surely to be more than an entertainment session.

"During the earlier part of your life," Lalji continued, "you spent much energy accommodating others, which can be a good thing. You have attained enough discipline in this area and now it is time to move on. Your earlier years of 'giving in' are finished. The strength of your individuality is taking over."

How does he know these things? Or are they statements that he might say to anyone? I suppose most people would feel they have accommodated others. Doesn't everyone want to be more independent and start putting his own needs first for a change?

Lalji leaned back in his chair. "Very possibly this shift in your life is coming because of some convictions in the area of philosophy or religion. You have very strong opinions in these areas, though you have enough flexibility on the surface to go along with the status quo, to survive and not antagonize others. But deep down, you are evaluating your position. And, once you have decided what your convictions or beliefs are, they will be very solid and stable in you."

This was me. These were not comments that would apply to just anyone coming in off the street, and although Lalji knew nothing about me except my name, he was describing my inner world so clearly I was short of breath.

"Now, a few sources of conflict for you." Lalji spoke in a matter-of-fact manner, and did not seem to be measuring my facial responses. "Sometimes others see only the surface that you choose to present to them and so are not aware of your depth. This will lead to some misjudgment on their part, and a challenge on your part to show your inner world and feelings more." That clearly rang true.

"Your personality has a number of curious twists," Lalji continued. "One is that while you like comfort very much, being almost luxury-oriented, nevertheless you are able to go through much discomfort for a short period if adventure is involved. And when your adventures tire you, you need a home base to come back to."

Lalji had not only described my inner life perfectly, he had just described my lifestyle in the India-Nepal mission. Several American friends had written to me wondering how I could handle the constant discomforts of life in Asia. I knew that the challenges of the mission were tiring, but still, India-Nepal was the most exciting adventure of my life so far.

As impressed as I was with Lalji, I squirmed in my chair, feeling naked in front of this man who had read my soul secrets through a magnifying glass he had aimed at my palm. But it was Lalji's next statement, made rather casually, that caused my heart to beat even faster.

"Mr. James, you must prepare yourself for a major change in your mid-forties. There will be some major climactic change, as in leaving a geographic area you are used to, and going away from a familiar style of life. The change in style of life does not mean the geographic change. It is something deeper, something related to values and beliefs."

I wanted to ask specific questions, but my mouth was dry. I was forty-three. Lalji was describing my near future. A geographic change? Might I be coming to the end of my stay in Asia? Going away from a familiar style of life? If that meant leaving the brothers, I hesitated to think about it much for it would be too earth-shaking. But really, I couldn't start believing in fortune telling. Surely my life was not determined by what Lalji said. That would mean I had no free will. Or was that an illusion too?

"So, are you predicting the future? How can you do that?" I finally spoke.

"Oh no, Mr. James, I am not predicting the future. I am telling you the likely outcome of what is happening right now in your life. It is like this. If you put a cup of water in your freezer at night, you can say that the most likely outcome is to have ice in the morning. Now, anything can intervene. You can change your mind and take the water out, the electricity may go off and the water will not even get cold, any manner of thing might change the expected course.

"I am seeing the present energies in your life. They, and your past energies, are written in the lines of your hand, etched there from brain impulses. If things continue the way they have been going, the outcomes will be similar to what I have described. You can, of course, change your thinking and your actions."

"What would that mean in my hand? Suppose I take a different course. Will my hand look different?"

"Quite so. You can change the lines in your hands within six months. I want you to keep your palm prints so you can see in a few years how they have changed."

The lines in my hand could change? Fingerprints too? I didn't know much about forensic science, but I knew that a person's fingerprints never altered. Obviously, palm reading was an inexact or even spurious practice. Why was I giving any credence to the process? I had been pulled in by the lure of esoteric knowledge coming from an Eastern wise man. How could well-fed Lalji, a smelly ashtray on his desk, really offer me anything? My mind could find multiple objections to taking a palm reading seriously, but my stomach was churning, a sure sign that genuine emotional issues had been addressed.

The wall clock said four-thirty. I had another half-hour. "What else? Things to be careful about?" I asked.

"As I said earlier, you must learn to show your inner world more to others or they will perceive you as shallow. It is similar with your emotional life. You have very deep feelings, but you are hesitant and passive in this area.

"In daily life, you can be quite impatient. You want things done right away, and handling the details of a project may be difficult for you because of this. Following through on things is a good discipline for you. Of course this is the other side of your ability to see the big picture, to have broad vision. The two go together, and you must not be discouraged when you see this negative side. Engage in self-discipline, patience, and follow through in projects that matter to you.

"But, I must come back to an important point. Since you are likely to enter a major shift sometime soon, be patient first of all with yourself. Do not aim at a complete synthesis of your life and beliefs at this time. Simply let yourself be. You do not have to know where everything is leading. Do things that are cathartic for you, especially physical things such as walking in the hills, meditation exercises that are more expressive than mental, like yoga or whatever. Trust in yourself. Your soul will lead. Let your ego follow. It will be the right thing."

My mind wasn't spinning anymore, just locked in place by the shock of seeing myself. The magic mirror of my hands had spoken.

TO KILL THE BUDDHA

IN FATHER DAVE'S office in St. Louis, I sat across from him and spoke about our growing number of candidates, the need for more staff for the mission, and the situation with Benedict. It was disappointing that Benedict had suddenly changed his mind and had needed a dispensation from vows. I had known we'd have our losses, but it was nevertheless a sad day when I finalized his departure.

Now Father Dave's fingers gently drummed on his desk while he waited for my response on a different topic. He had wanted to know how I was *really* doing, and my glib "just fine" had not satisfied him. An innately perceptive man, Dave had known me for years, had followed the India mission closely, and no doubt could discern subtle shifts in my attitude.

"You look deeply tired, and not just physically," he said.

"It's true, I'm weary at every level. Sometimes my mind is terribly confused and even my dreams are crazy. The other night I dreamed I gave birth to a child. Don't ask me how, I just know I did."

"The India mission is your 'baby,' isn't it? Sounds like a wonderful dream to me. The mission has come a long way, and you've stuck with it. However, you don't have to return to Asia if you feel you're worn out."

"Oh, no, I want to go back."

"Then, is there anything else you want to tell me?"

If anyone would understand what I was going through, Dave would. He was broad-minded, caring, and insightful. But if I told him everything and sought his advice, I might have to follow it, and the usual plan for someone with serious religious doubts was to take a year, in America, for theological renewal. My spiritual journey needed to be worked out on the soil of the Indian sub-continent, that I knew. I needed to return to Asia for *me*, for my own soul work.

"Yes?" Dave waited.

"I see so much wisdom in all religions…" I chose to be vague.

"And?"

"But religions separate us from each other. Isn't something terribly wrong here?"

"That's a pretty big question. What's the question for you personally?"

I hesitated, then went on. "Dave, sometimes I'm not sure what I believe anymore. I don't know whose authority to accept."

Dave paused, then sat back in his chair. "We have a solid religious tradition behind us for guidance. Evidently that authority doesn't answer your questions right now, does it? Neither can I, but since the East has influenced you so much, take this saying from among its best. 'If you meet the Buddha on the road, kill him.'

"What it means is that, ultimately, all authority outside your-self is inadequate and you must follow your own deepest call. I know this may sound contradictory to Church teachings, but even the official Church has always honored the primacy of conscience. And in the matter of spirituality, certainly the great Christian mystics understood this point."

We sat in silence a few more minutes. Dave had given me the support and encouragement I needed whether he knew it or not. It wasn't egotistical to search for your own answers. It was the only authentic thing to do.

I assured Dave I wanted to return to Asia, but that I had a feeling the next two years would be my last "round of duty" there. He agreed, though I caught a hint of sadness in his eyes as I left.

In October I arrived in Milwaukee to visit my family just as the crisp air of autumn was turning leaves bright red, gold, and orange. How I had missed the vibrancy of this season! India and Nepal lacked the expanses of deciduous trees that splashed color over the countryside in Wisconsin. "Do you remember," my younger sister said one day, "those trips years ago to the Mississippi to see the fall colors?" When I said yes indeed, my mother reminded me that the last time we had taken such a trip together was actually in summer, when I had entered the novitiate located not far from the Great River. "You know," she said, "it's almost twenty-five years since you first went in. Next year you'll celebrate your Silver Jubilee. Will you come home for that?"

"No," I replied, "we only come back from the missions every two years." When I saw her disappointed look, I added, "I told Father Dave I'd return here for good in two years, so we'll have another celebration when I get back then, a bit belated, that's all." I doubted if my words softened her disappointment, and even I had to admit they sounded half-hearted. Lalji's comments had made me wonder if I would still be a brother in two years. Whatever I did with my life, it would be based on my own convictions, not on someone else's rules or expectations.

ASSASSINATION

"MRS. GANDHI'S BEEN shot!"

The sound of sandals slapping along the cement floor brought me upright in bed. It was late morning but I was napping, my sleep schedule still disrupted by my recent return from the U.S., and it took a few seconds to remember that I was in the brothers' apartment on the outskirts of Delhi. William peered in through the curtain that separated the large room into sleeping cubicles and added breathlessly, "It's very serious. They don't think she'll live." And then he was gone, back downstairs.

I slipped into my sandals and headed downstairs, where everyone was gathered around the radio, silent. Reporters were describing the crowds gathered in front of the hospital where Mrs. Gandhi had been taken. A doctor announced that seven bullets had been removed from her abdomen and that surgery was continuing, and a newscaster informed the public that Mrs. Gandhi's own security guards, "now in custody," had fired the shots.

The numbness that often goes with dramatic and unexpected news crept over me. I had no response other than shock, though I knew the situation was serious for the whole country. What enemies did Mrs. Gandhi have? I had not followed her career closely, nor the vagaries of India's politics.

I looked at my fellow brothers, who themselves gazed blankly at the radio—Father Florian, about my own age and recently arrived in India, the Superior of the community, and John, Johnny, William, Stephen, and Sylverius, now college students. All of us sat immobilized.

"Shot by her own bodyguard? How could that happen?" I finally asked, to no one in particular. Between William, who was knowledgeable in political affairs, and the radio commentator, the story emerged.

The bodyguards were Sikhs. And it was the Sikh's holiest shrine, the Golden Temple in Amritsar, Punjab, which Mrs. Gandhi had ordered the Indian army to attack the previous June, hoping to flush out Punjabi separatists. The bullets had scarred not only the temple walls but the religious psyche of an assertive Indian minority who felt violated by the assault. Advisors had suggested that Mrs. Gandhi replace her bodyguards with men other than Sikhs, but she had remained firm in her trust of them.

"There's going to be trouble for sure, and Sikhs will not be safe," William declared, as we walked to the meal getting cold on the table.

We ate lunch with very little conversation, keeping an ear to the radio, though scant new information was forthcoming. Newscasters speculated that the security officers who had fired the shots, loyal until today, had been pressured by Sikh radicals. The bodyguards' families probably had had their lives threatened unless the bodyguards carried out the deed. At mid-afternoon, the chilling announcement finally came: "Our Prime Minister, Mrs. Indira Gandhi, died at two twenty-three this afternoon. Her death came as the result of gunshot wounds inflicted by two bodyguards as they greeted her in the garden of her home."

William and John left to visit other tenants in the apartment complex who had television, and I drifted into the courtyard, alone with my thoughts. Who was in charge of the country now? Would Indira's son and political heir apparent, Rajiv, take the reigns of government? The radio said Rajiv was away, in West

Bengal. Anything could happen in this time of chaos. India, I feared, was a country that could reel out of hand without a strong central government.

The courtyard was empty, so unusual in India. I surmised that people were glued to their radio or television. The apartment complex housed perhaps fifty or sixty units, many occupied by Christian families. The presence of so many Catholic families had been a reason I chose the location for the brothers. A sense of community support along religious lines was important for religious minorities, our brothers being no exception. Neighbors in the complex seemed friendly, spoke to each other from balconies, and sometimes gathered in the courtyard of the walled-in compound. But I was alone in the courtyard that October day, feeling like an observer of pending disaster.

"They're burning Connaught Place!" someone shouted from a balcony. I rushed back inside wondering if the downtown area was truly under siege. Rumor was to be expected in India in everyday life and certainly during a crisis. The radio announcer confirmed that a number of shops in New Delhi's downtown shopping district had been set on fire. All were Sikh-owned. No police restraining action was reported.

I returned to the courtyard, now filled with people, and heard a neighbor say that the Sikh taxi drivers whose taxi stand was located across the street had driven away. The men had doffed their turbans and cut their long hair, both distinctive signs of Sikh men. They had departed quickly and left the flimsy lean-to's they used as night shelters deserted and flapping in the wind.

The sky over central Delhi had turned dark from smoke, and pungent air assailed my nostrils. Surely I wasn't smelling that smoke from so far away. Besides, the wind was at my back, blowing in from further edges of the city. What was I smelling?

"Please don't go, it won't be safe for you," a woman's voice said, distracting me. I turned to see the woman addressing a Sikh family that lived in the apartment complex. Suitcases in hand, they were headed for the gate of the compound. The gentleman seemed bewildered, holding a valise in one hand and clutching a small child's hand in the other. His wife's eyes flashed both fear and anger, and she snapped back at the well-meaning neighbor. "What then shall we do? We shall not wait here and be killed in our very own home. No, we shall not!"

"But where will you go? You are an easy target for these mad people," the neighbor replied, glancing at the man's turban and full beard.

"What can we do? What can we do?" the Sikh woman wailed. "Our name and apartment number is on the list outside the compound, like everybody's, and they will come and get us." I had seen the name Singh, a common Sikh name, posted outside the gate.

"You do one thing. You come and stay in our apartment. If anybody comes and forces their way into your place, you will not be there. We shall tell them that you already left," the neighbor offered.

The acrid smell of smoke again blew into the compound, stronger than before. It had to be from a close source.

"Jim." William entered the compound, breathing hard. "I've just come from the Ring Road. I saw the smoke and investigated. No one must go out! They are stopping cars and trucks and if a Sikh is found inside, they beat him up, kill him, and burn the truck. And there's a mob headed this way."

The Sikh family raced for refuge in the neighbor's apartment.

Several men had returned early from work and stationed themselves at the gate and the walls of the compound, just as shouts from the street announced that the mob had arrived. About twenty-five men and boys, farmers and their sons from the outlying areas, gathered at the gate. Carrying picks, shovels, and sticks, barefoot and angry, they demanded that the Sikh man listed on the directory be handed over to them. Their blazing eyes announced they were on a crusade and there would be no stopping them. Their boldness surprised me. Under no other circumstances would farmers enter the city and speak threateningly to men of higher social and economic standing.

I edged closer to the gate. The farmers' clothing gave off the smell of both smoke and diesel fuel. I knew then that they had been involved in the truck burnings, and perhaps killings, on the Ring Road. I had no fear for myself. The only danger for me or any of us inside the compound was getting caught in the crossfire of the violence.

The men inside the compound stood firm. Yes, there was a Sikh family that ordinarily lived there, but no, they were not there now. And absolutely no, you may not enter to investigate. This is private property and we shall call the police if you try to enter. That summoning the police was a hollow threat was lost on no one. There were no police in sight and there would not be that night and the next day, as Sikh homes and businesses were burned and looted, and Sikh men slaughtered in broad daylight.

Most of the women had stayed inside the apartments or in the background as the men argued. Mrs. Pereira, however, an assertive school administrator, stepped forward, her dark blue sari wrapped tightly around her ample figure. "You are wasting your time here," she scolded. "Almost all families here are Christian, and the one Sikh family has left. You have missed them, and the Sikh taxi drivers who live across the street." The farmers looked stonily at the imposing woman, then glanced across the street in the direction she had pointed. With a few abrupt instructions to their sons, they moved on. The young boys attacked the abandoned Sikh camp, flailing their shovels and sticks to level the tents and cots, their faces, however, occasionally looking more playful than angry.

Evening came and a faint red glow of fire hovered over the city center, though our neighborhood was quiet. Nevertheless, the brothers joined the other men in keeping watch all through the night, which thankfully proved uneventful.

The following day, tenants milled about in the courtyard and gossiped, or remained in their apartments listening to the news. No one went to work. Fresh patches of smoke filled the sky. No doubt the torching of cars and buildings was continuing. Where were the police? The radio gave little news about the city's condition, but announced that Rajiv Gandhi had been sworn in the previous night as Prime Minister.

The next morning the government announced a curfew. No one was to leave their homes unless on official business, and the army had been called in to enforce the curfew and keep order. Liberal reporters and newscasters castigated the local government and police for looking the other way during the riots of the previous days. The police claimed they were overwhelmed, but reports of officers standing idly by while Sikh businesses were torched rang true to many of us. I was glad the army was on the streets.

The day passed slowly. At noon, I ran into Mrs. Pereira in the courtyard. "I can't believe it," she told me. "That Sikh woman told Mrs. Vincent, who took her in, that Mrs. Gandhi deserved what she got. What is the matter with these people? Brother Jim, is the whole world crazy?"

"It seems that way. Is the family still with Mrs. Vincent?"

"No, they have returned to their own apartment. Of course they can't go out to buy food, but then we can't either. Tomorrow is the cremation at Raj Ghat, so the curfew will have to be lifted."

I knew Raj Ghat, a serene park and memorial grounds on the banks of the Jumuna, not too far from our old house on Sri Ram Road. Mahatma Gandhi had been cremated in that spot and some of his ashes were kept there for veneration.

"I'm glad it will be lifted," I said, "because I'm scheduled to leave for Kathmandu the day after the ceremony. Now I'm not sure if I should go."

"There's nothing you can do here," Mrs. Pereira replied. "If the curfew is lifted for the following day you might as well leave. If the curfew is still on, come and see me. I may have an idea on how to get to the airport."

The following morning smoke particles still hung in the air, though the night had been a quiet one. The city was calm, and all hint of wind had disappeared, as if both the populace and nature were suggesting we be still for the cremation ceremony. The radio told us that the curfew was lifted, though people should leave their homes only if necessary.

"Which of the bikes is a sturdy one?" I asked John in mid-morning. "I think I'll take a ride around the city."

"Take the blue one. Where are you going?" John's eyes looked concerned. "Do you think it's okay?"

"I'm not sure where I'll go. I just want to get out. I've been cooped up in this compound for three days. And I want to see what's happened."

I let Florian know I'd be gone, and set out. The streets were deserted. No neighbors, no vendors, no police, no army. Had the radio not announced that the curfew was lifted, I would have thought it still in effect. Not a soul was astir. To see Delhi's day-time streets devoid of people was shocking, and that indelible image drifts back to me even today.

I passed the charred remains of a large truck next to a blackened taxi. Boxes of clothing were strewn on the pavement, some of them half-burned, evidently the truck's cargo. No bodies. Perhaps the drivers got away.

I caught the Ring Road on the north side of town and followed it to the eastern part, near our old neighborhood. In front of one shuttered storefront, a man was sweeping debris from the sidewalk. He glanced up at me. We stared briefly at each other as I moved on.

A ghost town. Empty streets, quiet. Another charred taxi. Two burned-out shops. No sign of a grieving public, only an atmosphere of fear and hiding. A woman, her sari pulled almost completely over her face, stepped into the street from an alley, saw me, then hurriedly turned back like a scared rabbit.

Grieving seemed absent. How could a nation not mourn its slain leader? The few that were permitted to view the cremation ceremony would surely grieve, but other public gatherings in Delhi were prohibited. The majority of the country, who apparently had supported Mrs. Gandhi, had little or no public way to express their loss.

I turned onto Boulevard Road, went past St. Vincent's Hospital, and arrived at Dr. Sundaram's house. Dr. Sundaram's wife, whom I knew well, answered the door.

"Come in, quickly. What are you doing out today?" Sheila asked.

"I had to see for myself what's been happening. Actually, the streets are very quiet. I don't think there's any danger."

Sheila offered me a chair in the living room. "It was so terrible the other night," she began. "The smell, that smell. I'll never forget it. I don't suppose you had it out your way."

"We had lots of smoke, all those shops and trucks burning."

"Oh no, not that. The bodies, the burning bodies. It was horrible. Of course I didn't go out, but the servants said they were burning bodies near the Ajmeri Gate and Old Delhi station. Trains had been arriving with their Sikh occupants butchered, some of them scalped, their heads hanging out the windows."

"Oh, Sheila."

"I closed all the windows, but the smell of death seeped in anyway. Ernest is out of town. I wish he had been here. The country has gone mad. The smoke from burning shops was strong here also, but the stench from the bodies was the worst."

I told Sheila about the mob coming to the apartment complex, then the conversation turned toward Indira Gandhi herself. "I still can't believe she's gone," Sheila said. "I thought no one would touch her."

"Why did you think that?"

"She was a widow. It's respect for the Mother. And she was a symbol of our unity, she gave direction to the country. She even consciously portrayed herself as Mother of India."

I remembered my first day in India, the crowds dancing in the streets to celebrate Indira Gandhi's victory in the elections, and the placards that read, "Mother India—Mother Indira."

"Also, she was Nehru's daughter," Sheila added, "so she had the prestige of that family behind her, and still she was murdered."

After more conversation on the political state of the country, I said goodbye. Sheila wished me a safe journey back home and hopefully, the next day, to Kathmandu.

Before returning to the apartment, I headed toward the Kashmiri Gate, just a few blocks away. The narrow street, usually clamoring with the sounds of vendors hawking their wares, lay silent. My eyes followed the street, through the narrow passage and into the Walled City, until the view was lost in smoke and dust. The area, shrouded by haze, was the place I had danced on the streets my first day in India. Where banners had once fluttered and men joyously danced, only trash cluttered the ground.

With my shoulders sagging, I turned away from the Kashmiri Gate and returned home through empty streets, feeling like the sole survivor of some cataclysmic event.

That evening at dinner, the community seemed less subdued than the previous night. Most had watched the cremation ceremony on a neighbor's television.

"So, tell me about the ceremony," I said. "Did her son actually crack her skull?"

"Oh yes," William responded. "It's to let the spirit out you know. But we couldn't see much of it. It may have been more of a gesture than a real blow, I don't know."

"It seems gruesome to me," I said, "even as a gesture. I couldn't imagine myself doing that to anyone, especially a family member."

"You'd do it if you were a Hindu and brought up that way," John added. "Besides, you'd have to do it, aren't you the only son? A son or male relative must perform the ritual."

"In India," Johnny said, looking down at his plate, "Christians bury the dead, but you remember that in Nepal where there are no cemeteries, the Christians are cremated. I don't think I'd like that. It's very Hindu."

At the end of dinner, Florian informed us that the curfew was indeed in force for the following day. A curfew meant there would be no taxis or buses on the street, no way to get to the airport. I would have to stay in Delhi.

The doorbell rang. William ushered Mrs. Pereira in.

"Good, I'm glad you are finished with your dinner. I didn't want to disturb you," she said. "It's all settled then, Brother Jim. Mr. Jacob will take you to the airport on his motorcycle. He says you definitely should go tomorrow since all other flights to Kathmandu are fully booked because of the trekking season. You please be ready at nine tomorrow morning."

"It's really okay with him to go out during curfew?"

"Yes. You see, he works for the airlines and has an airport identification badge. If they stop you, he will tell them he must report for work at the international section. You are a foreigner. They won't be concerned about you."

"I thank you so much, Mrs. Pereira. But if there is any danger, of course I can wait."

"It will be fine. At nine, then? He will be at the gate. Good luck." She nodded and left without further ceremony.

The next morning, John and Florian helped carry my suitcases downstairs to the gate. Mr. Jacob, a middle-aged stocky man, greeted me and assured me that the trip would be completely safe. I threw a leg over the motorcycle, and took a suitcase in each hand. As John opened the gate and wished us a safe journey, Mr. Jacob and I sped out. Once again, the streets were deserted. People were observing the curfew. In only a few minutes, we sped through the flat fields that surrounded Delhi. A lone man walked on the road ahead of us, but stepped into the field and was scurrying away by the time we passed him. Burned trucks dotted the shoulder of the road, most likely pushed to the side by the army. But the army was not in sight.

Mr. Jacob took the corner onto the airport road rapidly, leaning the motorcycle so far to one side that a suitcase scraped the pavement. The motorcycle wobbled and swerved while my heart pounded, and we crossed over to the opposite shoulder of the road. Just in front of a charred lorry, the vehicle stabilized itself and we surged back across the road. I held the suitcases higher, though ten minutes later I was certain the bags would slip out of my aching arms. Just when I felt I could hold them no longer, Mr. Jacob pointed to the right. A broad field had come into sight, affording us a view of the road that we would soon cross. Three army trucks advanced toward the intersection. If we kept up our current speed, we would reach the crossroads at the same time.

Mr. Jacob hesitated, and seemed to slow down. "Speed up!" I shouted, and he throttled the engine. We passed the intersection well ahead of the lumbering lorries, which had not increased their speed. I looked back and saw soldiers standing in the rear of the trucks, no doubt headed toward the city with more important concerns than a lonely motorcycle.

Just before the last turnoff to the airport, Mr. Jacob slowed down again. I peered around him to see several army trucks and a road barricade a short distance ahead. "I must stop," he called back. Near the barricade, rows of army cots, tents, and motor-cycles, lined the side of the road. Two soldiers walked toward the barricade. I was glad Mr. Jacob was with me. The soldiers would probably not understand English, and my Hindi would hardly suffice for questioning. The first soldier reached the bar-ricade, swung it open, and waved us through, hardly looking at us. If anything, he looked irritated that we had bothered him. He returned to a small table that held coffee cups. Apparently we had interrupted breakfast.

In front of the international terminal I thanked Mr. Jacob, wished him a safe return, and entered the building. Two hours later my flight left for Kathmandu, and we passed over Delhi cov-ered by layers of smoke and haze. With a heavy heart I thought of the assassination, the murdering of Sikhs, and the immense human suffering that lay below me. The very soil where I sought to find my own peace of mind was torn apart by violence. India, the land of holy men and sacred rivers, was a very unforgiving place.

AT THE BORDER

LIKE A SAFE haven of comfort and refuge, the brothers' house in Kathmandu welcomed me when I arrived from the tumult of Delhi. The regularity of our house schedule, the smell of incense in the chapel, the laughter in our living room—all these gave shape and meaning to my life. Mary still visited us to receive phone calls, though the calls were now more frequently from Egypt than the U.S.

"Mohammed wants me to return to Egypt! What do you think, Jim?" she said one evening.

"What do *you* think?"

"I'm ready to move on." In less than two weeks she was gone, and I lost another friend who was so easy to be around.

The new group of eight novices had settled into the house routine, which included English classes from Brother Paul, our new staff member from America. Paul, a tall, husky man in his late thirties, used games to teach English vocabulary and had started learning Nepali himself. He laughed easily and, with his round stomach and graying full beard, looked like Santa Claus with horn-rimmed glasses. I suggested that he visit our candidates in Bhopal soon and, though he agreed, he appeared reluctant to travel much. Later, I was surprised to learn he had not joined George, Del, and the novices a month earlier on a trek in the Himalayas.

"Oh, heavens no," he explained. "I saw the peaks from the plane on the way in. That's close enough for me."

"But it was wonderful!" the novices chorused. Both George and Del agreed that the trek to Lantang National Park had been an exciting experience.

"C'mon, Paul. Let's do it together," I coaxed. "There's adventure out there just waiting for us!" Danger too, perhaps. Though I had climbed the foothills of the Himalayas, I knew that the higher regions of the "Abode of Snow" carried their own risks of sudden storms in November, and altitude sickness with its attendant disorientation. Yet I was being pulled forward, fueled by childhood images of the "forbidding, foreboding" Himalayas, a place on earth I had never expected to see. And now, they were in my own back yard. I could not miss the chance to enter that realm more closely.

Paul rested his feet on a stool and sipped his afternoon tea, but was firm that an airplane view had been enough. Del encouraged me anyway. "It's a great opportunity even if you go alone, but you must go before it gets too cold." So, though just barely settled again in Kathmandu, I set out for a trek in the Himalayas.

THE ROOM, AT nine thousand feet, was icy cold.

During the previous week, the trek to Langtang, just north of Kathmandu, had been filled with spectacular views by day, but the nights had grown steadily more frigid with each increase in altitude. Howling winds now swept up a narrow valley and buffeted the tiny guesthouse I stayed at, and though my room had a bed, it had not a shred of warmth. The next destination, a Buddhist monastery situated at over twelve thousand feet near the Tibetan border, would be even colder.

I had been on the trek several days already, though not by myself. Hesitant to travel alone, I had hired a porter more for companionship and safety than for carrying the few items we needed. Kumar, a sturdy young man accustomed to mountain treks, turned out to be pleasant company. He conversed easily in English, introduced me to his friends along the trail, and joked readily with the proprietor and cook of every guesthouse we stayed at.

Early in the trek, I had told Kumar he could walk faster and precede me if he wished. "Oh no, James. I must remain close to you and assist if there is any need," he replied, as he took up his place several yards behind me and whistled softly. Only when the next village was plainly in sight would Kumar forge ahead to arrange for lunch, or for evening dinner and lodging. On those occasions, I could always count on finding him at the village edge, ensconced on a rock or squatting along the trail, waiting to usher me to our accommodations. I felt quite fortunate to have found Kumar.

Now, Kumar lay in a bed a few feet from my own. How could he sleep so well in this cold, I wondered? Wasn't he shivering like I was? And as cold as I was under the threadbare quilt, I would have to slip out of bed into the icy room, and force myself to run to the outdoor toilet a few yards from our door.

I slipped into my boots and jacket, and quietly opened the door. A nearly full moon cast its glow on the startling landscape before me—slate-gray slopes running down the mountainsides to the river below, with only occasional rock outcroppings to vary the desolate scene. Not a single piece of vegetation clung to the mountainside. The freezing night air stabbed my body like a thousand needles and numbed my cheeks and hands. Even breathing was painful as each intake of air scraped against my throat making me shiver almost uncontrollably. By the time I returned to the room, my shivering and shaking caused me to slam the door.

Kumar stirred in his bed. "James, is that you?"

"Yeah," I chattered.

"Are you sleeping fine?"

"Not really, I'm rather cold," I said as I searched in the semi-darkness for my sleeping bag.

"Cold? Come here."

"What?"

"Come here, sleep with me."

I didn't pause to weigh the matter but sat on the edge of Kumar's bed, pulled off my boots and jacket, and climbed in. In a flash I remembered my hesitancy to sleep next to the soldier on the train near Bombay, but that seemed like eons ago. Now, lying with my back toward Kumar, I could feel his breath on my neck and wondered if I had left him enough space.

"Come closer to be warm," Kumar said. He draped his arm over my shoulder and pulled me to his chest, holding my hand in his as men in Asia often do. In just a few minutes the chill that had invaded my bones began to slip away. I took several deep breaths and let myself sink into our warm cocoon. Hours later, dogs barked outside the door and I awoke. Kumar and I had changed positions in the night though I had no recollection of it. Surprisingly, I had slept soundly lying so closely to another person.

The following night Kumar came to our room with tea. We sipped the warm fluid in silence, and when I climbed into bed Kumar lay facing me. He smiled, moved closer and entwined his legs in mine. "Hold me very close tonight, James," he whispered in my ear. The smell of smoke lingered in his hair from the kitchen fire and his thin underclothes felt damp against his body. My own body, smelling of sweat and mountain air, warmed as I pulled him to myself and smoothed his hair. A small voice reminded me that such intimacy was not fitting for a brother, yet I yearned for physical touch, sensuality, sexuality. Kumar's warm chest and groin against mine fanned all those desires in me and when dawn broke on that intimate night I knew one thing clearly: I wanted my body back!

10 December 1984
Kathmandu, Nepal

Dear Dave,

Less than six weeks after Mrs. Gandhi's assassination, India has suffered another tragedy, as you must know from news reports. The poisonous gas that escaped from a chemical plant in Bhopal claimed over 4000 lives the night of the incident, and tens of thousands more are injured, many of whom will eventually succumb from their exposure. I don't know how the Indian psyche can absorb such constant battering.

You remember that several of our candidates are taking basic training at the Bhopal minor seminary, but that institution is actually about a two-hour bus ride from the city so people there were in no danger from the gas leak.

One of the candidates wrote immediately to assure us they were fine, and to give us more details of the tragedy. The gas leak occurred at night not far from where a convent is located, and the nuns had a close call. December can be a cold month in northern India, and apparently the air was quite cool that night. Right before midnight, one nun felt chilled and went around the convent shutting all the windows that had been left open. Just minutes later, as the sisters slept, the gas seeped across the town and into the area around the convent. The nuns heard nothing of the melee nearby—people running, trampling each other in their panic, choking to death, and being blinded by the gas.

In the morning, the sisters rose to find bodies strewn on the street, some dead, other people gasping for breath. Unscathed, the sisters immediately set to work bathing eyes, offering drinking water, and doing whatever they could. Because the nuns had been spared while living at "ground zero," word spread among the Hindus that "the Christian god of the sisters is a very powerful god."

We had our own somewhat close call. Brother Paul, who is spending his first few months here getting to know both Nepal and India, was supposed to visit our Bhopal candidates that very weekend, along with Stephen from the Delhi community. They were to return to Delhi on the night train, scheduled to leave about the time the gas leak occurred. At the last minute they decided to cancel the trip. I'm not sure why. Thank God for the change in plans!

Our candidates in Bhopal have been helping in the aftermath of the disaster, assisting in the food and clothing distributions. They say they cry when seeing the scorched eyes of the victims and hear the continued gasping of survivors. I'm sure I would too.

For all the good I hope our brothers will do in India, can we make even a small dent in that land's constant travail? I tell myself yes, to keep encouraged.

Peace,

Jim

DELHI AND THE VATICAN

DECEMBER IN KATHMANDU brought its usual chilly weather and, of course, Christmas. With all the activities surrounding the holidays, India's woes were pushed to the back of my mind. The Indian brothers from Delhi came up to celebrate the feast with what had become our traditions—a "Star of Bethlehem" shining brightly over the house, Christmas decorations throughout our home, evening recreation periods filled with laughter and games, and afternoon tea on Christmas Day for dozens of friends. The gathering of the brothers from the two houses was an encouraging sign to all of us that our mission was growing steadily.

After the New Year, the Delhi brothers returned home to their college studies, George geared up for classes with the current novices, and I traveled to India. There, once again, I would interview several candidates for the brothers and also attend the Conference for the Religious Superiors of India. At the annual conference, Superiors gathered and discussed current trends in the Church of India, information which I hoped would help give direction to our fledgling religious order. But first, I had business in Delhi.

At the New Delhi airport, I waited in line at the immigration officer's desk. When my turn came, the officer—a small wiry man with sunken cheeks—paged through my passport once, then a second time while he quite deliberately examined each page. What *was* he looking for? My visa for entry into India was in order, though perhaps hidden in the additional pages placed in my passport by the American embassy. I had needed the extra pages because of my frequent trips between countries.

The officer, who wore a dark brown uniform and an equally sober face, looked up at me from behind his desk, glanced at my luggage, then paged through the passport once again. I hoped he didn't want to inspect my luggage. I was traveling lightly as I always did, but I possessed papers I didn't care to have examined. Father Antu, the administrative head of the Church in Nepal, had visited me the previous day in Kathmandu and asked me to make a delivery to the Apostolic Nuncio, the Vatican's ambassador to India. "These papers," Father Antu explained, "contain information about Nepali Catholics, their names, where they live, sort of a census. I don't want to send this through the mail. You know that this is sensitive information, and it would be better if the papers were hand-carried out of Nepal. Could you deliver this personally to New Delhi?"

Converting from Hinduism to Christianity was considered an affront to the king of Nepal—himself an incarnation of a Hindu god—and an erosion of Nepali culture. Thus, to change one's religion was against the law and revealing the names of those who did so could put them in jeopardy. Though we brothers were not engaged in conversion practices, I nevertheless felt it an individual's right to switch religious allegiances if one wanted to. And so I had no qualms about delivering the secret information to the Vatican ambassador. In fact, the task had felt a bit spy-like at first, slightly adventurous. Now, standing before a law officer scrutinizing me, I felt considerably less cavalier about the project.

The immigration officer stepped from behind his desk and looked at the name tag on my luggage, then returned to his desk. I guessed he was only verifying my name because immigration personnel didn't search luggage. Customs officers handled that duty.

"You must be liking India very, very much," the officer finally spoke. "You come here quite often."

"Oh yes, I enjoy India very much."

"And do you like Indian women? Do you want to marry an Indian woman?"

His questions caught me by surprise. I had often been asked my purpose in coming to India, to which I always replied, "More travel, there is so much to see in India." I preferred to keep religion out of the picture when dealing with official India. But I had never been asked such personal questions. How to answer? If I answered yes, he might think I was a lecherous man pursuing innocent women. If I said no, perhaps he would interpret that response as an insult. I tried to read the officer's face to determine what he wanted to hear, but his look was stony. He waited for an answer with the entry stamp poised in his hand. I knew that on a whim he could delay my processing through immigration.

"I'm not sure," I replied. "What would you advise?"

"No! No! You must not marry an Indian woman. You Americans treat women like old shoes. When you are tired of them, you throw them away!" He smashed the stamp onto my passport, and motioned me to pass through.

With a sigh of relief I stepped out of the airport. The air of mid-afternoon Delhi, heavier than in Kathmandu, carried the familiar smells of street cooking. The scent of "Bombay *channa*," chickpeas simmered in curry sauce, cooking near the taxi stand, smelled happily familiar. The taxi drivers who waited for passengers were mainly turbaned Sikhs, chatting comfortably with each other. The horrors of the days following Mrs. Gandhi's assassination had evidently been replaced by a certain return to normalcy, and it felt good to be seeing an India that was relatively at peace with itself.

My taxi delivered me to the Yatri Hotel in the downtown area where I had frequently stayed in the past. The location had proved convenient for the several tasks I usually needed to accomplish in the downtown area: confirming onward plane tickets—this time to the conference in South India—wiring for foreign currency, and securing a return visa to Nepal. On my return to Delhi in a month, I would stay several days at the brothers' house on the outskirts of the city. For the next two days, however, the Yatri would suit me. Billed as the "people's" hotel, the Yatri was simple. A foam mattress placed on a foot-high cement platform at one end of the room constituted the bed, no curtains covered the windows, no towels hung in the bathroom, and a thin door that gapped several inches from the floor let in hallway voices all night.

While I told myself that a hotel in the city's center was a matter of convenience, I knew in my heart there was another reason—my growing love of independence, a trait that Lalji the palm reader had noted. Staying at the brothers' house wouldn't permit me the same flexibility to stroll New Delhi's broad avenues or sip coffee and read at the Indian Coffee House. I liked getting up as the city awakened, setting my own schedule for the day, and especially taking a walk at dusk, a pleasure most often denied by the prayer schedule in the brothers' house.

At the hotel, the desk clerk explained to the man in front of me that the hotel was completely booked, but that the traveler could try the smaller hotels near the New Delhi railway station. The disappointed gentleman left, and the clerk looked up at me. "Mr. James! So nice to see you again." He lowered his voice and added, "For how many nights will you be here? Two? No problem. You do one thing. You leave your bags with the porter and come back in two hours. I shall find a room for you. Always welcome, Mr. James, always welcome."

My bag deposited, I walked the several blocks to Connaught Place, wondering what small gift I could present to the clerk. I decided on a pack of foreign cigarettes which I purchased from a street vendor, then entered the park in the center of the shopping circle. With a lighted fountain, paved pathways, and large trees, the park pulsed with late-afternoon strollers enjoying the pleasant air of mid-January. People constantly crossed the circle to bus stands on the other side, others lingered on benches and low stone walls and bought popcorn from persistent vendors. A few families still sat on the grassy lawn, but would move soon as the late afternoon cooled. A band, with trumpets and drums and xylophone, played near the fountain, attracting a sizable crowd. Indian tourists pointed at the taller buildings in the area, and sometimes at me. A massage wallah repeatedly solicited me, so I finally paid him to work on my feet.

An hour later, darkness had descended and the park was nearly deserted. Not even beggars remained. Yet, a few night sounds greeted me as I headed back to the hotel—the putt-putt of the last autorickshaws heading home, the clanging of a corrugated metal door closing over the last open shop, a man singing to himself as he headed to the bus stand. I felt at home. Delhi still charmed me.

The next morning, the taxi drove smoothly down the wide avenues of Chanakyapuri, New Delhi's diplomatic enclave, taking me to the Vatican embassy. Broad lawns in front of stately mansions, park-like roundabouts covered with flowers, and almost no pedestrians made this section of Delhi truly a foreign domain. I almost felt I wasn't in India. It was nearly nine-thirty, and since most embassies opened at ten I hoped to see the Apostolic Nuncio before his scheduled morning appointments. At the front entrance of the Vatican's pillared villa, a small brass plate announced that office hours began at eleven. How Italian, I thought, and vigorously rang the bell.

After several minutes, an Indian servant opened the door, his eyebrows raised. "Yes please, what is it?" he inquired in crisp English.

"I'm Brother Jim, and I have a special package from Nepal for His Excellency. I must deliver it in person. Would you please take my card to him?" I held out my card while making small movements with the package under my arm. He glanced at the package, then back to my card. After a moment's hesitation, he picked up a silver tray from a nearby table and placed it under my outstretched hand. "I will present your card to His Excellency. Please have a seat," he replied in a business tone, and waved me into a large reception area.

The room, hung with tapestries and lined with red velvet chairs, exuded a European flavor. Two other chairs of ornate carved wood and a circular table adorned with a vase of white flowers comprised the select, if limited, furniture. A large oil portrait of the Pope hung on the far wall, the small light above it already lit. Pastel frescoes of angels looking heavenward covered two walls, and several faux stone pillars reached for the ceiling. The shiny marble floor, however, looked real, hard, and cold. I recalled the time nearly twenty-five years earlier when I had prostrated myself on a similar chilly marble floor while taking my vows.

I glanced around the room again, feeling that I was out of place. A well-appointed Italian villa in the middle of poor India was indeed strange, but there was something else that bothered me.

Sadness began to fill me because I knew that a cornerstone of my life that had once served me had become a millstone around my neck and must now be left behind. It was a moment of profound knowing, but not one of commitment. But time was running out, and the heaviness of indecision could not be sustained for long.

The rest of the visit passed in a haze, as if I were a third person observing the event and not a participant. I was ushered into His Excellency's private quarters, offered coffee and conversation by the pleasant Italian emissary, thanked for the delivery of the material from Nepal, and wished "God Bless" on my departure. The meeting had been cordial enough. The Vatican prelate was gracious—it was I who was distant.

THE SEAT OF AUTHORITY

THE CAMPUS OF St. Ignatius College in the South Indian city of Trichy lay before me, its palm trees waving a gentle welcome. After finding my assigned room in a dormitory, I reread the literature that described the meeting of the religious Superiors. This year, the topic was bringing "our rather Western version of Christianity" into closer harmony with the best Indian traditions. For this purpose, one of the speakers was Father Bede Griffiths, founder of an Indian-style prayer center near Trichy.

I had heard of Father Griffiths. A British Benedictine, he had already spent several decades in India, adapting to local ways in dress, manner, prayer style, and lifestyle. According to many, he personified the bridge not just between Catholicism and Hinduism, but between East and West in general. His topic was just what I wanted to hear about!

The next morning, by the time I arrived at the campus auditorium, it was packed with over three hundred conference attendees. Many priests wore black cassocks and a surprising number of nuns were in full-length habits with starched veils and wimples. I considered it a small miracle that, in the heat of South India, the nuns hadn't passed out. Compared to similar gatherings in America where cassocks and floor-length habits were practically extinct, the attire was decidedly conservative.

Four bishops, whose black cassocks sported purple buttons and collars, entered at the last minute and took their reserved seats in the front row. Their presence signified the official Church, for they monitored the orthodoxy of new religious ideas as well as details of how rituals, such as Mass, were performed in their diocese. They even had the power to determine if someone who claimed he had visions was spiritual, psychotic, or somewhere in between. Clad in the official attire of the Vatican, they had been invited to give their views on making the Church more Indian.

After a lengthy opening prayer and the usual acknowledgments, the first speaker took the microphone. A thin Indian with a low-pitched voice, he droned on from a stack of notes for the next hour with catch-phrases I had heard all my life—the community of the faithful, the teaching authority of the Church, the universal or "catholic" nature of the Church—all overused expressions that signified less and less to me. Where was *insight*? Where was a way of looking at our lives that truly *enlivened* us? Just when I thought I'd have to leave to get fresh air, the audience broke into polite applause. Thankfully, it was time for tea.

During the break I ran into an old acquaintance, Sister Stella, a Swiss nun about my age and one of the five or six foreigners at the conference. "Well, what did you think of the presentation?" she asked.

"It was extremely boring and you know it. I don't think I can take another minute of such talk."

She patted my arm and said, "I think you are tired and weary. It's in your eyes."

"Oh, I'm fine," I protested.

"Jim, the body reveals the spirit."

Back in the auditorium, Father Bede Griffiths appeared on stage. He wore a *lungi* and simple shirt, and his long white hair surrounded a thin and kindly face. Though he was scheduled to speak for an hour he carried no notes.

He began by speaking about the retreat center he had founded. "Meditation is the cornerstone of life in the ashram," he began. "Our whole day revolves around this priority. What struck me many years ago, when I first came to this country, was the gift India had to offer the world, the image of individuals in deep communion with God."

Griffiths acknowledged the value of communal prayer and group ritual, but we depended on it, he said, for our main connection with God. We needed to claim our personal access to God. India was a country of ordinary people seeking God directly, and was indeed seen as a "spiritual" country *for that very reason.*

In the audience, we stopped fanning ourselves with our programs and listened carefully. He claimed his spiritual authority from his very personal internal work, not from his priesthood. This was the very path I wanted to follow!

Father Griffiths continued, saying that large numbers of Christians, disappointed in the traditional Church, were coming to his ashram to discover the mystical dimension of their lives. Then he straightened his back and broached a sensitive topic. He admitted that the hierarchy was not altogether enthusiastic about his center, and he had difficulty obtaining Church endorsement.

The audience grew more quiet. The bishops, he said, actually appeared wary of his center. More than once he had felt defensive while explaining its goal—everyday mysticism—to bishops. He chose not to elaborate on the tension, but moved on to describe details of the ashram's day. He concluded by opening the floor to questions.

After several questions were asked about the ashram's physical setting, and one about meditation practices, I raised my hand. My question might be bold, and I was nervous about asking it.

"Father, you've made some striking statements today," I began. "At your ashram private prayer is given more priority than the Mass, the ritual that embodies the essential doctrines of the Church. I'm not surprised that some bishops are not supportive of your work. Because it's a ritual, the Mass can be regulated, but contemplation cannot. Could it be that the hierarchy's hesitancy is basically a distrust of personal religious experience?"

In the silence that followed, two of the bishops in the front row turned pointedly to see who had spoken. Father Griffiths let the silence linger as he pondered a response, then said in an even voice, "Yes, I think you have a point." As he paused again, the chairman quickly announced that it was time to adjourn for lunch, though my watch said we still had another ten minutes.

I made my way alone to the dining hall where I spied Sister Stella and sat down across from her. "Well spoken," she said, looking at me intently. "Organized religions don't trust the individual. You have said aloud what many of us know. Thank you."

I found I wasn't hungry after all, so I excused myself and headed out of the dining room. Near the door I passed Father Griffiths in conversation with another priest. He took a moment to look up and smile at me, and say, "God bless." I made namaste to him in return.

As I climbed the stairs to my room, my legs felt heavy and the humid air seemed to hold me down physically, almost suffocating me. Another day of the conference remained, but I found that I could not. My hands reached for my travel bag, and I tossed clothes inside without care. Nothing mattered except to get away from the oppressive atmosphere. I soon began to collect my belongings faster and faster, with a new sense of urgency. I simply had to leave. And I didn't mean South India.

THE SHEPHERD'S TOMB

THE HOUSEBOAT I was about to stay on for a week contained one large bedroom, a small kitchen, and a spacious living room. I might have thought I was in a miniature Persian palace—with patterned carpets, billowy drapes, ornately carved ceilings, and large floor cushions—if it weren't for the gentle rocking of the boat. The movement calmed me, creating an inner peace that I would need to accept the next surprise in store for me.

I had come to Kashmir, India's northernmost state, to rest and bring down high blood pressure that had lingered for the previous two months. After the conference in Trichy, I had spent another six weeks traveling and interviewing candidates, then arrived at the brothers' house in Delhi. Unable to sleep well, I sought medical help. The doctor prescribed relaxation, "Perhaps in the beautiful Vale of Kashmir," and a supply of pills, if needed.

A houseboat on a peaceful lake promised to be an ideal place to relax, although Kashmir's beauty and serenity had seemed quite distant earlier that afternoon when I arrived. Drizzly April weather hid most of the lush valley. And, adding to the dismal atmosphere, guards backed by rifle-toting soldiers had meticulously checked all passengers at the airport in Srinagar, Kashmir's capital. The intense security measures reminded me that Kashmir was a land torn apart by factions: some wanted the state to be independent, others fought for it to be part of Pakistan, and still others wished to keep it part of India.

The conflicts in Kashmir had their origins in the Partition of 1947 when the Indian subcontinent had been split into secular, though Hindu-dominated, India, and Muslim Pakistan. Kashmir, never part of British India but rather an independent princely state, had been ruled by its own maharajah who hoped to keep his small state independent from both India and Pakistan. Pakistan, knowing that the majority of Kashmir's population was Muslim, expected Kashmir to join its side.

Kashmir's maharajah, however, was Hindu, and when he eventually realized he could not remain independent, he decided to align with India. As an absolute ruler, he saw no need to consult his people in the matter and unilaterally invited India to send in its troops to secure the land. India eagerly agreed, promising to eventually hold a plebiscite for self-determination. The referendum never took place. Instead of self-determination, the India-Pakistan War of 1948 was waged, stale-mating in a divided and disputed Kashmir, and continued unrest and periodic bloodshed over the years.

It occurred to me that Kashmir's internal strife, in nature if not in scale, was not unlike my own. My quest for self-determination, my own move toward greater independence and away from a heart divided because of religion, had involved a clash of loyalties for some time. But now I was clear. I was leaving the Church and the Brotherhood. Bede Griffiths' words had been a catalyst, and Sister Stella had seen the weariness of my current state in my eyes. I was definite in my decision, but I needed to simply *be* with that decision for some time, let it sink in.

Outside the houseboat, slight rain had turned to mist and fog, obscuring even the closest houseboats. I didn't mind. A few days inside a cozy houseboat, sitting in front of the fire and reading a book, was surely an antidote to high blood pressure. I mentally thanked the British, who were not allowed to own land in Kashmir, for building dozens of houseboats in the nineteenth century as their home base while hunting or vacationing in Kashmir. The boats' current owners rented the vessels to tourists, and I felt quite pampered in my own floating home. I didn't even have to leave for meals. Ravi, the young man who managed the houseboat and who had ferried me to it just an hour earlier, said all meals could be served on the boat.

A knock on the door told me that Ravi had returned to check on me.

"Everything is just fine, Mr. James? Very good. Now, you see this ladder? It reaches to the roof where you can sit enjoying the sun all day. It will absolutely be sunny tomorrow. Absolutely."

He explained that he could take me in his small skiff, called a *shikara*, directly to many points of interest in the valley, including the famous Shalimar Garden, and even to places of interest in Srinagar itself, which was laced with rivers and canals. "We are the Venice of the Orient, you must be knowing." Ravi threw another log on the fire, then added nonchalantly, "And one day you may want to visit Jesus' tomb in the city. Many Westerners are interested."

"Jesus' tomb? Are you serious?" Surely Ravi meant no affront, but his statement sounded irreverent. Though I was stepping away from the institutional Church, Jesus as a divine being who had died on the cross and risen from the dead was deeply embedded in my psyche. The idea that he could be buried in a tomb in northern India was unacceptable. I was certain the tomb was just a tourist attraction, of interest to Christians primarily for its astounding claim.

Ravi informed me that the tomb was an important shrine and that indeed many Muslims prayed to the prophet Jesus. We could visit there anytime, even in the rain. And, switching topics, he wanted to know if the accommodations suited me.

Yes, they suited me. It all suited me, even the rain which had picked up again. Its hypnotic drumming on the roof was already lowering that pesky blood pressure.

The rain continued for two more days, and I was content to spend my time in the houseboat, reading or occasionally taking the small boat to shore for lunch. By the fourth overcast, mist-filled day, however, I was indeed ready to venture further, so when Ravi brought my breakfast I said, "Maybe this afternoon would be a good time to visit Jesus' tomb."

"Oh yes, how very perfect. We shall take the *shikara* to the city and the mosque. The tomb is in a mosque, the Roza Bal, you see."

After lunch, Ravi guided the boat across the lake, through city canals, under arched wooden bridges, and finally pulled up at a landing that led to our destination. The Roza Bal, the mosque containing the tomb, had simple white stucco walls, shuttered windows, and a slightly unkempt appearance. It looked peaceful that afternoon, and the few bowed figures entering the building seemed genuinely intent on prayer. One vendor offered a pamphlet for sale entitled "Jesus in India," which I bought and paused to read before entering the mosque.

According to the pamphlet, Jesus spent his "hidden years," those between the ages of twelve and thirty, in India learning the spiritual traditions of the East. It claimed that he had been highly influenced by Buddhism, and it went on to make an even more astonishing claim: Jesus didn't die on the cross at all, but somehow survived and returned to India, settling in Kashmir where a colony of exiled Jews already lived. These Jews were one of the Lost Tribes of Israel dispersed throughout the world after the Assyrian conquest of Israel in the eighth century B. C. For years they had wandered the earth and eventually settled in Kashmir.

Linguistic evidence, the booklet asserted, connected the ancient Hebrews with modern Kashmiris. In Kashmir, Jesus lived out his days as a teacher, well-loved and accorded the affectionate name, the Shepherd. After his death, far from ascending into heaven, he was buried like other mortals. For two thousand years his tomb was venerated as that of a holy man, and at one point a mosque was built over the site. The pamphlet concluded with, "May all who visit the Shepherd's tomb receive a blessing from the great prophet lying therein."

Even though I questioned many Catholic practices, the pamphlet's story still shocked me. It went against my most fundamental beliefs, against everything I had been taught and had treasured and lived by for decades. Who *were* these people who so flagrantly offended millions of Christians? I noticed that the pamphlet's author had an Islamic name. Of course, he's just promoting his own version of history. He blindly accepts the Koran's assertion that Jesus was only a prophet. And he believes this preposterous story about the tomb.

But if the tale was so preposterous, why was I reacting so strongly? I needed to calm down and figure things out in the quiet of the tomb, so I entered the mosque though my feet were dragging.

The mosque held a smaller structure within, a filigreed wooden room. In the middle of that room, a high rectangular object covered with heavy quilting was the object of veneration. Three mute figures swathed in gray shawls circled the tomb, pausing frequently to murmur prayers and touch their hands to the tomb and then to their foreheads. I forced myself to rationally assess the situation. The Muslims in front of me considered Jesus a prophet, though not divine, for the same reason I believed the opposite—we had both been *instructed* to believe differing statements. Hindu children were taught to believe in hundreds of gods. Buddhists didn't believe in any god. Countless other religions had similar dogmatic beliefs. Suddenly, standing in the Shepherd's Tomb with its own unbelievable claim, every belief of mankind seemed completely and absurdly arbitrary. Perhaps we were all right in our own way, or perhaps we were all equally blind and ignorant. The bottom line was that none of us really knew anything.

Could I really face the possibility that Christianity's, and *my*, most basic belief might have no basis in reality? The prospect felt overwhelming. Jesus as God was so ingrained in me that I couldn't imagine letting that go. But, since I was jettisoning so many other beliefs lately, I had to ask myself, why did I really need a divine Jesus? That precept was essential if you believed that you needed to be "saved" by God dying for you. Saved from what, hell? Every article of faith needed another gratuitous belief to bolster it. It was an endless cycle, one I now desperately wanted to free myself from. With every passing second, I was grasping more clearly the futility of blind belief and its false promise of peace of mind.

Yet Jesus' face was so familiar to me. He embodied love of neighbor, forgiveness of enemies, sacrifice for others' sake—a way of life I aspired to. I didn't want to lose that.

Somewhat shaken, I stepped into the line moving around the tomb and a few minutes later found I was the only pilgrim remaining. Who *was* buried in the tomb? The question was like a koan from a Zen master. Perhaps there was no answer, but it was important to ask the question because it opened oneself up to possibilities.

I was startled to hear the next question that raced across my mind. Could Jesus be in the tomb? Though by habit I wanted to say "of course not," those words didn't come. A deep shift inside me had taken place. I didn't need to believe *anything* about the place I stood in, or about Jesus, or about any of the religious doctrines I had been taught.

I looked around the dimly lit room. Its rectangular shape and deathly silence made me feel as if I were in a large casket—my casket. Indeed, a part of me—the believer—was dying in that remote and most unusual place. I wasn't angrily casting down beliefs. They were all just dropping away, falling through my fingers like dry sand.

I touched my hands to the tomb, then to my forehead. A spaciousness began to fill me, and I felt more free and at peace than ever before. The Shepherd in the tomb, whoever he was, had blessed me. I had lost religion, but gained my soul.

JUBILATION

ON THE PLANE back to Kathmandu, I had to confront an issue I had pushed to the back of my mind the last several months. In just a few weeks I was to have my Silver Jubilee, the celebration of twenty-five years as a brother, and now I had to look at that event in the light of my recent decisions. I was definitely leaving the Church and the brothers, but I didn't really want to do it immediately. I was not at odds with my religious community, and after calling it home for twenty-five years, I was in no hurry to rush out the door. I would be living with my brothers for a while yet, including the time set for the jubilee. However, with my religious loyalties so shifted, I was uneasy with going through with the ceremony.

Paul met me at the airport and announced, "Most of the plans for your jubilee are in place, and you can let me know of anything special you want. I'm organizing the whole celebration."

There was no backing out of the event, and in fact deep down, I knew that I really *did* want to celebrate the jubilee. I simply needed to get my reasons clear, so I began with taking stock of my whole religious situation. Though leaving the Church and its doctrines, I would always have Christian and Catholic roots. My past wouldn't disappear. Ritual and sacred song would always be dear to me. Christianity, with its icons etched deeply in my mind, was my religious mother-tongue. The images of Jesus,

Mary, and the saints would always evoke in me a sense of the transcendent, a feeling that I was part of something greater than myself. The images themselves had power, though the underlying theology no longer carried weight for me.

That was the big picture, and I knew my mind about it. But the jubilee? How could I go through with it when I was leaving the brothers? I needed to talk to someone about it.

Later that day, Paul appeared at my bedroom door. "I'm going to pick up some clothes at the tailor's. Want to come along?"

I said I did, and remembered that the tailor shop was just a block from Ananda Ashram, where I might find Swami Jyoti. No doubt he had heard many stories before from people disenchanted with organized religion and might have counsel for me. I chuckled to myself wondering what Del and George would say if they knew I was going to the swami for spiritual guidance.

While Paul waited at the tailor's shop, I knocked at the ashram door and found Swami Jyoti at home. He welcomed me into his room and sat patiently, fingering the beads around his neck, as I poured out my story. "So," he finally asked, "the question is about this event you called a jubilee? It's really quite simple, you know. You've said what is important about it several times the last few minutes."

When I paused to think, the swami continued, "You always call it a jubilee 'celebration.' You want to *celebrate* your past twenty-five years. Do it. Laugh, dance. Above all, drop any negative feelings you might have and *enjoy* the event."

I hurried to the tailor shop where Paul was waiting for me, and we walked home together. "Paul, I do have something special I want for the jubilee celebration and I want you to help me with it." Paul listened as I described a skit I had decided to perform.

THE SILVER METAL cup engraved, "Brother Jim, God's Pioneer – Congratulations," awaited me on the dining table. A round of applause from the gathered staff and novices, and afternoon tea with an excess of cookies and sweets began three days of festivities for my Silver Jubilee. The following day, colored streamers scalloped across the dining room ceiling, a wreath of silver paper with a large "25" in its center hung in the living room, and large silver letters spelled out, "Twenty-Five Years in God's Service," on a wall in the study hall. The house buzzed with activity. Several novices helped Maela in the kitchen, while others dusted, swept, and told me they were doing "super cleaning," a term I had taught them. George and I planned the Mass celebration for that evening, and the brothers who had arrived from Delhi made sure all the invitations for the next day's Mass at the parish had been delivered.

That evening after the banquet prepared by Maela, we gathered in the living room and sang songs, and watched the novices imitate me. They accurately mimicked the way I fanned my mouth and called for water after eating hot chilies, and how I bobbed my head up and down while playing guitar at Mass to keep the other guitars in time with me. William imitated my attempts at pronouncing Hindi nasal sounds, and according to his version, I sounded as if I had a bad cold.

"I have a skit too," I announced. I placed a table in front of the gathering, and on it arranged a toothbrush and tube of toothpaste, a razor and a can of shaving cream, a breakfast bowl, and a small washbasin. Paul came up to sit close behind me, draped a sheet over his head, and stuck his arms out around me, as if they were mine, as I hid my hands behind my back. I had done what I called the "Brother Jim Getting Up in the Morning" skit before in the States, and wondered how it would look to this group.

With Paul's large and long, hairy arms, obviously not mine, rubbing my eyes, I pretended to yawn and to begin my "morning wash-up." At first, stunned silence greeted the spectacle of Paul's arms splashing water on my face and up my nose, then inexpertly toweling me off. But just a few seconds later, silence gave way to laughter at Paul's efforts to brush my teeth—most of the toothpaste lay glued to my mustache and the brush scrubbed more of my chin than my teeth. Vincent, a new novice, gasped when Paul's arms wielded the razor over haphazard patches of shaving cream on my face, but I was safe—the blade had been removed. By the time Paul's arms tried to feed me oatmeal, most of which ran down my chin and neck, no one in the room had maintained his composure.

"Jim, I laughed so hard my face hurts," Vincent said. "I've never seen anything like that. You know, an Indian Superior would never play a joke on himself like that. This is wonderful."

Johnny added, "Yes, I will always remember this."

"Good, please do," I said. "Some day you may be a Superior, and I hope you will find space for laughter, especially at yourself!"

The following afternoon, friends crowded against each other on floor cushions, and others perched themselves on small stools at the back of the parish church. The warmth of the May afternoon had pushed through the church's brick walls just enough to take nighttime chill from the room, yet not too much, and the flower garlands around my neck remained fresh. As I waited for the ceremony to begin, a sense of awe and contentment flooded over me when I thought of the twenty-five years I was celebrating. The years had given me many things to be happy and proud about, and so few regrets. I regretted almost nothing, except perhaps my failings against compassion. Regrets were for people who lived in the past, who wanted things to be different. I felt content with the present, with who I was. And I knew that "who I was" was the result of every thing that I had ever done, everything that had ever happened to me, every single thing, pleasant or not. And for all that, I was grateful.

I stepped forward to address the gathering.

"At celebrations like this one today, or at weddings, birthdays, or family gatherings, you have heard over and over people saying they are grateful. And indeed, that is what I most deeply feel right now. But, what is gratitude?

"Gratitude is that feeling that steals upon us when a stranger returns a lost article to us, when we finally appreciate the lessons we have learned from a strict teacher, or when we see that all our blessings have come to us through other people. Gratitude is what surrounds us like a warm shawl when we ourselves help another person, for we know that the two of us are made from the same earth.

"I feel gratitude now as I look over the past twenty-five years as a brother. I think of the brothers who help shaped my life. I think of the students who made me into a teacher, of the teachers who have stretched me to look at life in new ways. I see you before me, your gifts of song, laughter, and love, and that makes me feel at home with you.

"So, gratitude is nothing more, and nothing less, than the experience of being profoundly connected to others. Let me say that again. Gratitude is our deepest self, our inmost being, telling us we are intimately connected to every other being—and that is what all religions call spirituality.

"So when we feel gratitude, we have entered the spiritual realm. You and I do that often, though sometimes without knowing it. That is my wish for all of us, that we claim the spirituality of our daily lives, that we fully accept that the most important events are happening right here and now.

"Namaste."

19 May 1985
Kathmandu, Nepal

Dear Dave,

In our conversation last summer I said I would stay in Asia another two years. Yes, I will stay here until next year and get things in order for my successor. After that, I'm definitely returning to America. I have much to tell you, but prefer to do it in person.

Jim

THE LAST JOURNEY

"TODAY IS NEPALI New Year's Day, a good time for a new start," Del said as the taxi arrived at our gate. Eleven months, almost a full year, had lapsed since my jubilee, and it was time to return to America. Spring had arrived and the magnolia tree at the end of the driveway was in bloom again. The bushes near the gate drooped green and lush from the recent rains, and the sun cast distinct shadows on the brick driveway. Lined up on those bricks were my American and Indian brothers. Each in turn wished me well, gave me a farewell embrace, and said "God Bless." Maela placed a garland around my neck, and I climbed into the taxi for the ride to the airport. I didn't look back, only forward.

How quickly the previous year had passed. The usual events had occurred—the annual "Come and See Program," trips to India for recruitment, long evenings with the brothers in Kathmandu. I had thrown myself into each activity with my usual energy, but I was simultaneously detached, and at peace.

I had been at peace even when interviewing young men who wished to join the religious order I knew I was leaving. The Brotherhood had served me in many ways and it could do the same for the young men seeking admittance. Each of them had to follow his own path with all its unique twists and turns.

The previous year had afforded me time not only to complete my duties, but also to travel and mentally say goodbye to the Indian subcontinent and its people.

The people of the great subcontinent! How many lessons had I learned, or not learned, from living among them? During my recent travels, the tired soldier on the train out of Bombay kept appearing to me, like a visual mantra, whenever I felt irritation at the crowded conditions of India. Seeing him sit quietly on the edge of my bed, not invited to lie down and rest, reminded me to be more compassionate. His patience reminded me to slow my hurried pace. His simplicity chided me to seek only what was important. Many times I said a short prayer for him. He never knew, I was sure, that he had been a teacher of mine.

So much of India had been a teacher of mine, from its mountains where my body had shivered to its southern coasts where I had sweated day and night—and come home to my body. Part of my new life would be the search for integration of body and spirit, a process already begun, but only glimpsed at. There was a long road ahead in that matter.

Along the seacoast in South India, I had been startled to see a towering, stone gothic church rising above the palm trees, dwarfing the modest homes—some practically shanties—in the surrounding neighborhood. But the fishermen who pointed with pride at the edifice reminded me of the importance of "sacred place" and of visible shrines that helped one rise above the daily toil. The spirit needed external support. The spirit needed community and ritual.

Where would I find those soul-nutrients outside of the Church? How would I find like-minded and supportive fellow-seekers, when, with dogma dismissed, I served no particular religion? I would have to clarify my convictions, create ritual as needed, and find community—all of it a bootstrap operation, but the final great journey. Nevertheless, I had no deep fear concerning what lay ahead for I carried close to almost every waking thought the words I had chosen for my jubilee holy card: "For those who love God, all things work together unto good."

How strange that this quote had been my favorite bible passage over the years, for I never felt that I had really "loved God." I never understood those who told of becoming a monk or nun for love of God. I had joined the brothers because a life of service in a community setting had given great meaning to my own journey. Over the years, I must have been translating that passage in another way. My "love for God" was the energy I poured into seeking truth wherever it might lie. That "all things" would work toward good was a trust that the universe continually supported me—I had often used the term "Providence" in that regard. It was a conviction that I could go forward despite mistakes. Indeed, the more solitary spiritual path I was taking was fraught with chances to go astray, but at least the mistakes would be my own, not those foisted on me by others.

In any case, I was not forsaking the wisdom in the Christian tradition, nor that of any of the world's great religions. I had learned, and would continue to learn, from the religious lore of the ages. I wanted the richness that was available. And I might even find larger, more universal truths than could be discovered in any one system. To me it was worth the chance.

Over the previous year, the faces of my Indian brothers had floated before my eyes many times as I waited, sometimes patiently, for buses and planes. Sylverius, serious eyes and steady demeanor; John, jaw set, solid and dependable; Johnny, smiling and helpful; all of them. Would they feel somehow betrayed when they found out that I left the brothers? I hoped not. Would it affect their commitment? I would never know, but their reasons for remaining brothers should have nothing to do with me.

Each of their vocations must stand on its own. But leaving them, and all my brothers—my home of twenty-five years—was the hardest part of all.

The previous night I had pulled my old suitcase out of storage and packed my few clothes, leaving behind the best shirts for the novices and Maela. Several souvenirs—a small oil lamp, a sandalwood letter opener, and the broken pocket watch I had purchased one summer—were the last items to be packed. As I slipped the watch into a side pocket of the suitcase, it struck something metal. My gold ring.

I picked up the ring, smoothed over its edges with my fingers, let it rest in the palm of my hand. A bittersweet symbol. It represented my life as a brother, satisfying in many ways, but ultimately too limiting. It reminded me of a commitment made, but not fulfilled. Father Dave could ask for the ring when I left the brothers, but he probably wouldn't. And I certainly wouldn't offer it. I would keep the ring as a symbol of a life that was, of a time when I was part of the Brotherhood.

At the airport, the immigration officer stamped my passport, and I noted the April date. I recalled that date from documents I had recently perused and was leaving behind. Exactly seven years earlier, to the day, the other India pioneers and I had held our first planning meeting for the mission. How could that event simultaneously seem so recent and yet so long ago?

As the plane taxied down the airstrip, it faced the Himalayas. Then slowly, it turned one hundred and eighty degrees. In that revolution, all of Nepal and India and a dozen cherished faces flashed across my mind, still pulling at me. For a single moment, I wanted to stop the plane.

India and Nepal—the smell of sandalwood in the bazaars, the sight of dazzling saris and *lungis* gracefully wrapping its people, the aroma of curry wafting from cooking pots, the melodic clang of multiple languages and dialects, the mountains and plains stretching to the horizon—all of this was in my bones now. I would miss the great subcontinent and its people, that was certain. But I was taking with me the lessons learned and the growth attained in the land where Shiva's fiery dance clears away the old world to make room for the new universe, even the universe we inhabit all by ourselves.

The plane raced down the runway and carried me into the air—and toward the next odyssey.

AUTHOR'S NOTE

THE PEOPLE, PLACES, and events in this story are real.

I have exercised the storyteller's device of telescoping time in order to bring events into focus, as well as creating and rendering dialogue which, though not necessarily verbatim, conveys my recollection of the event and my perception of the speaker's personality.

The official name for the religious congregation is the Society of Mary, and its members place the initials S.M. after their names. We used both our first and last legal names, though in the interests of simplicity and privacy, I have used only first names for the brothers and for most locals. Some Indian and Nepali names have likely changed due to the vagaries of memory. DeMello is not the name of the family in Bombay. Santosh's name is D. Showriah.

The letters in this narrative are composites, summaries, or excerpts of real letters, sometimes with information added to ensure clarity of the story line.

I have chosen, against convention but for ease of reading, to translate one proper name. "Light of Wisdom Seminary" is Vidyajyoti College of Theology in the Civil Lines area of Delhi.

Also known as Marianists throughout the world, the brothers in India and Nepal continue to grow and their works expand, affecting the lives of thousands. They have brought education to rural areas as well as to the cities' poor, and their efforts for the uplift of the urban "ragpicker" children have been lauded as model programs by the government of India.

Finally, an acknowledgment of gratitude must now go to those individuals, situations, and institutions with which I had conflict. Without them there would be no story.

ACKNOWLEDGEMENTS

To ENCOURAGE IS to "give heart," a grace much needed to write a book. I have been blessed with that gift from a list of accomplished and generous people.

High on that roster is writer, editor, friend, Betty Dietz. Her professional and personal support has been invaluable, and each page reads more smoothly because of her skillful editing. Other writing coaches include the insightful Jane Anne Staw, and the talented Amanita Rosenbush. Without them, I would have only sparse phrases, thin paragraphs, and no book.

Very early on, writers Jeremy Taylor and Greg Castillo offered crucial encouragement without which I fear this memoir would have remained a bundle of fading memories.

A host of others supported me in a variety of ways, and I must acknowledge some of them, and apologize to those whom I have left off the list. Sandy Krakowski, Dan Krakowski, Joseph Sheehan, John Murray, Coralie Murray, Kathryn Taylor, David Casuto, the Joseph Campbell Group, the Breakfast Club, and Brother Earl Leistikow, S.M. (Marianist Archives, San Antonio).

For support on the journey accounted here, a grateful *Namaste* goes to our original pioneer group, those who came after, those in the U.S. and Europe who supported this venture, the Indian brothers, the many nuns, brothers and priests in India and Nepal into whose communities I was readily welcomed, and the many acquaintances and strangers along the path who made the adventure all that more colorful.